FREE BOOKS

www.*forgottenbooks*.org

You can read literally thousands of books
for free at www.forgottenbooks.org

(please support us by visiting our web site)

Forgotten Books takes the uppermost care to preserve the entire content of the original book. However, this book has been generated from a scan of the original, and as such we cannot guarantee that it is free from errors or contains the full content of the original. But we try our best!

Truth may seem, but cannot be:
Beauty brag, but 'tis not she;
Truth and beauty buried be.

To this urn let those repair
That are either true or fair;
For these dead birds sigh a prayer.

Bacon

PASTOR PASTORUM

OR THE

SCHOOLING OF THE APOSTLES
BY OUR LORD

BY

REV. HENRY LATHAM M.A.
LATE MASTER OF TRINITY HALL CAMBRIDGE

SIXTEENTH THOUSAND.

First Edition printed May 1890
Reprinted with alterations
November 1890, *October* 1891, *July* 1892
Reprinted 1893, 1895, 1897, 1899, 1901, 1902
1904, 1905, 1907, 1908, 1910, 1913,

PREFACE.

OF the general purport of this book, and of what led to the writing, I have said all that is necessary in the Introductory Chapter. The ideas it contains were growing into distinctness during the five and thirty years of my College work, and to many of my old pupils they will offer little that is new.

But although the book took its source from teaching; and instruction—but instruction divorced from examinations—is in some degree my object still, yet it is meant, not so much for professed students, as for that large body of the public, who entertain the desire, happily spreading fast among the young, of understanding with as great exactness as possible what it was that Christ visibly effected, and what means He employed in bringing it about.

I have avoided all technical terms of Divinity or Philosophy, and where, as in Chapters II. and III., I have been led to touch on theological speculations, I have tried to present the matter in as familiar a form as I could. Frequently, I have explained in the notes some geographical and other particulars which a large majority among my readers may not require to be told; in this case I must be pardoned for consulting the interest of the minority.

A didactic purpose and a literary one, do not always run readily side by side. A teacher who desires to inculcate certain principles or ideas, is ever on the look out for illustrations and recurs to his topic again and again. So, having, as I thought, certain topics to teach, I have brought them back into view more often than I should have done if I had written solely with a literary view.

I have not commonly given accounts of what has been said by others on the points of which I treat, or criticised conclusions different from mine, for I know that this manner of treatment is not in favour with the present generation. I recollect the reason of an undergraduate, in my early days, for preferring the instruction of his private tutor to that officially provided—"The Lecturer tells you that Hermann says it is this, and Wunder says it is that, but Blank (the private tutor) tells you what it *is*."

With the same view of making the book read-

apologising when I have advanced a notion not commonly received. In my first draft I had made such apologies for what I say on the second and third Temptations, on the Mission to the Cities, the Transfiguration, the Denials of Peter and some minor points—but I afterwards thought it better to leave them out, and to disclaim here once for all, any intention to dogmatize, or to fail in respect toward the weighty authorities with whom I have ventured to disagree.

In many cases, however, the views that I have taken rather supplement than supplant those that are commonly received. Writers on Divinity have not so much opposed them, as failed to notice the points on which I dwell. There is however one topic—the parable of the Unjust Steward, on which I find myself at variance with all the writers on the subject I know of, excepting perhaps Calvin, who begins his Comment on Luke xvi. 1 by saying "The main drift of this parable, is, that we must shew kindness and lenity in dealing with our neighbours." He does not, however, follow up this view as I have done.

Though in so difficult a matter I cannot be confident of being right, yet I do feel convinced, that the accepted interpretation of the parable, viz. that it is intended to teach the right use of riches—"the really wise use of mammon" as Göbel puts it—is wholly inadequate. So simple a moral would have been pointed by a simpler tale. Surely the riches would have been made the giver's own. Moreover the salient point of the outward story, that which first catches attention, always answers in our Lord's parables to a cardinal matter in the interpretation. Here that salient point lies in the words "Take thy bond and sit down quickly and write fifty" and this has but a very oblique bearing on the true use of riches; the distinctive point of the outward parable is the exercise of delegated power, and the spiritual bearing must be in conformity with this.

I have everywhere followed the Revised Version, and I must warn readers that where italics occur in the *longer* passages they are not *mine*, except in passage on p. 101. They are introduced, not to mark words important for my purpose, but simply because they are found in the Revised Version where they indicate, of course, that the corresponding word is wanting in the Greek. For the course of events I have generally followed the Gospel of St Mark up to the time of the feast of Tabernacles; and after that the Gospel of St John. Of the great historical value of the latter I have, like most biblical students, become more deeply sensible, the more closely I have studied it. Speaking of the absence of miracles wrought in public during the week of the Passion, p. 430, I have not noticed Matt. xxi. 14, because I believe the Evangelist to refer to miracles that had taken place during earlier visits to Jerusalem. It was beyond the scope of my book to discuss the differences of character of the different Gospels.

In a few instances I follow an order of events different from that which is most commonly taken. This order I have shewn in a Chronological Appendix, in which I have tabulated the chief events of our Lord's Ministry, taking them month by month from the time of the Baptism to that of the great day of Pentecost. I have made this Appendix more full, in point of reference and arguments in support of the dates, than would have been quite necessary for readers of this book, because I thought it might be made useful generally to students of the Gospel History.

I have to thank several persons for their assistance and advice, especially Canon Huxtable, without whose kind encouragement at the outset the book might not have been written. I must note that I have made use of an idea on Luke xii. 49, which I first came upon, many years ago, in a small publication of the Rev. A. H. Wratislaw, then one of the Tutors of Christ's College; and that I was in like manner set on a track of thought by a sermon on the Temptation, by T. Colani, published at Strasburg in 1860. I have acknowledged my obligations to Bishop Ellicott's "Historical Lectures," and Edersheim's "Jesus the Messiah." Many members of my own College, and many other friends have assisted me greatly with advice and corrections.

Although my book is not written with any thesis about the Gospels to support, still I trust that I have cleared away difficulties here and there, and have shewn, in small matters, how one account undesignedly supports another. If what I have said shall lead to discussion on some of the questions raised, or if I shall induce younger men to apply themselves, in some of those directions towards which I have pointed, to work of a literary kind waiting to be done, I shall not have spent my time and pains without result.

TRINITY HALL LODGE,
May 1st, 1890.

CONTENTS.

CHAPTER I.

	PAGE
INTRODUCTORY	1

CHAPTER II.

HUMAN FREEDOM 28

CHAPTER III.

OF REVELATION 52

CHAPTER IV.

OUR LORD'S USE OF SIGNS 74
   (1) *The attraction of hearers* . . . 77
   (2) *Selection* 79
   (3) *Preparation* 80
   (4) *Setting forth the Kingdom of God* . . 82
   (5) *Teaching wrought by Signs* . . . 84
   (6) *Miracles as a practical lesson to the disciples* 91

CONTENTS.

CHAPTER V.

	PAGE
THE LAWS OF THE WORKING OF SIGNS	112
The Temptation to turn stones into loaves	127
The Temptation on the Mount	134
The Temptation on the Pinnacle of the Temple	139

CHAPTER VI.

FROM THE TEMPTATION TO THE MINISTRY IN GALILEE	147
Outset of the work	147

CHAPTER VII.

THE PREACHING TO THE MULTITUDES	188

CHAPTER VIII.

THE CHOOSING OF THE APOSTLES	228

CHAPTER IX.

THE SCHOOLING OF THE APOSTLES. THE MISSION TO THE CITIES	270

CHAPTER X.

TO THOSE WHO HAVE IS GIVEN	311
The Teaching by Parables	311
Resumption of the Narrative	328

CONTENTS. xi

CHAPTER XI.

PAGE
FROM THE MOUNT TO JERUSALEM . . . 349

CHAPTER XII.

THE LATER LESSONS 373
   Different cases receive different treatment . . 373
   Parable of the Unjust Steward . . . 386
   Our Lord refusing to judge 398
   Our Lord's action prospective . . . 411
   Christ washing the Apostles' feet . . 419
   Use of signs in the later Ministry . . . 425

CHAPTER XIII.

THE LESSONS OF THE RESURRECTION . . . 437
   The Ascension 457

CHRONOLOGICAL APPENDIX 473

INDEX OF TEXTS 491

GENERAL INDEX 495

INTRODUCTORY CHAPTER.

IN this opening chapter I propose to lay before the reader the leading ideas which will be developed in the book. This will necessitate some repetition, but many readers want to know at starting whither the author is going to take them, and whether his notions are such that they will care for his company.

In the course of lecturing on the Gospels, being myself interested in questions of education, my attention turned to the way in which our Lord taught His disciples. Following the Gospel History with this view, I recognised in the train of circumstances through which Christ led the disciples, no less than in what He said to them, an assiduous care in training them to acquire certain qualities and habits of mind. I observed also method and uniformity both in what He did and in what He refrained from doing. Certain principles seem to govern His actions and to be observed regularly so far as we can see, but we have no ground for stating that our Lord came to resolutions on these points and bound Himself to observe them. A man sometimes sees his duty so clearly at one moment that he wishes to make the decision of that moment dominant over his life and he embodies it in a resolve, but we must suppose that Christ at each moment did what was best. So that what I call a Law of His conduct is only a generalization from His biography, and means no more than that, in such and such circumstances He usually acted in such and such ways. I can easily conceive that He might have swerved from these Laws had there been occasion.

I have fancied that I got glimpses of the processes by means of which the Apostles of the Gospels—striving among themselves who should be greatest, looking for the restoration of the kingdom to Israel, and dismayed at the apprehension of their Master—were trained to become the Apostles of the Acts,—testifying boldly before rulers and councils, giving the right hand of fellowship to one who had not companied with them, and breaking through Jewish prejudices, to own that there were no men made by God who were common or unclean. The shape which much of the outward course of Christ's life took, His choice of Galilee as a scene of action, His withdrawal from crowds and His wanderings in secluded regions were admirably adapted to the educating of the Apostles; while His sending them, two and two, through the cities was a direct lesson in that self-reliance which reposes on a trust in God. Were not these courses ordered to these ends? The training was wonderfully fitted to bring about the changes which occurred.

That this fashioning of the disciples should have been a very principal object with our Lord is easy to conceive. For what, except His followers, did He leave behind as the visible outcome of His work? He had founded no institution and had left no writings as a possession for after time. The Apostles were the salt to season and preserve the world, and if they had not savour whence could help be sought? Is it not then likely that the best means would be employed for choosing and shaping instruments for the work; and can we do better than mark the Divine wisdom so engaged?

On many sides the work of Christ stretches away into infinity. God's purpose in having created the world, and put free intelligences into it, as well as the changes which Christ's death may have wrought in the relation of men's souls to God, belong to that infinite side of things, which we cannot explore. But we *can* follow the treatment by which Christ moulded the disciples, because the changes are not wrought in them by a magical transformation, but come about gradually as the result of what they saw and heard and did.

Changes are brought about in the disciples by an education, superhuman indeed in its wisdom, superhuman in its insight into the habits of mind which were wanted, and into the modes by which such habits might be fostered, but not superhuman in the means employed. We can analyse the influences which are brought to bear, judge what they were likely to effect, and estimate fairly well what they did effect, because they were the same in kind as we now find working in the world. Christ's ways, therefore, in this province of His work fall within the range of our understanding. The learners are taught less by what they are told than by what they see and do. They are trained not only by listening, but by following and—what was above all—by being suffered, as in the mission to the cities of Israel, to take part in their Master's work.

They are altered by their companionship with our Lord, insensibly, just as we see the complexion of a man's character alter by his being thrown into the constant society of a stronger nature. But Christ works on them no magical change. Our Lord never transforms men so as to obliterate their old nature, and substitute a new one; new powers and a new life spring up from contact with Him, but the powers work through the old organs, and the life flows through the old channels; they would not be the same men, or preserve their individual responsibility if it were otherwise. God's grace works with men, it is true, but it uses the organization it finds; and as much cultivation and shaping of the disposition is required for turning God's Grace to account, as for making the most of any other good gift.

Christ's particular care to leave the disciples their proper independence is everywhere apparent. They come to Him of their deliberate will. They are not stricken by any over-mastering impression, or led captive by moving words. They are not forced to break with their old selves; their growth in steadfastness comes of a better knowledge of their Lord, and the more they advance in understanding God's ways and therefore in believing, the stronger are the grounds of assurance which are granted to them; the more they have, the more is given them; the most attached are granted most.

Christ, we find, draws out in His disciples the desired qualities of self-devotion and of healthy trust in God, without effacing the stamp of the individual nature of each man. He cherishes and respects personality. The leader of a sect or school of thought is often inclined to lose thought of the individual in his care for the society which he is establishing, or to expect his pupils to take his own opinions ready made, in a block. He is apt to be impatient if one of them attempts to think for himself. His aim very commonly is

"To make his own the mind of other men,"

and a pupil who asserts his own personality, and is not content with reflecting his master's, is not of the sort he wants.

But our Lord was a teacher of a very different kind. He reverenced whatever the learner had in him of his own, and was tender in fostering this native growth. He was glad when His words roused a man into thinking on his own account, even in the way of objection. When the Syrophœnician woman turns His own saying against Him, with the rejoinder, "Yes Lord, yet the dogs under the table eat of the children's crumbs," He applauds her Faith the more for the independent thought that went with it. Men, in His eyes, were not mere clay in the hands of the potter, matter to be moulded to shape. They were organic beings, each growing from within, with a life of his own—a personal life which was exceedingly precious in His and His Father's eyes—and He would foster this growth so that it might take after the highest type.

Neither did He mean that what He told men should only be stored in their memories as in a treasure-house, there to be kept intact. They were to "take heed *how* they heard." With Christ, the part that the man had to do of himself went for infinitely more than what was done for him by another. If men had the will and the power to turn to their own moral nutriment the mental food which was given them, it would be well; but if His words merely lay in their memories, without affecting them or germinating within them, then they were only as seeds falling on sterile spots.

The training of the disciples was partly practical, turning on what they saw our Lord do and were set or suffered to do themselves, and partly it came from what they heard. I want the reader to go along with me in marking how this training of the Apostles was adapted to generate the qualities which the circumstances of their situation demanded when Christ left the world; and it is in the practical part of the work that this is most readily traced.

The selection of the Apostles may serve as an instance of what I mean. They were to preach a gospel to the poor—the movement was to spread upward from below. This will be found to be the law of growth of great moral principles which have established their sway among mankind. The Apostles therefore were chosen from a class which, though not the poorest, had sympathies with the poor. Again the Apostles were to be witnesses of the resurrection to after times; it was important, therefore, that they should possess qualities which would make men trust them; had they been imaginative, had they been enthusiasts, this would have been a bar to the accepting of their evidence; but the Apostles were singularly literal-minded men, so little suspecting a metaphorical meaning in their Master's sayings, that when He told them to beware of the leaven of the Pharisees, they thought it meant that, having no bread with them, they would be constrained to eat some not made in the proper way. We see no exaggeration in them, no wild fervour, nothing that belongs to the religious fanatic. Our Lord never employs the force that such fanaticism affords; when He meets with what seems the result of emotion, as when the woman breaks out with "Blessed is the womb that bare thee," He always brings back to mind that doing is more than feeling.

We shall have to note, moreover, the progressive way in which our Lord taught His followers self-reliance and faith, and the tender care with which He lets His hold of them go by degrees. Wandering along with our Lord, they grow into a capacity for marking greatness, and trusting themselves to a superior nature. When they are sent, two and two, through the cities of Israel, they learn to use responsibility, and to feel that His power could still protect them even when He was not by. They lacked nothing then, for Christ provided for them; but the time should come when they would complete their training and have real work to do, and then they would have to employ all gifts which had fallen to them. For the real conflict, both the purse and the sword are to be taken; prudence and judgment and courage must be brought into play in doing God's work as they are in doing that of every day life.

And when Christ leaves the world, the disciples are not for long exposed to the revulsion which the crucifixion would cause. They are not suffered to feel their Master's loss and miss Him all at once. They are not left to suppose that He had altogether gone, that His cause had failed and all was over; so that they had better wake from their delusion and go back, with blighted hope and faith, to Galilee and their boats and nets. Soon comfort came. The work for which they had been trained was still to go on, only not in the way they had expected. Their following Christ was not to be a mere episode in their lives: they had not been wrong in thinking that they should serve Him all their days. Christ is near them still, and they see Him now and again. For forty days or more they felt that He was in their neighbourhood, and might at any time appear; any stranger who accosted them might turn out to be He. Thus they are carried through the time when the effects of shock on their mind and moral nature was most to be feared, and they are brought one step nearer to the power of realising that Christ is with them. After the Ascension, He is withdrawn from the eye of sense altogether, His presence will henceforth be purely spiritual, but no sooner do they lose sight of Him in the body than the Comforter comes to their souls. So long as men walked by the guidance of one whom they saw by their side, they would not throw themselves on unseen spiritual aid. The Comforter would not come unless the Lord went away, but as soon as He was gone the comfort came.

I now come to the oral teaching. Here we note the same fitness of the means to the end, but the purpose in view is a more abstract one: a quality very essential for Christ's purpose is *expansiveness*. The truths which He revealed and the commandments He gave were to be accepted by different nations, and in various states of society: they belonged therefore to what is primary in the nature of man. It is in this that Christ's doctrine differs from all systems. It does not belong to one age or one nationality but to all. Whether this character of Universality was due to prospective wisdom or to chance, I do not now discuss; I only say that the substance of Christ's teaching is suitable for men in different conditions; that the form in which it is put makes this teaching easy for the ignorant to retain; and that the circumstances which accompanied it were singularly conducive to its spread. Christ arose amongst a nation which was the most strikingly individualised of all peoples, but He transmitted the type of Humanity in its most general form. We mark in Him no trace of one race or of one epoch; He was emphatically the Son of Man.

In all His sayings and doings, our Lord was most careful to leave the individual room to grow. Some of the "negative characteristics" of our Lord's teaching arise out of this universality. If we go to Him looking for a Social system or an Ecclesiastical polity we find nothing of the sort. Humanitarian theorists have turned in disappointment from His word; but a system suited to our age must have been unsuited to Gospel times. Christ gave no system for recasting Society by positive Law, and no ecclesiastical Polity, for men could make laws better when the circumstances which called for them arose. He gave no system of philosophy, for such systems are only the ways of looking at some of the enigmas of life, which suit the cast of mind of the nation or the generation which shapes the system. So different nations and generations should be left to make their systems as of old, only a new truth was declared, and a new force was set to work, which systems would henceforth have to take into account.

Again, the next world is what all want to know about. If the founder of a religion would win men's ears, he must set this before them. But, as we cannot conceive a life under conditions wholly different from that we lead, any description must be misleading. False notions besides engendering devotees and fanatics, would sap human activity and arrest progress. Hence Christ speaks to the fact of a future existence, but says nothing of the mode. He assures us that eternal life awaits those accounted worthy, but of the nature of this life He says nothing. He gives no details on which imagination can dwell.

Farther, Christ leaves no ritual. For a ritual belongs to those outward things which must change; it would in time symbolize a view no longer taken, and if some should still cling to it from the idea that it had a magic worth of its own, then it would stand in the way of the truth it was meant to set forth.

Laws, Systems, and Ritual, then, were raiment to be changed as times went on; with them therefore succeeding generations were left to deal. The form must come of man, so to man the shaping of it is left. But Christ gave what was more than raiment and more than form. "The words that I have spoken unto you," said He, "are Spirit and are life." He gave *seed thoughts* which should lie in men's hearts, and germinate when fit occasion came.

These thoughts were clothed in terse sayings, such as a man would carry in his head and dwell on the more because he did not see to the bottom of them all at once. Moreover some of these sayings, for instance, " For whosoever hath, to him shall be given[1]," will startle the hearer as being contrary to what he would expect; and the more he is perplexed, the more he is provoked to think, and thereby a greater impression is made.

Other truths are wrapped up in parables. The form of the parable, not the matter it conveys, concerns me now. It is a form of speech which imbeds itself deeply in the memories of men and was admirably suited to preserve a genuine record during the time when the Gospel should subsist as an oral tradition. It put what was most important into the shape which made it most easy to recollect,

[1] Matth. xiii. 12.

Nothing except proverbs takes hold of men's memories so firmly as tales. The most ancient literary possessions of the world are, probably, certain stories containing a moral. Of course our Lord's teaching in parables answered greater ends than this of making His lessons easy to retain: but this form of teaching agreed wonderfully well with what the circumstances required. Next to tales in respect of being easily remembered, come narratives of detached striking acts. So the materials of the Gospel History, sayings, parables, narratives of signs and wonders, are cast into the forms best calculated for safe transmission through a period of tradition.

We find the same suitableness of the form to the needs of the case, in the shape in which the whole Gospel has been delivered to us. I refer to its being narrative instead of didactic, and coming from the Evangelists instead of from Christ. If our Lord had left writings of His own, every letter of them would have been invested with such sanctity that there could have been no independent investigation of truth. Its place would have been taken by commentatorial works on the delivered word. When writings are set before us and we are told, "All truth lies there; look no further;" then our ingenuity is directed to extract diversities of meanings from the given words; for matter must be set forth in human speech, and human speech conveys different meanings to differently biased minds.

The Jews regarded their sacred books as the actual words of God; hence came that subserviency to the letter, and that stretching of formulae which brought them to play fast and loose with their consciences. The Scribes looked on their Law as a conveyancer on a deed: they were bound by the letter, and this led them to regard the Almighty as One dealing with men under the terms of a contract. This drew them out of the road which led to a true knowledge of God, and helped to make them "blind leaders of the blind." Our Lord breaks down this slavery to the letter of the Scripture which He found existing, and He is careful not to build up a new bondage to His own words.

When matter has come down by oral tradition, men can hardly worship the letter of it. We possess only brief memoirs collected by men, the dates and history of the composition of which are far from certain, so that room is left for criticism and judgment. The revelation of God is, therefore, not so direct that men will be awestricken and shut their minds at the sight of it; but human intelligence can be brought to bear on the records, whereby their meaning is brought out, and men's intellects are braced by the exploration of lofty regions. Men may without irreverence raise the question, whether the narrator had rightly understood Christ's sayings, and properly connected them with the circumstances out of which they arose.

Our Lord, in Galilee at any rate, spoke Aramaic,

and we have merely the Greek; we have only fragments of His teaching; we possess different versions, agreeing indeed in essentials, but with such differences, that we are forced to admit in the writers a human possibility of error. We have our Lord's words it is true, but not in the order, or in the connection, in which they were spoken. There is not only room for human judgment but a necessity for it. Hence the form in which our Lord's utterances have come down to us is suited to the plan which seems to run through all our Lord's teaching; it calls for the free play of the human mind, and leaves room for the admission of a certain choice as to what we accept as revealed truth.

It is true that some Divines have endeavoured to do what our Lord was careful not to do—they have, by theories of verbal inspiration, endeavoured to put our Gospels in the position that actual writings of our Lord would have held; and, so far as they have succeeded, they have brought about the evils which attended the notions of the scribes. But the form in which we have the Gospels does not lend itself to such a theory. If men go wrong in this way they have only themselves to blame.

There is another way in which this form of the Gospels answers to the plan of Christ's teaching. He impressed men, above all, by His Personality, and the record of His life is preserved to us in that form which is best adapted to preserve personality and store it up for the future, viz. the form of memoirs put together by contemporaries, or by those who were familiar with contemporaries.

History and literature furnish many instances of men who have made their mark in virtue of a striking *personality;* whose reputation rests, not on any visible tokens,—not on kingdoms conquered, institutions founded, books written, or inventions perfected or anything else that they *did*,—but mainly on what they *were.* Their merely having passed along a course on earth, and lived and talked and acted with others, has left lasting effects on mankind.

This may serve to put us in the way of understanding what was wrought by the Personality of Christ: for our Lord's disciples followed Jesus of Nazareth for this above all,—that he *was* Jesus of Nazareth. Those of His own time had felt this Personality working on them while they saw Him and listened to Him. It is consistent, then, with what we gather of His prospective care, that He should so provide, that after generations should have as nearly as possible, the same advantages as that with which He lived upon the earth. This is effected by His being presented to them in the Gospels, not as a writer is in his works, not as a lawgiver is in his codes, but as the man Christ Jesus, mixing with men, sharing their feasts, helping their troubles, going journeys with them, and in all these occasions turning their thoughts, gently, with a touch that is scarcely observed, towards that knowledge of God which He came to bring.

Which is it that sways us most? Is it the teacher who tells us,—This is the way you are to think, this is what you are to believe and what you are to do? Or is it the friend who blends his life and heart and mind with ours, with whom we argue and differ, but take something each from the other, which assimilates with what is most our own? Surely we yield more freely to the one who helps to foster our particular personality than to him who would thrust it aside, and replace it by his own.

Now Christ, as portrayed in the Gospels, is such a friend. He trusts to men's believing that the Father is in Him, not because He has declared it in set dogmas, but because He has been "so long with them." He is a friend who lifts us out of our common selves, and helps each one of us to find his own truest self: we catch fire from the new light which he kindles in us, and we become conscious of a new force, a spiritual one. When the narrative brings us to the sacrifice on the Cross, we see what the spectators saw, and something more, for we see this new inward force transcending all outward violence. When we turn to the Sufferer on the Cross, we say "after all, the Victory is there."

But not only is our Lord's Personality presented to us in the literary form in which it can best be put forth, that of the informal memoir, but we are given *four* such memoirs, each regarding its subject from a different point. We have then four different projections of what we want to construct. The help of this is obvious; and it is worth mentioning that hereby there is more scope for man's mental action than if we had only one Gospel. By diligently comparing and fitting in each with the other, we cultivate our mind's eye to catch the lineaments of Christ's figure. A painter, who has to produce a portrait from four photographs, has a less simple task than if only a single photograph existed; but his work will be more intellectual; it will do him more good, and the result will be more of a conception and less of a copy.

I believe that the education of man to a knowledge of God is part of the Divine purpose running through God's ways, and I detect in the narrative form in which our knowledge of Christ has been delivered to us, a wise tenderness for the spiritual freedom of man and a help to keep his faculties alive.

I spoke just now of Laws of Christ's conduct. The more we look at Christ's life and teaching as a whole, the more we discern in it the observance of certain Laws, which give it unity and order. When we stand near some large painting, or masterpiece of Art, we are taken up with the portion of it just under our eye; we scan this or that group and admire its finish and its truth.

INTRODUCTORY CHAPTER. 19

But when we go a little way off, and again look, and give our minds to it, we become aware of a different order of perfections in it, namely those perfections which belong to it as a whole, as the completed conception of a gifted mind.

So it is with the Gospel History. While we read chapter by chapter we see what answers to one group in the great picture; but when we have the whole in our mind, we see a consistent purpose holding it all together: we find that our Lord always acts along certain lines, and carries out certain principles. One of these, which lies at the root of His ways of dealing with men, is His carefulness to keep alive in each man the sense of his personal responsibility, and of the dignity of such responsibility. He would seem to say to each man, "It is no small thing to have been entrusted by God with the care of a soul which you may educate for fitness for eternal life." We find in our Lord, indignation, once, at least, even anger[1], towards men and their ways, but never contempt or scorn. A man is, merely as a man, entitled to be treated with respect. The enforcing of this on the world is, among all the "Gesta Christi," perhaps the most noticeable now.

The simple fact of His dealing directly with men *themselves*, shews that He owned their free agency more or less. If men had been merely puppets moved by strings, Christ could only have

[1] Mark iii. 5.

benefited them by swaying the powers who held these strings, and there would have been no meaning in His addressing Himself to the puppets themselves and giving His life for them. Now, if men are free they must be at liberty to go in a direction different from that which is best for them —that is to go wrong; and so it must needs be that "occasions of stumbling" come, and cause suffering. I mention these principles now, because they are the bases of the Laws of which I am going to speak. They will come before us again further on.

The marking of uniformities in Christ's conduct, and in His modes of conveying instruction, is serviceable in this way. We perceive the Laws (defined as in p. 2) by regarding Christ's career as a whole; and in return, the Laws, when perceived, help us to grasp its unity and completeness in a more thorough way; and, besides this, we strengthen our critical faculty, and arm it with a new criterion which may become an effective weapon in arguing on questions of internal evidence. For if we find in any newly-discovered fragment, or even in the Gospels themselves, that which runs counter to what we think we have established as a Law, then we have to ask ourselves whether it is likely that the passage is spurious or imperfect or put out of its right place; or, on the other hand, whether our Law has been framed too narrowly, and ought to be restated or enlarged.

Again, when we find a Law constantly observed, and are sure that the narrative cannot have been written up to the Law, because the narrators knew nothing of such a Law; then we come on a new variety of internal evidence. 'If, in matters which only a student would observe, our Lord is found to adhere to certain ways, this favours the view that the materials for the portrait came from life; for an artist drawing from description or following an idea of his own must have missed these delicate details now and then. This consistency uniformly observed forms a sort of undesigned coincidence ramifying through the mass, and holding it all together. The notion of Laws underlying our Lord's action, and shewing their traces on the surface from time to time, will be best illustrated by an example. I shall take the rules which our Lord observes in the working of Signs and Wonders; and so I must here anticipate something of that, which I shall make the subject of a whole chapter further on.

Our Lord is set apart from all other teachers by His use of Signs and Wonders. We shall enquire, how He regarded them? What use He designed to make of them? And, what more especially concerns us now, what Laws He observes when He employs them? These Laws we shall find—wrapped up as it were—in our Lord's answers to the Tempter in the wilderness. The narrative of the Temptation, which seems, at first sight, to be a fragment unconnected with the course of the action of the Gospel History, becomes, when the Laws are noted, the key to the interpretation of much. Isolated phenomena fall into system. I will relate the Temptations in the order given by St Luke, and briefly state the Laws indicated in the Tempter's suggestions together with our Lord's replies.

I. Christ will not turn stones into loaves to appease His hunger in the wilderness. This refusal contains two principles to which our Lord will be found to adhere.

(1) He will not use His special powers to provide for His personal wants or for those of His immediate followers.

When our Lord provided food for the five thousand, the loaves and fishes the Apostles had with them were enough for their own party[1].

(2) Christ will not provide by miracle what could be provided by human endeavour or human foresight.

Our Lord will not even make men better by action on them from without; He will not change their being by any spiritual action without their cooperation. When the Apostles said "Increase our Faith," He worked no sudden change in them, but He pointed out to them the efficacy of Faith, in order that by longing for it, they might attain to it.

II. Christ will not purchase the visible "kingdoms of the world and the glory of them" by

[1] St Matth. xiv. 17.

worshipping Satan—that is to say, He will not do homage to the Spirit of the world to win the world's support. He will not ally Himself with worldly policy. He will not fight the world with its own weapons, and become its master by giving in to its views and its ways. In addressing the people He runs counter to the notions they cherished the most. He would not proclaim Himself as the Messiah, or allow Himself to be made a King though thousands, who were looking for a national deliverer, would have rallied round Him if He had done so[1]. He would not conciliate the favour of the great. He would not display His powers, for a matter of wonderment, to satisfy the curiosity of Herod, nor would He use them to repel violence by open force. He would not hearken to the temptation which said, "Use your miraculous powers to establish a visible kingdom upon earth; and when this is done you can frame a perfect form of society by positive Law."

III. Christ will not throw Himself from the pinnacle of the Temple. The Temptation must have been to do this in the sight of the people. Else, why is this pinnacle chosen rather than any other height? The refusal points to the following important Laws.

(1) No miracle is to be worked merely for miracles' sake, apart from an end of benevolence or instruction.

What appear to be exceptions to this rule cease to be so when fully considered.

The walking on the waters, as we shall see further on, was a step in training the Apostles to realize His nearness to them, when He was not before their eyes. The withering of the fig-tree, which had leaves before its time, but no fruit, was an acted parable bearing on the Jewish people. These are miracles of instruction. We shall find others of the same kind.

(2) No miracle is to be worked which should be so overwhelming in point of awfulness, as to terrify men into acceptance, or which should be unanswerably certain, leaving no loop-hole for unbelief.

As, in the second Temptation, our Lord refused to allow physical force to be used to bring men to adopt His cause, so here *He refuses to employ moral compulsion.* The miracles only convinced the willing, men might always disbelieve if they would. They might allow the fact of the prodigies, and yet set them down to magic or witchcraft: it was with many an open question whether to ascribe them to God or to Beelzebub, for the latter had, it was supposed, a share of power upon the earth. But one popular criterion there was of the power being God's: in heaven, said the Jews, God reigned supreme and alone. A Sign worked there would carry with it the autograph of God. When Joshua would convince their fathers, he had wrought a Sign in heaven; he had made the sun and moon stand still. Let Christ do this and they would believe. No such Sign will Christ work. If the world was to be converted *nolens volens* it might as well have been peopled from the first by beings incapable of error.

If the end of His coming had been to gain adherents, His purpose would have been furthered by granting a Sign which would have struck the imagination of the masses; but to raise a large immediate following was *not* our Lord's design. He wanted only a few fit spirits as depositaries of His word.

He came to educate men to know God. In this knowledge lay the assurance of immortality. The knowledge reached through this education could not be imparted by any mere telling or express communication, but had to be unfolded from within the learner's self. Belief was to grow and not to be imposed. It had two elements, a perception of a Divine agency at work in the world, and a personal trust in Christ who manifested God, —a trust based on something like the devotion of a soldier to his chief. That the probability that His mission did really come from God, should be made to exceed by a little the probability that it did not, and that this balance of arguments should lead people to acknowledge Him, was not what Christ had in view. He sought only the homage of free, loving, human hearts.

The Laws above mentioned will be found to

regulate the course of our Lord's actions as regards the performance of Signs and Wonders. They are frequently violated in the Apocryphal Gospels, never, I think, in the Canonical ones. There are other Laws which I shall have to trace; one, which is very important, is stated on at least two occasions; I have referred to it as being paradoxical in form, and the more fitted to force itself on men's minds on that account. It is the text, "For whosoever hath to him shall be given, but whosoever hath not from him shall be taken away even that which he hath." This looks as if it would fall in strangely with the Law of Natural Selection and the Survival of the Fittest, in the organic world. What I believe our Lord to have meant by it will be discussed in its proper place.

I shall have also to speak of the *prospective* bearing of much that our Lord says and does, and to shew how this gives us a greater assurance of our Lord's being "with us always to the end of the world." Christ seems to me to look over the heads of the generation about Him far into the future; His eye is fixed on the distance, but it does not look out vaguely into space; it is turned in a direction that is precisely determined. He walks with the assured step of one who marches to a goal. But what that goal is He never tells men, and when He designedly keeps men's curiosity unsatisfied, we may conjecture that no answer could be given without touching on conditions of spiritual existence beyond our ken. There may be such conditions which we could no more conceive than we could imagine space with another dimension, beside length and breadth and height.

The history of the Church and of the workings of men's minds may disclose the existence of Laws, lying under the events of ages and operating through them, analogous to those laid down by our Lord for his own conduct; and we may look along the direction in which these Laws point. Some have thought they descried, at the end, a time, in which peace and righteousness should reign over the whole world. But Christ Himself doubted whether He should find faith upon the earth when He came[1]. However, if He should not, still He will not have failed, we can be sure of this. What He meant to effect, whatever it was, will have come about. Righteous souls may be garnered elsewhere, and this earth may be only a school of life, a training ground for the education and selection (for these two go together) of beings who shall be fitted to enter into the Kingdom of Heaven.

[1] Luke xviii. 8.

CHAPTER II.

HUMAN FREEDOM.

I HAVE spoken in the foregoing chapter of certain characteristics of our Lord's ways of dealing with men. In considering these ways we find ourselves, at almost every turn, face to face with the great enigmas of life which underlie all Theology. Questions about Divine government and human freedom will, I see, force themselves upon us.

It would keep this book more close to its purpose, if I could proceed at once with the examination of what our Lord says and does, and leave all these difficulties on one side, taking it for granted that all my readers had arrived at their own views about them; or if I were to refer them to works in which they are formally discussed.

But I trust my readers will forgive me, if I suppose that it may be with them as with those I have been used to teach—that is to say, that they will be attracted by these perplexities, and that they will be impatient at being told that just what they want to ask lies outside my province. Many too, I know, would never turn to any of the learned works on these matters, of which I might give them the names.

I have resolved, therefore, to deal with these matters once for all, in as familiar a way as I can. I cannot, of course, give my readers solutions of these questions; I can only tell them how I manage to do without a solution myself, and put before them the view of these matters which I hold till I can get a better, so that they may more readily enter into my views of Christ's Laws of action, and understand what I write.

The characteristics of our Lord's ways which particularly bring us in contact with these mysteries, and which therefore concern us most now, are (1) His care to keep alive in His hearers their sense of being free and responsible agents; (2) His tolerance of the existence of evil in the world.

These questions of free will and the existence of evil have been for ages the battle-ground of divines, and they come before us every day. "Why did not God make every one good?" is a question which occurs to every intelligent child. He runs to his first teachers with it, and finding himself put off with an answer that is no answer—for a child is quick in detecting this—he gets his first notion that there are matters which even grown-up people know nothing about.

So, that I may not serve my readers in this way, I give them all I have myself. I can no more tell them "How" or "Why" God brought about the present state of things, than I can solve the great mystery which is at the bottom of all mysteries: "How, or Why, God and the world ever existed at all?" But I think I can shew that free agency in men, and the existence of evil, and also a reserve in the revelation of God's ways—a question I shall have to deal with next—are consistent with our situation in this world; supposing that the mental and spiritual development of God's creatures is the proximate end and aim of the Spiritual Order. Some hypothesis we must make as to a purpose in the world, if we regard it as the work of a *mind;* and this is the purpose which most seems to fall in with what I observe.

Our Lord speaks of Divine action as "The mystery of the kingdom of God[1]." He directs the thoughts of His disciples to these ways by telling them, not what they are, but to what they are *like*. We shall never, while on earth, perfectly know these ways, but Christ thinks it well for His disciples to strive after this knowledge, and to look for lessons in all they see to help them towards it.

Not only does Christ give us what I have called *seed-thoughts* on these matters, but He puts us in possession of a unique method for leading men towards the truth about them. He takes an incident of familiar life, and uses it to set forth spiritual verities. So when we must discourse of these hard matters our safest course is to follow

[1] Mark iv. 11.

our Lord's way. No doubt, He meant to shew us *how* to teach, as well as to tell us *what* to teach; so if we begin with a sort of allegory or parable, we cannot be far wrong in point of *form*, however feeble and faulty the execution may be. I believe that the relation of a parent to his household affords likeness enough to that of the Father to His world, to be used as the ground of a parable on God's Will and Human Freedom.

Let us suppose that the father of a family, a man of strong will, and steadfastly abhorring evil, should conceive the project of forcibly shutting it out from his home. We will suppose the household planted in a spot remote from human intercourse, in some self-supplying island or dale among the hills; and, as I do not mean to touch on physical evil, let us suppose that no external calamity comes nigh the dwelling. Here, let us suppose, the children grow up, uncontaminated by ill, knowing no temptation, reared in love and kindness, treated wisely and with such even justice that envy and jealousy find no room to enter.

The parent proposes to himself to do away with all temptation, all chance of individual aberration, and to cast his children's character in a perfect mould. He would have them merge themselves in him as much as possible, repeating his thoughts and accepting his views without questioning them, or supposing they could be questioned. All society, all books, but what he approves, are banished from that house, so that no whisper of evil, no pernicious notions can possibly intrude. Evil is by him regarded as a pestilent weed, which only exists, owing to some oversight in the making of the world, for which he is at a loss to account. It is at once to be eradicated whenever it is espied.

Let us suppose that all goes well in our imagined household—that the children love their father and believe implicitly in him; that they are so happy in their home and home pursuits that they do not look beyond; and that the healthy labour, which their common wants necessitate, gives room for all their energies. Hence, there is no repining at their narrow sphere, no longing for more strenuous activity or more varied life. Each does his daily work, and returns to pleasant rest and a happy home, and no more asks himself whether he is happy than he asks whether the valves of his heart are opening and closing as they should. The father, then, looks around him, and sees his ideal accomplished. He has a family of which no member does anything but what he approves, or has a thought but what he shares with him: not one of them sets up an opinion different from what he holds. It never occurs to them to doubt the wisdom of any injunction. Life presents to them no moral difficulties, because, as soon as any question occurs to them, they run with it to their father, and on receiving his reply put aside the matter, as being decided and disposed of for good and all.

We might suppose the parent would look around with unalloyed satisfaction. But a moment comes when he finds something wanting. He is not so thoroughly satisfied as he had expected to be with the ideal which he has worked out. Some misgiving obtrudes itself. He asks himself—Is this condition, this merging of my children's wills in mine, what is best for them or what is best for me? Is not this goodness of theirs too negative? Is it not rather the absence of evil than the presence of good?

Further he asks, am not *I* substantially *alone*? Is not mine the only independent mind in the place, of which all the rest are mere reflections? Am I not intensifying my loneliness and all the moral disadvantages that attach to it, by thus rendering all who surround me merely portions of myself? For my children are not separate persons, but bits of *me*. Are not whole provinces of moral activity shut out from me, by the very fact of my having everything my own way? Are there not virtues which require opposition to call them out? Is it not good to have to ask ourselves whether we are dealing fairly with opponents? Is it not good to forgive wrongs? Is it not good to reach out a helping hand, and lift one who has stumbled, back into his self-respect? I engage in no struggles. In my world there are no misdoings to forgive and no misdoers to restore. Have I not closed against myself whole worlds of moral action and of moral life?

Then, as to my children, "Have I not been wrong in supposing that they must *be* good because they have never *done* wrong? They have been so kept from the suggestion of evil that they could hardly help going right. But could they resist temptation if it came? They have never been braced by a struggle with it, nor marked the ill fruits of evil. They take it on trust from me that evil brings sorrow; but it usually comes in disguise and declares itself harmless, and how should they recognise it if it came?" So, question after question suggests itself, all destructive of his satisfaction. "Can it be," he says at last, "that I have brought up these children so as to be fit for no world but that which I have carefully constructed for them? I used to delight in their goodness; but since I have suspected it to be mainly instinctive—an innocence that is the outcome of ignorance—my satisfaction in it is half gone.

At length, he is harassed with the idea that he may have given up his life to a mistake, that what he has done has cramped his own mental and moral expansion, and that the excellence of his blameless family is only fair-weather goodness after all. He casts about to think why it is that they have "neither savour nor salt," and concludes "What they want is *personality*—and how should they have got it, living in a household where I have taken care to be all in all?"

Then his thoughts run upon *evil*, which he has been at such pains to shut out, closing against it every cranny and chink. "God," he may say, "has let evil into His world—was I right in keeping it forcibly out of mine? May not the resisting and assuaging of evil give occasion for good to grow up, and feel its own strength? Are there not many kinds of goodness, brought out in this way, which we could no more have without evil than we could have light in a picture without shade? If there is no room for my children to go wrong, what moral significance," he asks, "is there in saying that they go right?"

So he is disheartened with his project, and gives it up. He abandons his isolated way of life, and gives his children freedom. He encourages them to act and judge for themselves. Henceforth they can choose their own books, their own friends their own pursuits, and go forth into life, outside their charmed circle.

Of course this involves the giving up of his absolute power; this is inherent in the nature of things. A man cannot be an autocrat and have free people about him. If he would have intercourse with free intelligences, in order to get the advantages to his own cultivation and expansion of character which spring from such intercourse; this must be purchased by abdicating some of his powers, or putting them in abeyance. So the parent forbears using his power, in order that his children may learn to be free, and that he may hold communion with free, loving hearts, and engage in discussion with unfettered minds.

Soon, he finds that he has to encounter opposition. The children are free to go wrong, and wrong some of them will go: evil appears in that household where it was not known. The father sorrows over this, but when he reviews his condition he finds that he has a countervailing comfort; the good that is left about him is now real good. It is the good of persons who have known and resisted evil. Besides this, there is more life and greater vigour of character in his family, than there was before. They no longer sit with folded hands always waiting for direction; they have the air of persons who see a purpose before them; and they move along their way "with the certain step of man." So he concludes that it is better that all should engage in the struggle with evil, even though some should fail, than that they should move along paths ready shaped out for them, shewing a merely mechanical goodness.

A great change has come over his life in another respect, he is now no longer *alone*. Other wills come into contact, sometimes into collision, with his will; a host of qualities, which had been folded up and laid by for years, come again into use. He is no longer among echoes of himself, but there are real voices in his new world. His views may still prevail, but it must be, not merely because they are *his*, but because they stand on solid ground. He may still lead in action; but it must be because he has the leader's strength, because he will venture when others waver, and decide when others doubt.

Here we must leave him, and say a word or two before making the obvious application of the parable. We must not press the application too closely or draw conclusions from the mere machinery of the parable: it must not, of course, be supposed that I conceive God to have dealt with man as the father does with his children; that is to say, to have kept him at first in tutelage, and then found it desirable to enfranchise him. The sole object of the story is to familiarise the reader with the need of freedom in moral growth. It shews that for education to be carried out, the *will* must be free to act. When we have brought this home to his mind, we shall be the better able "to justify the ways of God to man" in some important particulars.

The parable is designed to apply to the condition of men on earth on the supposition, that their education—in the largest sense of the word—is the main work held in view: all depends on the hypothesis that man is placed on earth to develop his powers. The need of freedom for members of the imagined family depends on their being in a state of growth. The parable would not apply to spiritual beings, if we could conceive such, whose qualities and character were unalterable. *Perfected* beings have done with growth and struggle, and have attained to the highest condition, viz. existence in unison with God. But for *imperfect* beings, struggling on to their goal, freedom is required and the opposition of evil is indispensable, in order that the moral thews and sinews may harden.

Whenever we come upon an objection to the ways of God's ordering of the world, which is put in the form of a question, such as "Why was not the world made in this way or that?" we shall find it a good plan, to follow out the line indicated in the complaint, and see what would have come about, supposing that God *had* made the world in the way which is suggested.

From the imaginary case here put, we see to what the common child's question leads us—the question "Why did not God make all people good and keep them so?"—If people had been "made good and kept good," that is to say if they had been constructed by God so as always to act as His will prompted, then they would not in the proper sense of the word have been people at all; they would have been mechanisms worked by God, and so they could not have been "good" in the sense in which we use the word of a man, but only in that in which we apply it to a watch. There could be no moral life without freedom; there could be no growth of character without temptations and difficulties to overcome; no heroism, no self-denial, no sympathising tenderness, no forgiving love, without suffering or wrongdoing to call them forth.

Moreover if not only people on earth, but all created intelligences had, in like manner, been constrained to respond to every motion of the Divine will, God would have been the one spiritual being in the world and would therefore have been absolutely *alone*.

Let us now suppose, and the supposition falls in with what our conscience and the Bible tell us, that in God all goodness dwells. This goodness cannot lie stored away as in a treasure-house, so as to be merely an object of contemplation, it must be active and in operation. This is essential to our idea of goodness, and it agrees with the view of God which Christ presents to us, which is that of a being ever *operating*. "My Father worketh hitherto," says our Lord, "and I work." For good to unfold, and advance toward perfection in its manifold ways, an arena is wanted. The world we know of affords the arena required; in this, God has been working from the first. One kind of His work we can conceive to be the suggesting thoughts to men; but if it be so, He leaves the will free either to entertain or to reject the suggestions, as we might those of a friend.

That we may not lose ourselves in the immensity of God and eternity, we will withdraw our gaze from the rest of the Universe, and fix it on this planet of ours, when organic life first began to appear upon it. The spiritual and material world might, before this, have been going on, each apart, through countless ages; but a moment came when the spiritual and the material were wondrously blended, and life began upon the earth. Different orders of being succeeded each other, and fresh forces came into play. We may suppose that God sympathised with all His creation, and that the qualities that appeared in it reflected something in Himself. God may have rejoiced in seeing the animal creation happy. The animals were in a degree free, but they were not self-conscious; they did not know that they were happy, or that they were loved, and God may have required for the full unfolding of His infinite capacity for sympathy and love, to be in relation with beings who could know Him and love Him, and know that they loved Him.

Mr Erskine of Linlathen, in his excellent book on the Spiritual Order, says " Is there not a comfort in the doctrine of the eternal Sonship, as a deliverance from the thought of a God, whose very nature is Love, dwelling in absolute solitude from all eternity without an object of love?" We may extend this observation to other qualities besides love, from the exercise of which, a being who is alone in the world is necessarily debarred. Is it not likely that a God of mercy, truth and justice would frame a world of beings, in His dealing with whom all these qualities should find scope and exercise? Without self-conscious beings having free wills, how could this be done?

Close by the side of this question of free will, lies that of the existence of moral evil, in a world made by a being who, by the hypothesis, is perfectly good. When we supposed the world to be formed for the evolution of moral goodness, we, perhaps without knowing it, introduced the idea of moral evil, implied in that of goodness; for actual good is evolved in resisting evil and repairing the mischief it has done; indeed many forms of it can no more exist without evil as an antagonist, than a wheel can turn without the friction of the road.

Now, as I have said, if men be left free, they must have liberty to go wrong. For if they had been originally made so perfect that they *could* not go wrong, this would only mean that they were like watches very excellently fabricated; they could only move in one particular way, viz. the way in which they had been designed to move by God. Inasmuch as such beings would not be persons, we could not feel gratitude or anger towards them, nor influence them in any way. If men were like this, there could be little or no growth, little or no action of man on man. If, to take another supposition, man had been so made that it would be possible for him to go wrong, but that he had been sedulously kept out of temptation and placed in an abode where innocence reigned undisturbed; then we come to a case very like that sketched in the foregoing parable.

There is a third case possible. God might make men capable of going wrong, but might watch over them and protect them, whether they craved His help or not, whenever temptation approached. This constant supernatural interference would soon have destroyed all self-helpfulness; men would never have formed habits of avoiding or resisting temptation. "God," the man would say, "will not let me sin—I may go as near to danger as I like, and need take no care of myself, because I am sure of God's protection." We know that a child does not learn to take care of himself, so long as he feels that it is the nurse's business to see that no harm happens to him. We come then to this result. God requires free self-conscious beings, for the full exercise of the moral goodness in Himself and for its development and manifestation in the world.

But He cannot give others freedom, and at the same time provide that they should act only in the way that He approves: because this in itself would be a contradiction, and a contradiction not even Divine power can effect. Hence these free, intelligent beings must be at liberty to go wrong, and God must, in exchange for having free wills about him, forego part of His absolute prerogative:

and so He must allow evil a place in the world because this is involved in the "liberty to go wrong" just spoken of.

This brings us to the mystery of the "origin of evil." I shall not lay myself open to the charge made against divines, "That they no sooner declare a subject to be a mystery than they set to work to explain it." I can see that if man is to be left free, evil must needs come, and that without evil in the world none of the more masculine virtues can be brought to the birth—that is to say, I see that evil, being in the world, serves to discharge a function—but I do not pretend to say how it came. I do not maintain that it came, solely, from man's misuse of his freedom.

From what we see in the world arises a fancy that every thing must have its opposite, that light presupposes darkness, and pleasure pain, and so good may presuppose evil; but this fancy is not substantial enough to build upon. Our Lord's words on the occasions when He deals with evil, are, to my judgment, most easily reconciled with one another, and with the circumstances which call them forth, by supposing Him to recognise a personal spiritual influence, presenting evil thoughts to the minds of men; the man remaining free to choose whether he will entertain these suggestions or not.

I return to my immediate subject—the function that evil performs in the existing moral world. We read in the Book of Genesis that the earth was to bring forth "thorns and thistles," and that man was "to eat bread in the sweat of his brow[1]." This is the result of a change worked, we are told, "for man's sake." It was indeed for man's *sake*—though in a different sense—that this was so. He would have remained a very poor creature if the earth had produced just what he wanted, without any labour of his. This illustrates the function of evil in the ordering of the world. Man's qualities, moral and physical, are developed by it. It subserves the progress of the human race.

We should have less heroism, without cruelty and oppression from without; and could have no self-restraint, without temptation from within. Piety and love indeed. when they had once come into being, might exist without evil; we may believe that they satisfy the souls of the saints in heaven; but among men they commonly owe their birth to a feeling of shelter against evil, and to a sense of pardoned wrong.

Another office which evil performs is this. The contention with it helps to bring out the difference between man and man. If any members of the family of my parable had possessed the germs of a strong character, they could hardly have brought fruit to perfection: the conditions of their innocent life tended to uniformity. But as soon as temptations came, latent differences would forthwith

[1] Gen. iii. 18, 19.

appear; the strong would grow stronger and the bad worse. Now there is need of strong men for human progress. They form the steps in the stairway by which the race mounts. If life were smooth and easy, men would, as it were, advance in line, and the stronger men would not so surely come in front of the rest. It is in times of trouble that men are most apt to recognise worth and capacity, and make much of them. So that the trials and difficulties of human life which come of evil, have this good effect among others, they help to pick out the men who are fitted to be the leaders of human movements and of human thought.

It may have struck us as strange that Christ does not deal directly with these perplexing questions which trouble so many minds. We shall see, later on, that His not doing so is quite consistent with the uniform "tenour of His way." But though our Lord does not lay down dogmas on these points, yet His own actions and expressions would, of course, accord with what He knew: if, then, when we hit upon some view of this "riddle of the painful earth," which commends itself to our minds, we find that it clashes with what our Lord does or says, then we may throw it aside at once: and, on the other hand, if we arrive at a way of looking at the matter which seems to harmonise with what falls from Him; then, we may hope, not indeed that we have found a solution of the riddle, but that our hypothesis will not mislead us, so long as we own it to be an hypothesis, and nothing more.

We may be supposed then to have arrived at this position. We assume the existence of a mighty Divine being, in whom all goodness dwells. We suppose that this world is an arena in which a struggle is to be carried on between good and evil by the agency of free intelligent beings; that by means of this struggle the better natures will be strengthened and developed, and come more and more into action; we suppose also that God whispers counsel and comfort on the side of good. Further than this we need not now go.

As regards the presence of evil in the world, there are several sayings of our Lord which might be noted. I must confine myself to one or two of the most important.

First let us consider the following passage from St John's Gospel[1]:

"And as he passed by, he saw a man blind from his birth. And his disciples asked him, saying, Rabbi, who did sin, this man, or his parents, that he should be born blind? Jesus answered, Neither did this man sin, nor his parents: but that the works of God should be made manifest in him."

Here the disciples take it for granted, that the blindness was a punishment for sin, either on the part of the man or his parents. It is our Lord's prac-

[1] John ix. 1--3.

tice—and a practice so uniform that we may call it a Law of proceeding—not to enter into controversy about wide-spread mistaken views on merely *speculative* subjects: He usually gives a hint, and leaves it to work in the hearer's mind.

Our Lord's answer in this case means, *not*, of course, that the man and his parents had never committed sin, but that the blindness was not the result of that sin; and He passes rapidly on to state His view of one purpose answered by this infliction.

In His few words of answer our Lord lets fall one of those hints, *seed thoughts*, as I have called them, which lie so thickly in the Gospels.

Our Lord tells us, that the works of God were to be made manifest by this man's infirmity. A light is thrown by these words on one of the "uses of adversity." Suffering gives room for moral goodness to come into play. The world is full of instances easy enough to note. Does not a sick child in a family educate all around it to tenderness and self-denial? What more touching lesson in patience can be given than the sight of the little sufferer, grieved at nothing so much as the trouble it causes, making the most of every alleviation, grateful beyond measure for every look or word of love. Rough brothers learn forbearance and gentleness; and to all the household it becomes natural to think of something else before, or at least beside, themselves. Wordsworth tells us of a half-witted boy whose helplessness and simplicity fostered a spirit of kindliness in all the poor of the village, and taught them to respect affliction.

Again in the parable of the Prodigal Son, we are taught how there is "a soul of goodness in things evil." The wickedness of the prodigal is made a means of revealing to him and to all the bystanders the Divine beauty and efficacy of forgiving love.

We will now[1] turn to the history of the cure of the Dæmoniac in the country of the Gadarenes. I take the history in what seems to me the plain literal sense, and I must suppose that our Lord recognised some real evil existence, which had possessed itself of the man, and which, by its presence in him, had unhinged his whole mental or nervous organisation. This existence is separable from him, but it requires, it would seem, some body to inhabit and to work upon. The dæmon begs not to be suppressed or annihilated, and our Lord grants his petition and lets him go among the swine. He saves the *man*—what other evils this dæmon may work in the world, so that he lets men go, is no concern of His. The Son of Man is concerned only with lives and souls—not with property in any way.

The point for us to note is this: Our Lord does not *annihilate* evil. He does not regard it as an outlawed intruder who had eluded God's notice,

[1] St Luke viii. 26; St Mark v. 1.

and who, as soon as he is discovered, is to be expelled from the universe at once. His Father has suffered evil to be, and He, Christ, follows in His Father's ways: evil may still do its work, only not on men. This evil influence, we must observe, is something external to the man; it would seem to belong to an order of existences, engaged in working ill as their congenial business; whispering bad counsel, something in the way that God's Spirit whispers good, only, of course, not in such deep authoritative tones; and, in these cases of possession, it masters the whole being of the sufferer. *Why* this was allowed to be, is of course a mystery, but yet it is hardly a greater mystery than why evil in its other forms should be allowed to exist, and without evil in some shape, as we have seen, this earth would be a very imperfect exercise-ground for mankind.

To represent this case to our minds, let us imagine some malignant "germ" that has caused a plague amongst men, and which in time takes a slightly different form, so that it is no longer adapted to human beings, but finds its prey in cattle instead. Then the plague among men is exchanged for a murrain among cattle, which, as a matter of fact, has been known to happen: this answers to the allowing the dæmon to go to the swine. Evil is not forcibly exterminated, but it is transferred from man to the lower animals.

So our Lord is gentle even with the powers of

evil. They had their function, or they would not have been there, and they were not to be crushed out of existence before the time.

If it be, as I have argued, that evil had a function in the world, then we can see why it could not be removed by a *universal* decree. But a *single* act of relief might be admissible in order to testify to the presence of an exceptional power; this would not engender in people the habit of helplessly throwing themselves upon God. For instance, Christ cures the son of the centurion merely by speaking the word, but if He had abolished all fevers by one decree, this would have been to disorganise the existing order in the universe. A King going on a royal progress relieves the misery that comes in his way; his own kindliness, his royal dignity, and the need of impressing on the people that their King delights in doing good, and can do it, require him so to do. But a regal donation for the relief of all distress in the kingdom would turn it into a nation of paupers. So our Lord bestows His bounty on those who fall in His way.

He who asks, Why did not Christ suppress evil? may naturally ask also, Why did not Christ sweep away all human error as to the relations of God with man? And why did He not so vouch for the authenticity of His communication that any doubt about it should be impossible? Now we believe, that God has revealed Himself to man, and yet has left men in some degree free as to what they will think about Him, and as fully at liberty to examine the credentials of those who have claimed to be His messengers, and to judge of their authenticity, as they would be in a purely human matter.

We find, as a matter of fact, that men who have accepted Christ's revelation are not fettered in mind by it; but are most often enterprising, energetic and bold searchers after truth. I believe that it would have been unfavourable to the preservation of this vigour of mind and to the temper which should "try all things and hold fast those which are good," if the full and absolute revelation which some demand had been delivered to mankind, and all the problems which beset human life had thereby been settled once for all. To the questions "Why we are told what we are told?" "Why we are not told more?" and "Why doubt and ambiguities are not all cleared away?"—we cannot hope to give *answers*, but we may find ways of looking at them which shall help in some degree

"To justify the ways of God to man."

It will be best to discuss this subject in a separate Chapter.

CHAPTER III.

OF REVELATION.

IF I took the word Revelation in its widest sense I should not attempt to treat of it here, for it would comprise nothing less than God's education of the human race. We talk of Natural Religion and Revealed Religion, but all Religion has in it an element of revelation from God. If God had not provided man with a mind's eye suited to see Him by, and also something that shadowed Him forth which that eye could behold, we could have no religion at all. Of the processes by which belief has come about in men not the least notable is this. Men have recognised in some new tidings what they seemed to have been looking for, without being aware of it. Some new teacher has become the spokesman of thoughts which were lying in them in a state too vague for utterance. Thus "thoughts out of many hearts may be revealed[1]." Now it is God who has planted these thoughts in men, and He brings about the occasions which reveal them.

[1] Luke ii. 35.

There are for man two worlds, that which is without him and that which is within. Some races from temperament or circumstances have been most taken up with the former, with the workings of nature and with active social life; while others have looked within rather than without;—their minds have found most congenial play in the contemplation of their own natures, and in brooding over the mystery of how they came to be what they were. Corresponding to these two leading diversities of the human mind, there are two modes by which men are brought to recognise a great spiritual agency in the world.

The man of Aryan race, the type of the first variety, caught sight of an infinite force underlying all the workings of nature, and so conceived Deities, with a personal will like his own, animating the physical world. For the people of the Semitic race on the other hand, the surpassing wonder was their own selves—their minds turned to contemplating their own nature. In so doing they noted this; they found something within them which caused them to be happy when they acted in one way—when they had done a kindness for example —and made them unhappy when they had behaved differently. This was so, even when no one knew of the act, and when they looked to no consequences from it. They called such actions right and wrong; but they asked, Where can this notion of right and wrong come from? This conscience too which witnessed of it—which strove with them just as a friend might, and seemed to be something outside them—Where did that come from? They were led by this to conceive a spiritual personal Being in the world who had left some trace of himself in men's hearts, and kept up some communion with them through this voice of conscience. Thus men of different stamps of mind were led along different roads, to the notion of something Divine in the world; and we may say that God revealed himself to man in these two ways. Now for knowledge to be sure and solid two elements must go to the making of it. One from outside the learner, and the other supplied by him. This outside element is in physical science provided by observed fact, and what answers to it in theology is authoritative revelation. Men can never feel fully assured about what is wholly spun out of their own brains, and has no external sign or testimony to lend it support.

Revelation, in the sense in which I have to do with it just now, means an authoritative communication from the Almighty, vouched by some outward sign, or manifestation. It is with this outward sign, and with the difficulties attending the ways of bringing it about, that I am now chiefly concerned.

For the present we will suppose that among the elements of human knowledge are *truths revealed by God*. How is this element of absolutely certain knowledge to be made to fit in with that which is only matter of opinion or provisionally true? Here we come on the great problem of Revelation. How can the infinite be brought into the same account with the finite? We know that if we give one term in an algebraical expression an infinite value, all the rest go for nothing; so likewise do probable judgments vanish in the face of absolute authority. But if Revelation is delivered *in such a mode* that its declarations admit of no question whatever, then its statements possess *absolute certainty*. Compared with such certainty all our judgments would be doubtful and dim, like candles in the presence of electric light. Would not this sharp contrast discourage man from using his own powers? But is it not by regarding this world as an exercise ground for these same powers that we come most near to understanding it? Is it consistent with God's ways, such as we make them out to be, that after giving us faculties which would find their amplest field in the consideration of spiritual problems he should preclude the investigation of them by solving them all Himself.

Again the truth delivered in any Divine Revelation of the problems of the Universe would come into contact with views based on supposed facts drawn from History or Geology, or with truths discovered by the human mind, and difficulties would occur all along the line of demarcation between what was infallible and what was not. For instance, if the history of one nation were absolutely revealed, much of that of the nations contiguous would be revealed too; more particularly the results of the wars between them: and if isolated facts belonging to science, such as those relating to the formation of our globe, were communicated on Divine Authority, then systems of Natural Philosophy, starting from these facts as axioms, might claim, upon religious grounds, acceptance for every one of their conclusions. If an independent system essayed to rear its head, it would be crushed by coming into collision with some statement that brooked no question. Such scientific investigation as would be possible could only proceed by deduction from truths authoritatively delivered. Observation and induction, which have led up to the knowledge of nature we now possess, would find no place. Man would be discouraged from using his own endeavours to understand the problems of the universe, and instead of so doing, he would only pray the Almighty to tell him all he wanted to know.

These ill effects do not follow in the case of Christ's religion for two reasons. First, because Christ does not reveal what man could find out for himself; and therefore this revelation does not come, so to say, into competition with human investigations. Secondly, because the genuineness of the revelation is not vouched for by evidence which is *overwhelming* and which finally settles the question; but is only supported by just enough external testimony to command attentive consideration and respect. The evidence that the Sign is of God is not so cogent that there is no escape from it. If it were so, it would silence all discussion about the fact of Revelation having been given, in the way in question, and would narrow the area for the exercise of religious thought.

Reason may agree to bow to Revelation as being God's declaration; but she has a right to satisfy herself that it *is* God's declaration, and she will call in learning and rules of criticism to help her in determining the question. Even when Reason has satisfied herself as to the credentials of this Revelation, there comes another question which gives play for human intelligence. It is asked "What does this Revelation mean?" Language is the outcome of the human mind, and all statements made in language, this Revelation among the rest, must be subject to the laws of the human understanding.

We see then, that both as to its credentials and its meaning Revelation must always be open to question; and that a man is as much bound to exercise his judgment upon these points as upon the other problems of life. This would seem a very natural state of things, yet it causes dismay to some persons when they first begin to look into these matters for themselves. They had expected, moreover, to find such a balance of evidence on their own side, that no one except from wilfulness and perversity could decide the other way. Examination shews that, regarding the question as one of historical evidence, and putting all prepossessions apart, the two sides are more nearly in a state of equipoise than they had been supposed to be; and it is remarkable that this kind of equipoise has been maintained, as far as we can make out by history, from the time of the Apostles till now. Arguments and testimony have, from time to time, appeared on one side, and have been answered from the other; and now and then some discovery has been made turning the balance on this side or that; but soon some new idea has been started which has put another complexion on the matter. So that positive evidence has never been so complete and decisive on either side as to prevent a man's habits or the bent of his mind from swaying his verdict.

When young men first look into these matters for themselves, having heretofore taken certain notions on trust, they are apt to be aghast at the unsettlement, and at the call on them to use their own judgments and make up their minds. Unhappily they have often been led to suppose that to hold a particular set of opinions, *merely as opinions*, without any effect being produced in their character thereby, gives them a claim to some degree of favour in the eyes of the Almighty: while to question these opinions, or to enquire too closely into the grounds on which they rest, is dangerous, and calculated to bring them into disfavour with Him. I cannot stop to combat this notion now.

But whatever the reason may be, the fact is certain, that when persons begin to investigate for themselves the bases of their belief, they find that many statements which they had regarded as true beyond all question are found to stand on less sure ground than they had thought; and since they fancy that if the authority of any word of the Bible is shaken they will soon have no standing ground left, they become much disturbed.

Then it is that we hear the outcry: "Why cannot all be made clear? Or, if we cannot be told every thing, why, at any rate, is not that which we *are* told put so plainly, that there can only be one way of looking at it? Why were not things so written that one who runs may read? Why are we not given quite positive assurance of the truth of what is revealed? Why have we not a Sign in Heaven as the Jews demanded, or, what would suit our times better, an incontestable demonstration of the truth of Christianity?" "Why, in short," to use the words of the objectors of the last century, "If God desired to make a Revelation to man, did He not write it in the skies?"

To none of these "Whys" can we supply its proper "Because." We cannot give the reasons of a man's conduct unless we can enter into his mind; and as we cannot enter into God's mind, we cannot give His reasons for having made the ways of the universe such as we find them. But though we cannot give the enquirer what he asks, we can do something to help him all the same.

We may be able to shew him that it is better for him only "to know in part;" and we may also be able to explain to him that a certain fringe of shadow must needs encompass those portions of truth which are revealed; for if they had clear-cut edges and hard outlines, when we had to fit them together, like pieces in a dissected map of knowledge, we should meet with all those difficulties about a line of demarcation between truth absolute and beliefs of opinion of which I spoke just now. The service of all Revelation is to supply our craving after infinity; and if our demand to have this infinity presented to us in a finite form—for that is really what we are clamouring for—could be approximately gratified, then we should find that, though a certain portion of the infinite field lying outside human knowledge had been enclosed and added on to our intellectual possessions, still we were as far as ever from having what we wanted: this new possession would have become *finite*, and what we wanted was the *infinite*. We should have got a new science in exchange for our old religion, but the craving after infinitude would still remain. The very definiteness introduced into these matters we should find destructive of their fascination for us.

To take one point at a time, I will begin with a side of the question which fits on to the subject of the last chapter. These cries after certitude are, in fact, petitions to be relieved of free will and responsibility in deciding religious matters for ourselves. What the complaints come to is this: Why am not I and every one else compelled to believe certain truths about God's dealings with man *whether we like to do so or not?*

The point of the matter lies in these last words. If we had no part of our own to perform in accepting this belief, if it were no more a matter of our own choice and feeling whether or not we admitted the revealed truths, than whether we admitted some indisputable fact in history or some proposition in science; then this belief would not be religion for us at all, it would be a branch of science and nothing more. It would have no more moral significance than a proposition in Euclid. To admit that a certain system may be built up from premises that are undoubted, is merely a matter of intellect. One man may have a head to follow the steps and another not, but conscience has no part in the matter.

It was distinctive of the Son of Man that His Gospel was to be preached to the poor; and a system which addressed only minds capable of clear reasoning, could not be suited to all mankind; in fact, it would necessarily set up a Hierarchy of intellectual culture. So our Lord did not speak to the understandings but to the hearts of His hearers. He dealt with His disciples on the supposition, that there was in them a germ which would respond to the quickening influences of His teaching, and grow into a capacity for eternal life. Just as the dormant seed germinates when warmth and moisture reach it, so would what was dormant in their hearts burst into life and growth, when the required vivifying influence was brought to bear. Our spiritual life is made to depend not only on what is delivered to us, but on our recognising the truth we want, and seizing on it as what we are craving after: so that we say, "I have always felt that there was something I was in want of; now I know what it is, and I have it here."

The Jews, who would not believe, wanted to be shewn a Sign from Heaven. They said, "Give us a proof which is beyond contradiction, and we will believe," which comes to saying: If we cannot help believing, believe we will. But they did not mean the same thing by the word "believe" as our Lord did. Our Lord did not call on His disciples to accept notions *about* Him, but to believe *in* Him, to trust Him as a child does his parent, or a soldier his commander. What the Jews meant was that they would give credence to a particular kind of evidence, as to the fact of His being their Messiah.

The demand for additional proof is dealt with by our Lord in the parable of Dives and Lazarus. The drift of a parable is usually pointed out in the concluding words; and the verse "If they believe not Moses and the prophets, neither will they believe though one rose from the dead[1]," spoken of the rich man's brethren, is, I believe, the key to one intent of this parable[2]. The state of mind here pointed at is a common one enough. It is that of the man who is rather uneasy at his own want of belief; but thinks the blame should be laid, not on any defect in himself, but on the want of proper proofs and external light. He thinks that his difficulty comes from the scanty evidence offered him; he has no idea that what he really wants is a better moral eyesight to see it by. So he begs for a little bit more of proof. If he could only be satisfied, he says, on this point and that, he would believe. But what would his belief be worth? Our Lord's answer goes to this: —No amount of external testimony can supply what you want, because the defect is within you. If a man *did* come to you from the dead, you might be terrified into acquiescence in everything he told you—you would probably be stupefied into the most abject submission—but instead of being elevated into trust in God, you would, very likely, be so cowed and paralysed, as to be incapable of any feeling of a noble or spiritual kind.

In the present day people do not ask for Signs from Heaven, or that men should rise from the dead—but the same spirit shews itself in the same

---

[1] Luke xvi. 31.
[2] Trench, Parables, 4th Edition, p. 453. "The rebuke of unbelief is the aim and central thought of the parable."

way. The corresponding demand is, "Give us an undeniable philosophical proof òf the truth of Christianity." "Shew us this," say men, "and we will believe." Accept the demonstration of course they must, if it be irrefragable; just as they must accept the truth that the three angles of a triangle are equal to two right angles; but such acceptance is a mental act of a wholly different order from adopting a religious belief—from feeling for instance that "Christ is with us to the end of the world." Much confusion has arisen from this difference not being properly marked.

From what I said at first, as to the nature of a revelation it appears that there are two elements in it, one within us and one without us. We must have "ears to hear" when God speaks—a faculty that discerns His voice—and also we must have some outward sign cognisable by human senses, or by such judgments based on experience as we form about historical evidence. I have just shewn that the first requisite is essential for any religious belief, and that it is a quality different from the logical understanding. But when we come to the attestation of the Sign which vouches the revelation, then the understanding assumes its ordinary jurisdiction. We are to judge by the common rules of evidence as to the authenticity of this Sign and the genuineness of our information. Reason and instructed judgment are to be used in these matters as in all others, and external evidence is allowed its weight by our Lord. When the Baptist sends his disciples to enquire, our Lord works cures before them, and bids them report what they *saw*.

A man wants some testimony to which he may turn, which is independent of himself. There are times when the surest believers mistrust themselves and their intuitions and ask, "How am I to know that this persuasion of mine is not a creature of my own brain, due to my temperament and mental conformation." "How can I call on other men to accept it?" Men are not left, unaided, to the distress of this kind of doubt. The Apostles were allowed to witness the Transfiguration and the presence of Jesus risen from the dead that doubt might not overcome them in moments of physical weakness or distress of mind. They could always turn to these recollections and say "We know the glory of God; for we have seen it."

We are not to expect that the Sign which attests a Revelation shall be guaranteed by a standing miracle; because such a standing miracle would be out of harmony with all God's ways as revealed in the Universe. For a standing miracle means that God is always, in one particular direction, visibly displaying the power elsewhere concealed. If such a miracle existed there would be one set of facts in the world not of a piece with the rest. If instead of working the world as He does by self-acting machinery, God were to reserve one department for His personal management, He might as well interpose in all, and direct all the movements in the world; in which case, as I said in the last chapter, the world would cease to have any independent existence, and would become merely a portion of the Divine existence.

So when it is demanded "That a revelation should be written in the skies" we may ask, How would you have God's autograph attested? The Jews, it will be said, had the visible Shechinah, the light between the Cherubim; but if this light existed now, there would be no proof of its being Divine: it would only be another phenomenon, and science would take cognisance of it. If we had an oracle declaring future events, all human enterprise would perish—for enterprise rests on hope and fear. The Delphic oracles would have paralysed action, if they had been unerring, unambiguous, and easy of access. A series of prophecies, it may be thought, fulfilled from time to time, would serve to authenticate revelation: and this aid is, indeed, admissible in attestation of the Sign we speak of; but it must be subject to the same condition which must attach to all external testimony: it must not be too clear or too strong. Men must always be able to reject it, if they like: either by ascribing the coincidences to chance, by declaring that the prophecy brought about its own fulfilment, or by some similar argument. If we had a series of prophecies all of which, up to the present time, had been fulfilled with due regularity, so that no one could doubt but that the rest would punctually come to pass, human action would be very much paralysed.

The miracles of our Lord's life serve us for our "Signs;" and our assurance that they occurred is to be based both on the external evidence, which in this case is the testimony to the authenticity of the record, and on the internal probability, which comes out of the conformity of the miracles with the Laws of Christ's action and the declared purpose of His coming. The miracles could always be referred to Beelzebub in old days, and they can always be disbelieved or explained away now.

Since the external evidence is not conclusive on this side or on that, the judgment formed must depend partly on the degree in which the Scriptures establish their own authority; and this degree depends on the mind and heart which the investigator brings to his work. One critic will see nothing but difficulties. Another will say, Our histories are photographs, imperfect no doubt, but what they show must have been there when they were taken: we see the main figures under different aspects, but we know them for the same. Some will feel as much convinced, from the character of thought and expression, that certain sayings came from our Lord, as a connoisseur in art might be that a certain picture came from the easel of a great master whose works had been the study of his life: he knows the touch.

Christ's great Revelation was not given in a book, not in a history or a treatise, but in a Life and Death. He shewed the world a Man who knew not Self, and He also shewed it the Force that came from God. Men will realize this Revelation in different ways in different ages; part may come to light at one time, part at another. Sayings which have long lain hardly noticed are one day found to be keys to unlock a treasure, and give insight beyond what we dreamt of. But besides this Revelation, personal to individuals, broad Truths are conveyed which we should not otherwise possess.

Some of the leading Truths are these. That Jesus came from the Father. That the Father loved men who believed in Him, and owned them as sons, and sent into their hearts[1] a filial spirit which should enable them to lay hold more firmly of this Revelation. Christ tells them that He came to manifest God to the world[2], and that, whether they chose to believe it or not, the kingdom of God was drawn nigh to them[3]. He tells them that to know God is eternal life[4], and that they who are counted worthy will attain a resurrection to such a life[5]. Above all he tells them—and this is the very charter of the Christian Church, without which her Doctrines would be only a set of notions, destitute

---

[1] Galatians iv. 6.   [2] John xvii. 6.
[3] Luke x. 11.   [4] John xvii. 3.
[5] Luke xx. 35.

of real vital power—"Lo, I am with you alway, even unto the end of the world[1]."

There is no clashing with human knowledge here, nothing that can tie the hands of the enquirer. The advance in spiritual knowledge is not brought about, simply by the communication of a new truth from without, which had never been dreamt of before: men feel rather as if they were reminded of something they must once have known. There appears, if I may so say, a tenderness of God in dealing with man, a carefulness so to reveal himself as not to obliterate a man's own personality, but to leave him to feel that any resolution he has reached is his own, arrived at, no doubt, by listening to God's prompting; without such prompting superseding the action of his proper self. No two men represent God to themselves quite in the same way: He was not the same for Peter that He was for John.

I believe that a revelation of God is needed for the education of what is highest in man, and for bringing him to the highest point he can reach; and that God has been always revealing Himself in one way or another. But the revelation of every age must be suited to the character of that age. Man must be educated up to it, or he cannot receive it. Our Lord tells his disciples "I have yet many things to say unto you but ye cannot bear them now[2]." Later generations are taught in this same way. The events related in the Acts, and the labours

---

[1] Matth. xxviii. 20.   [2] John xvi. 12.

which came upon the Apostles fitted them by degrees for fresh revelations. If our Lord had declared to St Peter when he first joined him in Galilee that the Gentiles should have as full a share in Him and in the Kingdom as he would have; might not he too have turned away? Or if, as is likely, he had been personally drawn to Christ too powerfully to quit Him, yet such a sudden shock to all his notions might have closed his mind spasmodically against new ideas? For when a man recoils from a view which unsettles him and turns him giddy, he clutches at his supports with iron grip. Many have been made bigots in this way. Our Lord is careful to avoid for the disciples all turmoil of mind; the new seed must be left undisturbed that it may take firm root; so that for our Lord to have disordered all St Peter's convictions by a premature disclosure, would have been contrary to His ways of acting.

An age must be ripe for the truth, and the truth must be ripe for the age for the last to profit by the first. If the theory of gravitation had appeared ten centuries ago, it would have passed unregarded away, for then, nobody thought the outer world worth scrutiny. On the other hand the neo-Platonic philosophy which once moved masses of men has now become so many words. How then is Christ's revelation to last for all time? It is enabled to do so, because there is *life* in it and *growth* along with life; because Christ does not deliver propositions about God which men are passively to receive once for all, but his sayings fall upon the human heart, and are quickened there, some in one generation and some in another: each generation seizes on its proper nutriment, and brings out of His sayings the special lesson it requires.

St Paul, to recur to the quotation which is, in fact, the burden of this chapter, speaking of the effect produced by the preaching of the word on the hearers says—

"The secrets of his heart are made manifest[1]."

Christ's words reveal for a man the secrets of his own heart to himself. They interpret to him his own confused and dreamy thoughts. This was what drew men so mightily to Him. It was not so much the novelty of what He told them that attracted them, as that they recognised in His teaching old familiar puzzles, which had come and gone through their minds, times without number, only in such shadowy guise that they could not fix and scrutinize them. Christ spake and then men said "This is what has been always troubling us." Here is what we have always been wanting to say, and could not put into plain words—and now these floating impressions of ours are found not to have come by chance but to belong to truths set in our

[1] 1 Cor. xiv. 25. This is commonly referred to a sense of guilt, which is included, no doubt, but the words bear a wider meaning.

being. God has "sent forth the Spirit of His Son into our hearts crying Abba, Father[1]." But He would not have done so if we had not had the capacity for being sons, to begin with.

We shall see too, when we think of it, that a revelation to men can only come by man, or in a voice or words like those of a man. Man's understanding is fashioned in a certain way; his language is the creature of his understanding; ideas could not be conveyed to him unless they were clothed in language which he could understand; Revelation therefore must express itself in terms of human notions because they alone can be made intelligible in human speech. If God speaks, He must speak after the fashion of men, or His words will be an unknown tongue.

To take an illustration: If a man, owing to something abnormal in his vision, became aware of a new colour, something which had nothing to do with red or yellow or blue; he could not communicate his new sensation because he could find no pigment which would in any degree represent it, and he could not describe it in words, by likeness to anything in the world. So God can only reveal to man about spiritual existence what man can conceive, that is to say only that to which he finds something analogous in his own being; for all must be put into that form with which man's understanding can deal; and the

---

[1] Galatians iv. 6.

only spiritual creature he can conceive is *man;* the only ideas he can conceive are human ideas; his mind must work on the lines along which men's minds move; the only creature with whom he can sympathise, and whom he can believe to sympathise with him is *man*, and so—since there can be no real teaching without mutual understanding—by *man* he must be taught. Christ's revelation meets this need. It was as the Son of Man that Christ declared Himself, and in this character He conveyed to men the germs of all the spiritual enlightenment they can receive. Does not this throw light on the words, " No one knoweth who the Father is save the Son, and he to whomsoever the Son willeth to reveal Him[1]," and again, "No man cometh to the Father but by me[2]?"

[1] Luke x. 22.   [2] John xiv. 6.

CHAPTER IV.

OUR LORD'S USE OF SIGNS.

It has been already observed that there is one feature of our Lord's way of revealing truths to men which distinguishes Him from all teachers before or since. This is the use of Signs.

Miracles may have been attributed to those who have promulgated creeds at various times, but these miracles did not form a constituent part of the teaching; they were not blended with it as those of our Lord were. They are introduced only to serve for credentials, so that an appeal to them may silence incredulity; they convey no lesson they only serve for proof. I hope to shew that it was otherwise with the signs wrought by Christ.

My especial concern in this chapter is not with the nature or the credibility of miracles in general but only with the purposes for which Christ introduced them; and with the questions of how far they were performed with a view to draw men to listen and to set forth God's kingdom, and how far for the purpose of working conviction. In the first chapter I have stated certain Laws, which our Lord observed in working Signs. These I shall presently discuss; but what I am concerned with now is the general question "Why did our Lord work Signs?"

I use the word "Signs" instead of miracles because it is our Lord's own word. The latter expression fastens attention on the wonderment which these deeds raised in men. But our Lord uses the word "Sign," which implies that these acts were tokens of some underlying power which, in these instances, passed into operation in an exceptional way. To our Lord, they of course were not *wonders*, and He never dwells on their wondrousness.

In the accounts of St Matthew, St Mark and St Luke, the word "Signs" is that most commonly employed by our Lord when speaking of His own working of miracles; while in the Gospel of St John, the term "works" is generally found in the like case, though "powers" sometimes takes its place. The expression "Signs and wonders" means, not two separate sorts of works, but signs that make men wonder: it means prodigies, worked to shew a divine commission, taken on the side of the *awe* they inspire. Our Lord only uses this expression twice—once when He says that false prophets shall come and "shew great signs and wonders[1]," and again in His answers to the noble-

[1] Mark xiii. 22; Matth. xxiv. 24.

man whose son was sick at Capernaum, "Unless ye see signs and wonders ye will not believe[1]." On these occasions the term refers to the popular conception of the form which Divine interposition would take. The expression "signs and wonders" occurs very frequently in the Acts of the Apostles.

When, as here, we are in search of the purposes which our Lord had in view, in something that He did, it is of service to ask, "What purpose or purposes did it actually fulfil?" What He did would not be likely to fail in producing the effect intended, or to bring about a result not contemplated by Him. So we must try to unravel the complex effects of these signs, and to discriminate the several ways in which they worked.

Some were witnessed both by the people and by the disciples, and some by the disciples and apostles only. The function of the miracles may have been different in the different cases. But, besides their effect on the actual witnesses, the record of these mighty doings has had a prodigious effect on generation after generation, from the time when our Lord walked in Galilee to the present day; and we may suppose that this posthumous effect was included in the Divine design.

The character of our Lord's miracles we shall find to be determined by the nature of the work He came to do. The work and miracles were adapted each to the other, and, owing to this, the study of

[1] John iv. 48.

the miracles throws a light on His purpose, and the more insight we get into His purpose the more reason we see for the miracles being of the kind they were.

We will consider, under different heads, the various functions which Our Lord's miracles fulfilled. That which comes naturally first in order is

(1) *The attraction of hearers.*

One effect of signs on the beholders lay on the surface. They awoke attention; they caused men's eyes to be turned to the Son of Man. Jesus won a mastery over men's souls both by what He did and what He said; but the doing had to come first, because without this He would not so soon have gained a hearing. From a district of small towns and scattered hamlets a crowd was not drawn together without some cogent influence. It was the rumour of the things "done in Capernaum[1]" and of other mighty works that caused the crowd to gather, and attracted the multitudes who listened, both in the synagogue and on the Mount.

The works of healing would be attractive enough to draw within the reach of our Lord's influence all who were likely to profit, as well as some who were not: while His words and the influence of His presence would *attach* to Him as true disciples those, and those only, who had "ears to hear:" in this way the crowd would be sifted.

[1] Luke vi. 23.

OUR LORD'S USE OF SIGNS.

One of the characteristics of our Lord, which puzzled His followers, and which also strikes us, was His seeming indifference about the number, or the worldly position of His adherents. He does not aim at gaining converts; when His popularity seems at its height He withdraws from the people. A warrior Messiah, or a prophet seeking to convince the world, would have displayed signs suited to attract the blind devotion of the multitude: he would have wanted to prove his pretensions by the striking character of his signs and wonders. Such was the Messiah whom the Jews were led to expect; in general they imagined no other, and for no other did they care: so we find that it surprised the disciples and the brethren of Jesus, that He should content himself with healing poor sick people in hamlets of Galilee, instead of confounding Herod in Tiberias, or the scribes in Jerusalem.

And if we regard our Lord as a leader looking to an immediate purpose and depending for success on His influence with those of His own day, his conduct is indeed inexplicable; but the whole tenour of it falls in well with the view which regards Him as setting afoot a movement which was to go on working to the end of the world. Hurry belongs to the mortal who wants to see the outcome of his work, while eternity is lavish of time[1].

[1] A friend recalls to me St Augustine's words, "Deus patiens est quia æternus."

We shall see later on that it is foreign to our Lord's ways to inflame the feelings and blind the eyes of men by kindling speech.

The overmastering influence of a great leader will "take the prisoned soul" of the people and make it follow his will. But Christ's first care is to leave each man master of his own will—the man who is no longer so, ceases to count as a unit. Just as this is seen in our Lord's teaching, so is it also in the miracles which set that teaching forth—they are not worked in the ways or the place that a Thaumaturge would have chosen—people are not invited to a spectacle—nor are the wonders so overwhelming as to cause a whole population to fall prostrate at our Lord's feet. The rumour of them is sufficient to make those who "have ears to hear" enquire further and "come and see;" and a further function of "Signs" is then called into play.

This function is that they should serve to select from the multitude those fitted to follow our Lord.

(2) *Selection.*

I have said in a previous chapter that education and selection are inseparable. Any process that unfolds the powers which lie within men, emphasizes, so to say, the differences between them.

The witnessing of wonders, declared to be wrought by the finger of God, must have stirred men's minds, and so brought about in them a species of education, well calculated to winnow out the chaff from the grain.

But the quality, which this kind of education seizes upon and develops, is not intellectual ability, but the capacity for "savouring the things of God." The miracles served as a touchstone for detecting this. Many would look, and wonder, and go their way—they had seen a strange sight, *that* they would allow, but it did not touch their souls: while to a few others it would seem as if they had lighted on what they had been watching for all their lives. They had always seen dimly that there must be in the world a living power; not a dead God in the keeping of the scribes, but a living God who should speak *in* their hearts and *to* their hearts, and they had found Him now. The minds of those who were worth rousing were put on the alert, and the sense of God's kingdom being near them, the sense that this every day world was His and worked by Him, was expanded within them.

(3) *Preparation.*

We have a distinct instance of the use of "Signs" to produce *preparation*. The seventy were sent working these Signs, "in every city unto which He Himself would come." This preparation would consist, partly, in the drawing out from the mass those who were likely to profit. When our Lord Himself came, these latter would be eager to hear

Him, and the great announcements He made would not strike them as altogether strange. The district over which these messengers were sent probably lay outside the country where our Lord's ministry had been chiefly carried on, and was only visited by Him on this one occasion. This made it the more important that the right men, rightly prepared, should form His audience. His truths were not to fail of taking root, from want of the soil having been loosened beforehand. We shall see, over and over again, how careful our Lord is to prevent the opportunities He gives being lost. He never neglects or underrates the need of properly preparing men for receiving new truths: He employs the ordinary means for effecting this, and He would have the Children of Light be as wise in their generation, and as judicious in the use of such means, as the children of this world.

Again, the display of the miracles roused some, the Scribes and Pharisees in particular, into active hostility—they watched the Signs to find ground for charges of blasphemy and Sabbath-breaking. Priesthoods, occupied with the externals of their function are aghast at the assertion of a living and working God. The worldly are terrified also and with the terror that awakens fury. These classes answer to those servants in the parable who said, "We will not have this man to reign over us." Whenever a vital religion has been proclaimed it has found opponents of both characters.

History witnesses to this, from the stoning of the prophets to the assaults on religionists in modern times. The miracles divided men into three great sections: there were those who were for Christ, and those who were against Him, and between these came a body who were not wholly indifferent or unaffected, but who quieted themselves with saying that such weighty matters were no business of theirs.

This breaking up of men into friends and foes was a kind of preparation for the Apostles' work. When men begin to take sides their minds cannot lie torpid: evil passion and selfishness mix with their doings, no doubt; but in the storm and stress men get to the bottom of their own hearts and find out their true selves; and men's truest selves were wanted by Christ.

So far we have spoken of miracles as means of rousing attention and drawing out from the mass those who had ears to hear. We will now consider them as practical illustrations accompanying the preaching, and

(4) *Setting forth the Kingdom of God.*

They shew not only how close this Kingdom is to us but they also convey visible lessons, to help men to conceive it aright.

We learn from our Lord's own lips that one purpose for which He wrought Signs was to make men sure that the Kingdom of Heaven was come upon them. When He was charged with casting out devils through Beelzebub, He says, after disposing of the accusation,

"But if I by the finger of God cast out devils, then is the *kingdom of God come upon you*[1]."

Whether Our Lord preached in the villages Himself, or the Apostles or the Seventy, going two by two, did so in His name the burden of their preaching was always the same. They call on men to change to a better mind, and declare that the Kingdom of God is come nigh. The seventy are bid to say to those who rejected them, "Howbeit know this that the Kingdom of God *is* come nigh[2]." Whether men chose to own it or not, God's Kingdom *was* near them even at their doors. St Mark, at the outset of his history of our Lord's Ministry, tells us[3]

"Now after that John was put in prison, Jesus came into Galilee, preaching the gospel of the kingdom of God,

"And saying, the time is fulfilled, and the kingdom of God is at hand: repent ye, and believe the gospel."

Christ declared that God was working underneath the ordinary agencies, which seemed to men to be working of themselves. God had been so working all along from the very beginning, but now Christ had come to reveal God—that is to say

[1] Luke xi. 20. [2] Luke x. 11.
[3] Mark i. 14, 15.

to make men sensible of the Divine presence and Divine agency in all that went on both within them and without. This revelation He would effect in the ways best adapted to make men understand it. And as the unlearned are most readily taught by what is set before their eyes; and as the teacher is much helped by having something to shew; so Christ declares the Kingdom and its nature, not only in parables and discourses, but by practical instances and illustrations as well; namely by the Signs He wrought. It was as though He had said, "I have told you that God's power was lying close about you: Behold it operating here." The combination of the word and the Sign, as the two essential elements of the teaching, is expressly put before us in one passage: we read,

"And they went forth, and preached every where, the Lord working with them, and *confirming the word with signs following*. Amen[1]."

(5) *Teaching wrought by signs.*

The Signs shew us, not only that the Kingdom *is* God's, but something also of the nature of that Kingdom as well.

Our Lord speaks of the power displayed in miracles as God's power working through Him. It is "by the finger of God" that He casts out devils and the man who is healed is bidden to tell his friends what God has done for him[2].

---

[1] Mark xvi. 20.   [2] Mark v. 19.

Christ nowhere claims the power as His own. It rests in God's hands; but it is granted to His prayer, because His will and God's are one.

Moreover the Signs set forth God's love and goodness to men, and thereby they tell us something of His nature. All the Signs worked by our Lord before the people at large, and all the works which the Twelve and the Seventy performed in their mission among the cities of Israel, were works of healing; with the exception of the two instances of the feeding of the multitudes, which also were works of Divine beneficence. There are other miracles of a different character, as we shall see presently, but those were witnessed either by the disciples only, or by a circle of private friends as at Cana of Galilee.

The men of Galilee had hitherto known the Lord as the God of Israel, who was especially concerned with the fortunes of their race and nation as a whole; but now they were told that He was the Father of every person in that nation, and was sent especially to the lost sheep among them. It was this declaration—that of the individual relation of each man to God, and of the preciousness of the very hairs of his head in God's eyes—that constituted, in great part, the comforting nature of the "good tidings of God." The miracles wrought in connection with the preaching could not bring this point very prominently forward: but so far as the miracles bear on the point they are in accord with the teaching.

They were worked, not upon masses of men at once, but on individuals, and our Lord addresses Himself personally to each particular sufferer, as though his case was considered by itself. I shall soon, for another purpose, notice two miracles recorded by St Mark which afford good instances of our Lord's sympathetic insight into individual cases. He does not, on entering a village, ordain that all the lepers in it shall be cleansed, or all the palsied restored to the use of their limbs. He condescends to take each case by itself.

There is hardly a case of healing narrated in St Mark, who, of all our authorities, gives the most detailed account, which does not shew traces of special attention on the part of our Lord to the spiritual and physical features of the particular case. We will take for an instance the cure of the sick of the palsy. The connection of what is spiritual with that which is physical is here very strongly marked. Our Lord begins by saying to the man "thy sins be forgiven thee." It is possible that the man's condition may have been due to imprudence or something worse; the thought of this may have rankled in his mind and the mental trouble may have aggravated the physical infirmity: the great physician cures both together. His restoration seems to come with the sense of pardon, but he does not shew himself aware of his recovery, until our Lord bids him arise.

The shewing that the Divine power worked

blessings on men one by one, contained in itself a lesson as to God's infinity; for a finite being would have been incapable of concerning himself for every unit of the world's population. Any supply of energy, short of an infinite one, would have been exhausted. Hence the notion of God's personal care for each soul is bound up with the conception of His infinity.

Christ does not begin with the abstract and say: "God is infinite and therefore He can find room in His heart to love men, every one;" but He begins with the concrete and says, "God does love you and every one else:" and He leaves it to men to arrive at the truth at the other end of the proposition: viz. that if God's strength is not lessened by drawing upon it, this can only be because there is no limit to it. From this infinity of God it also follows that the distinction between what we call great occasions and small ones—between occasions that we think would justify Divine interposition and those which would not—may not exist in God's eyes. In the presence of His infinity, the difference between great and small things may disappear; certainly His measure will be a very different one from ours.

This brings us to another point in the use of miracles to illustrate the ways of God's Kingdom: they exemplify the truth that God is no respecter of persons. Neither the persons on whom they are wrought, or before whom they are wrought, obtain this privilege by any merit or superiority. Men are not healed because they deservé it. As God sends rain on the just and unjust, so Christ cures the sick who come in His way, rich and poor alike—the son of the nobleman, and the blind beggar; for our Lord, worldly distinctions do not seem to exist. A man, *as man*, was of such transcendent value in the eyes of the Son of Man that, compared to this, little outer differences were but as the hills and dales of the earth, which scarcely roughen the surface of the globe when seen as a whole. Men, too, are not, except for very special purposes, picked out by Christ to witness the miracles; any more than they are in God's world to receive special mercies, or the lessons, or the afflictions of life. Those who were passing by saw the Signs, some profited and some did not: Herod and other great men would gladly have witnessed a miracle, but it was not granted them.

The Signs wrought by Christ harmonise with His teaching in another way: they never have the air of ostentatiously overriding and superseding Nature. His power, in its tranquil might, proceeded calmly along the homely track of every-day life; just as if it had always been present ruling quietly in its own domain, and might at any time have interposed without effort, if the Spiritual Order had needed it. A man is healed and an evil spirit is quelled by a word, and a multitude in the desert is supplied with food they do not know how,—all proceeds in a calm continuous way. Fresh energy is given to natural powers, and effects are produced of vast magnitude and with astonishing rapidity; but these powers seem to work through the organs and along the channels which nature provides: to our Lord there is one primary source of all life and movement and light and force, and that is God, from Whom all His power comes. He does not call certain visible manifestations nature, and refer others to God, as though nature and God were different powers. The Signs, accordingly, are worked in such a way that it is hard to mark the particular point where what is called the supernatural comes into play— to say, in fact, when nature ends and God begins. The cures, so far as we can trace them, are effected by the renewal of vitality in a disordered organ; this vitality would seem to proceed from Christ; just as the power which set life going on earth proceeded from God.

"For as the Father hath life in Himself, so hath He given to the Son to have life in Himself[1]."

Here, of course, we pass beyond the realm of the forces we can measure, but this imparted force only restores the organs needed for the cure; the optic nerve is reinvigorated or the absorbent vessels are stimulated to abnormal action, and the eye becomes again efficient. The man is not *enabled to see without an eye*, as was claimed to be done by

[1] John v. 26.

some workers of miracles in the middle ages; and there is no miracle in the Gospels like that mentioned in Paley's Evidences, where a man who had only one leg becomes possessed of two. Christ *restores* organs and withered limbs. He does not dispense with the proper organ or create new ones.

St Mark gives us full particulars of two cures, of which we can in some degree trace the process.

"And he took the blind man by the hand, and led him out of the town; and when he had spit on his eyes, and put his hands upon him, he asked him if he saw ought. And he looked up, and said, I see men as trees, walking. After that he put his hands again upon his eyes, and made him look up: and he was restored, and saw every man clearly[1]."

From this it appears that the eye was gradually restored, and our Lord's question shews that He did not expect an instantaneous cure. He speaks as a surgeon might who had performed an operation. He does not take it for granted that the man must have received his sight. He applies His hands, a second time and then the ill-defined dark objects which the man spoke of, become distinct.

The other case is that of one who was deaf and had an impediment in his speech.

"And he took him aside from the multitude, and put his fingers into his ears, and he spit, and touched his tongue; and looking up to heaven, he sighed, and

[1] Mark viii. 23—25.

saith unto him, Ephphatha, that is, Be opened. And straightway his ears were opened, and the string of his tongue was loosed, and he spake plain[1]."

The restoration of the disabled organs is clearly indicated here. I have referred to these two cases a few pages back. We now come to—

(6) *Miracles as a practical lesson to the disciples.*

So far, we have spoken of miracles as performed for the sake of the multitude; in order to draw them to listen and to sift from among them those fit to become disciples: I have remarked too how the "Signs" incidentally conveyed instruction, how they exhibited to the crowd the goodness and the power of God. But there were some miracles, as I have said in the first chapter, which were especially miracles of instruction, and I would say a word or two about those, before I pass on to miracles as means of assurance. These miracles of instruction were, in almost all cases, performed when but few of the disciples were by; and they are mostly wrought in the later period of our Lord's Ministry.

Among the miracles of this class are, The miraculous draughts of fishes, The walking on the sea, The stater in the fish's mouth, The withering of the fig tree, and the Transfiguration. The last named, is not usually classed among miracles

[1] Mark vii. 33—35.

or considered in books which treat of them, but a " Sign " it certainly was and it carries lessons with it which, bit by bit, the world is learning still.

That miracles should be employed as a means of impressing truths on the learner, we can well understand.

In no way could a great truth be presented so forcibly to the mind as by being clothed in the garb of a miracle. The wondrous circumstances would print themselves on the mind's eye at once and for ever; and as they recurred in lonely hours of thought, something more of their drift and purport would peep out every time. It is characteristic of our Lord's ways, that His teaching yields its fruit gradually; much as a seed-vessel driven by the wind, which scatters the contents, now of one cell, now of another, as it whirls along.

I trace in many miracles of instruction, a bearing on the great movement in which St Peter was the chief actor; namely, the calling of the Gentiles, and the taking from the Jews thereby their exclusive position, as the one people who knew God. Our Lord quietly, and by slow degrees familiarizes St Peter with this idea. He is not suddenly brought face to face with a notion which would cause a violent shock to his mind. With men like the Apostles new ideas want a little time to grow into shape: we know how easily a man is startled into shutting his mind against novelty when it is suddenly presented. St Peter

OUR LORD'S USE OF SIGNS.

could not have been instructed as to God's plans without a long course of explanation which it was not our Lord's way to give: so He lets the lesson lie in St Peter's mind till the circumstances shall come which shall be the key to it.

Of what I call miracles of instruction, I propose to consider two briefly, with a view chiefly to illustrating the way in which the instruction was conveyed.

There is this singularity about the Transfiguration, that our Lord *foretells* it, and in most remarkable words.

"And he said unto them, Verily I say unto you, That there be some of them that stand here, which shall not taste of death, till they have seen the kingdom of God come with power[1]".

This promise I understand to mean that some of the Apostles should, even while yet alive on the earth, be vouchsafed a glimpse of another world, and behold Christ in the glorified state which belongs to Him. The expression "in no wise taste of death," which occurs in all three accounts, must mean that they should not only have this experience after passing from this life to another, but even while yet in mortal frame. For six days these words are allowed to work in the minds of the disciples, and then:

[1] Mark ix. 1. Luke ix. 27.

"Jesus taketh with him Peter, and James, and John, and bringeth them up into an high mountain apart by themselves: and he was transfigured before them[1]."

During the six days and on the way up the mountain after they were taken from the rest, Peter, James, and John must have wondered what the "coming of the kingdom of God with power" would be. This prevented their being so stupefied with astonishment as to miss the lesson of the appearance. Here again we note our Lord's mode of *preparation* for the receiving of truths.

I do not discuss the nature of the vision, because I have now only to deal with the matter as to its educational effect. When the Apostles saw the glorified Lord with Moses and Elijah—their impression was not fear but joy.—"It is *good* for us to be here" says St Peter. He thought they had arrived in another world, and he proposes to build tents, as if he had landed in a strange island. He expects to be always there.

But what, in the view I am taking is the cardinal point of all, is the voice out of the cloud—"This is my beloved Son, *Hear ye Him*[2]." In these last words the old covenant is replaced by the new. Moses representing the Law, and Elijah the Prophets

---

[1] Mark ix. 2—8.
[2] Mark ix. 7. Compare Deuteronomy xviii. 15, "Unto him ye shall hearken."

—they who had been hitherto the spiritual teachers of men,—stood there to hand over their office to the Son. Their work in nursing the minds of a people set apart as the depositary of the knowledge of God was now at an end; now Humanity had succeeded to its heritage, and its teacher was to be the Son of Man. A religion which is shaped by the history and the mind of a particular people will be cast in a particular mould: its outward form must be rendered plastic if it is to become Universal. So Moses and Elijah the teachers of Israel lay down their functions in the presence of the chosen three, who hear their Master owned as God's own Son, to whom the world is henceforth to listen.

And when, many years later, the truth broke upon St Peter so that he said:

"Of a truth I perceive that God is no respecter of persons: but in every nation he that feareth him, and worketh righteousness, is acceptable to him[1],"

then a new light might illumine these recollections, which had been laid by in his mind, and they would draw a fuller meaning from the new idea by which he was impelled; and he would see how God's purposes, long entertained, work to the surface by degrees.

There is one miracle in which I can see no other intent, than that of the instruction of the

[1] Acts x. 34, 35.

disciples and, as it may not come before us again, I will say a few words on it now. The withering of the fig tree was, as I have said in the Introduction, an acted parable: the most circumstantial account is that given by St Mark.

"And on the morrow, when they were come from Bethany, he was hungry: and seeing a fig tree afar off having leaves, he came, if haply he might find any thing thereon: and when he came to it, he found nothing but leaves; for the time of figs was not yet. And Jesus answered and said unto it, No man eat fruit of thee hereafter for ever. And his disciples heard it[1]."

Of the next day it is related:

"And in the morning, as they passed by, they saw the fig tree dried up from the roots. And Peter calling to remembrance saith unto him, Master, behold, the fig tree which thou cursedst is withered away. And Jesus answering saith unto them, Have faith in God[2]."

When our Lord remarked from a distance one fig tree—probably one out of several, for Bethphage was named from its figs—which alone was in full leaf, He was drawn to it; whether this was because He saw occasion for impressing a lesson which He had at heart to give, or because He really expected to find refreshment, we cannot decide. The last motive is not excluded, for though the time of figs was not yet, still we are told that in Judæa the fruit of the fig is ripe by the time the leaves have reached

[1] Mark xi. 12—14. [2] Mark xi. 20—22.

their full size; and this display of foliage therefore gave prospect of fruit. We must not argue that our Lord would, of his superhuman illumination, have known that the tree was barren, for our Lord never uses this source of knowledge to find out what may be learned by ordinary means.

But whether our Lord approached the fig tree with the lesson in His mind or not, the aptness of the circumstance struck Him and the lesson it furnished was given on the spot. It was unusual for a tree to have leaves at that early season: by putting them forth, however, it held out hopes of fruit which it disappointed. This presented in a parable the situation of "the Jews' religion[1]." They made a show, and contrasted themselves with other nations, they dwelt on the fact that they alone worshipped the true God, and knew and observed His laws—they invited admiration on this ground—but of all this nothing came. So the fig tree seemed to say: "See I am green when other trees are leafless, you may look to me for fruit." It is said that this precocious putting forth of leaves shews that the tree is diseased and should be cut down, in like manner it was time that the Jewish Hierarchy should lose its office. It is to this Hierarchy that the words "No man eat fruit of thee henceforth and for ever" are really spoken. Mankind was no longer to draw its teaching from the scribes and priesthood of the Jews.

[1] ὁ Ἰουδαϊσμός, Gal. i. 13.

Individual Israelites might of course enlighten the world, as indeed they have done in a most remarkable degree; but the Jewish nation as a body was no longer to be the one recognised channel of God's communication with mankind. The leading people among them had wrapped themselves up in self-complacency and self-sufficiency; they had moreover enslaved themselves to the letter of their canonical books and to rabbinical traditions: they were therefore neither ready nor able to expand when expansion was needed. In other words, they were no longer fitted for a living world; which must, of its very nature, grow and change and discard all that will not change along with it; and so like the pretentious tree they were to wither away, and no man henceforth was to eat fruit of them for ever.

It would have been long before an Israelite could have brought himself to see this meaning in the words of our Lord; but St Peter must have thought over this last miracle, all the more from the apparent harshness of our Lord shewn in it—from its being the solitary instance of a final condemnation from His lips—and he must have asked himself; What did it mean?

There are many other miracles in which the instruction of the Apostles and notably of St Peter seems to be the leading aim. The walking on the water might have taught him how closely failure treads on the heels of impulse: the prophecy,

"Before the cock crow thou shalt deny me thrice," again conveyed this same lesson together with much beside: and the words "Then are the children free," which point the moral of the finding of the stater in the fish's mouth, must have recurred to St Peter when the Church at Jerusalem was debating as to how far she could free her Gentile members from the burdens of the Law. Of this I shall speak again. I have adduced sufficient instances to shew what I mean by miracles of instruction and the way in which they worked.

Lastly we come to the important subject of

(7) *Miracles as a means of proof.*

The signs, worked by our Lord, whatever other functions they fulfilled, had one office which in the eyes of some apologists is so important as to drive all other functions into the back-ground. They are regarded as the main ground of conviction. The Apostles, it is true, make little appeal to the Signs worked by Christ: this may have been because they worked similar Signs themselves, and knew that their enemies ascribed them to magic. Their favourite arguments were the fulfilment of prophecy and the resurrection of the Lord. The earlier hearers were Jews, and the question with them was, "Did Jesus of Nazareth answer to the prophetic notices of the expected deliverer of their race?" The Jews we hear "were mightily convinced" by Apollos, not because he declared Christ's works but because he "shewed by the Scriptures that Jesus was the Christ[1]."

But in time the early preachers addressed themselves to the Gentiles. The Jewish notion of the Messiah was strange to hearers, who had never heard of the prophets; while the idea that God should love the world and reveal Himself to it commended itself to them, and they would expect that such a revelation would be accompanied by manifestations beyond human experience. The consequence was that, after a century or two, less was made of prophecy and more was made of miracles: and if the question "What makes you believe that Jesus of Nazareth was the Son of God?" had then been put to all Christendom, the answer of an overwhelming majority would have been, "Because of the wondrous works which He performed."

We shall see, however, that our Lord does not Himself put Signs in the very forefront of His claims to the allegiance of men. He only appeals to them as subsidiary proofs; on which He would rest His cause when, owing to the situation or the disposition of the hearer, no higher kind of proof was available[2].

It will be asked, "If miracles were only a subsidiary ground on which our Lord claimed belief; What was the primary one?" We shall see that our

---

[1] Acts xviii. 28. [2] See next chapter.

Lord's first appeal was Personal; He claimed men's allegiance from what they had seen of Him and from what they knew.

There is a passage in St John's Gospel which brings this very clearly before us. The naturalness of it and its fidelity to character and situation are such, that I am as sure that these words passed between Philip and our Lord, as if they were found in all four of the Gospels, though they only occur in the last. They occur in the final discourse of our Lord when He and the Apostles are on the way to the garden of Gethsemane. Our Lord has said,

"And whither I go, ye know the way. Thomas saith unto him, Lord, we know not whither thou goest; how know we the way? Jesus saith unto him, I am the way, and the truth, and the life: no man cometh unto the Father, but by me. If ye had known me, ye would have known my Father also: from henceforth ye know him, and have seen him. Philip saith unto him, *Lord, shew us the Father, and it sufficeth us.* Jesus saith unto him, Have I been so long time with you, and dost thou not know me, Philip? he that hath seen me hath seen the Father; how sayest thou, Shew us the Father? Believest thou not that I am in the Father, and the Father in me? the words that I say unto you I speak not from myself: but the Father abiding in me doeth his works. Believe me that I am in the Father, and the Father in me: or else believe me for the very works' sake[1]."

[1] John xiv. 4—11.

In Philip's words we perceive an assurance of the reasonableness of what he asks, which is most true to the life. He never doubts but that God *could* be brought before his eyes;—he supposed that the clouds might be rolled away, so as to reveal a form of awful majesty clothed with resplendent light, and with one glimpse of this he would be content. He thinks that he makes a most moderate request.

Our Lord shews a sort of surprise, that after having been so long with them, going in and out among them, they should have missed seeing that God was in Him. It was perhaps this constant companionship that stood in Philip's way; that what was Divine should have mingled with his daily life was beyond his conception. God, he supposed, could only shew Himself in some strange and appalling manner. That God's presence is reflected, in the least broken way, in that course of things which is most normal and most ordinary, was an idea that did not belong to Philip's race or time; but Christ drops a germ from which it should arise.

It is the concluding verse of the passage with which I am most concerned—

"Believe me that I am in the Father, and the Father in me: or *else* believe me for the very works' sake[1]."

The first appeal is to that belief, which ought

[1] John xiv. 11.

to have grown up from personal knowledge; that failing, He points to the works. This belief was of the same order as that which we have in the rectitude of an honoured friend. In knowing a man, we get to a deeper kind of knowledge than we do in knowing an object : all we can tell about an object is what its properties are, we know nothing about what it *is;* but we do get nearer to knowing what a friend *is,* our souls interpenetrate, as it were, a little. So that if Philip had known our Lord as Peter did, he would, like him, have recognised the "Son of the living God." Supposing, however, that he was not sufficiently "finely touched" for such a knowledge, that he judged mainly from his senses, and needed proofs of which they could take cognisance; then—as an alternative course though a very inferior one—He might believe for the *mere Signs'* sake. Signs were provided to suit the cases of those who could not believe without them.

But while many take it for granted that Christ rested His claims on miracles and worked His Signs to provide Himself with credentials; others have gone to the other extreme, and have urged that Christ disparaged the belief that was engendered by the sight of wonders. No doubt the principle—"Blessed are they that have not seen and yet have believed" runs through all our Lord's teaching, but it was better they should believe from the sight of *such Signs as our Lord worked*—Signs which were not coercive—than not believe at all. Signs, certainly, have led men to believe, when, either from inward or outward causes, they would not have believed without. This effect I regard as a good one, and all good that has ensued from what our Lord did, I believe that He intended to do.

The chief texts adduced in disparagement of miracles are:

"Except ye see signs and wonders, ye will in no wise believe [1],"

and

"An evil and adulterous generation seeketh after a sign [2]."

If signs and wonders were the appointed means of bringing men to believe, "Why," ask the objectors, "are those blamed who cannot believe without seeing them?" "Our Lord," they say, "here shews that He sets little value on the belief that comes of seeing signs." This is, no doubt, quite true of the sort of belief that comes of the mere assent of a terrified man: but our Lord did not terrify men, and the belief that sprung from seeing *His* signs involved a will and a disposition to recognize God's hand.

I do not feel sure, however, that the first text really bears on the matter. I think it quite possible

---

[1] John iv. 48.   [2] Matt. xii. 39.

that the stress should be laid on the word *see*. The nobleman "besought him that he would *come down*, and heal his son; for he was at the point of death[1]." He thought that our Lord must go down to Capernaum with him and work the cure there; he cannot believe that it will be done unless it is wrought before his eyes. When he began to speak he had not the faith of the Roman centurion; he could not suppose that the power of healing could be exercised from afar; but he soon caught this confidence from looking on our Lord. If the text have this sense it does not touch the question before us.

The second text refers to a sign from Heaven. It is spoken of those who wanted an overwhelming miracle to be wrought, which should settle the question and compel assent in the unwilling. The generation is not called "evil and adulterous" for seeking after such Signs as our Lord wrought, for crowding to see the cures for instance, but, for challenging Him to produce a Sign of a very different character, a magical one, which, for reasons explained in the last chapter, He would not do.

Our Lord Himself on several occasions points

---

[1] John iv. 47. Mr Sanday considers this miracle to be identical with the healing of the centurion's servant, and that the "ye see" is addressed to the elders who stand by. With this I am not prepared to agree. See the Authorship of the Fourth Gospel, W. Sanday, M.A., Macmillan and Co., a well-known and excellent book.

to another result of His working of Signs. It rendered the rejection of Him a sin; this was because the will was called into operation to explain these Signs away. The leaders among those adverse to Him invented loopholes, such as referring the works to Beelzebub, and those who wanted to escape being convinced availed themselves of them. In this way, the acceptance or non-acceptance of Signs formed a touchstone for discriminating those who virtually said "We will not have this man to reign over us"—a section of people to whom I alluded in the earlier part of the chapter. Men were pardoned the unbelief of blindness and dulness, but not the wilful hatred which went out of its way to find grounds for rejection, and which would refer works of pure beneficence to the chief of the devils; this shewed innate aversion. The following are passages in point:

"Woe unto thee, Chorazin! woe unto thee, Bethsaida! for if the mighty works had been done in Tyre and Sidon which were done in you, they would have repented long ago in sackcloth and ashes[1]."

"He that hateth me hateth my Father also. If I had not done among them the works which none other did, they had not had sin: but now have they both seen and hated both me and my Father[2]."

Again, it is easier to convey to another by

---

[1] Matth. xi. 21; Luke x. 13.   [2] John xv. 23, 24.

OUR LORD'S USE OF SIGNS. 107

description an external fact than a personal impression : and thus the evidence from Signs is easier to transmit from man to man than that which arises from realising a Personality. Those who followed our Lord were subjugated by His influence; some of us too may extract from His memoirs a conception of His Personality: but it is only those possessing the gift of seeing the reality in the outline, who can lay hold of this source of belief; while in a miracle, all can perceive credentials given by God.

Our Lord's course of proceeding in a very important instance, the occasion on which John the Baptist sends his disciples to Him, is a most instructive instance of His use of Signs. These Signs furnished the kind of evidence most available in that particular case.

When the Baptist is in prison he sends two of his disciples to our Lord with the question, "Art Thou He that cometh, or look we for another[1]?" Many months had passed since the baptism of our Lord, and it seemed that nothing had been done. He was himself in prison, removed from the presence, and personal influence of our Lord. His recollections of Him were perhaps fading, and his faith growing low. He was then in the position for which the argument from signs is especially suitable—nothing would help him like facts. He was in the situation in which tens

[1] Luke vii. 20.

of thousands of Christians are still—believing, and yet having misgivings now and then whether what they call their Faith may not be fancy,—longing for something positive to cling to, some support outside themselves. Such support our Lord affords the Baptist; He puts him as nearly as possible in the position of a witness of the miracles.

We read:

"In that hour he cured many of diseases and plagues and evil spirits; and on many that were blind he bestowed sight. And he answered and said unto them, Go your way, and tell John what things ye have seen and heard; the blind receive their sight, the lame walk, the lepers are cleansed, and the deaf hear, the dead are raised up, the poor have good tidings preached to them. And blessed is he, whosoever shall find none occasion of stumbling in me[1]."

We have no other instance in which miracles are wrought in order to assist one who is in doubt. Our Lord does not give a direct answer to the words "Art thou He that cometh?" If He had said "I am He"—and yet had not restored the kingdom to Israel as the Baptist expected, He would only have led him into further bewilderment. So his disciples take back for sole reply, an account of "what they hear and see." The works are such as our Lord continually performed; but John's disciples are given a special opportunity

[1] Luke vii. 21—23.

OUR LORD'S USE OF SIGNS.

of witnessing them for their Master's sake. The Baptist is however certified of this; a great work of God was being carried on in the world, through Him on whom he had seen the Spirit descend when He rose from Jordan[1].

Of the two grounds, then, on which our Lord claimed men's allegiance—His personal influence and the signs He worked—our Lord rests preferably on the first, but the second has its place and it is an important one.

Our Lord is the great physician who deals with all according as the case and the constitution require. In different ages men's minds require different kinds of proof. I believe that such different kinds are provided—that there is lying ready for each generation and each type of mind the degree of evidence which is good for it and of the kind which it is fitted to assimilate. Miracles are not the sort of evidence most wanted now; but it was the sort which for many centuries was looked on as the most incontrovertible. It spoke to those who could understand nothing else. It was for many ages what men especially wanted, and there it was to their hand. A future generation may find their main ground of belief in Christ in a realization of His Personality; and they may in this way arrive at that kind of knowledge of Him which our Lord had hoped that Philip might

[1] John i. 32, 33.

have gained. This we can scarcely obtain without a careful study of our Lord's ways of influencing men.

I have not yet spoken of our Lord's miraculous knowledge of events or of His insight into men's hearts. There have been a few persons in the course of the world's history who have, in a wondrous way, discerned the ends towards which events were working; and others who have divined the thoughts of other men. These gifts in the fullest degree our Lord possessed; and when He needed stronger illumination for the purpose of His work these faculties were exalted beyond human range. The superhuman supervened, proceeding along the lines of human action; and this, like the powers whereby His other works were wrought, came from the Father in answer to prayer. By displaying this divining power He converts Nathanael, and He forcibly impresses the woman of Samaria. But effective as the display of this superhuman penetration was for bringing about conviction, it was much more than an evidence of Divine power. The knowledge of this insight of their Master into their hearts played a large part in the Apostles' Schooling. They were habituated by means of it to feel that their hearts were known, and this habit became so much a part of themselves that when Christ had left the world they could realize to themselves that they were under His eye still. This condition of mind was required for their special work, and Christ's training was directed to develop it within them as I hope to show.

In the next Chapter I pass to the discussion of the Laws which our Lord appears to follow in His working of Signs.

CHAPTER V.

THE LAWS OF THE WORKING OF SIGNS.

I HAVE already, in the introductory Chapter, given my view of the principles which guided our Lord in the exercise of His superhuman powers. He is tempted to employ them when He saw they should not be employed, and the Laws are drawn from His refusals. Consequently they all take the form that, for such and such a purpose, or under such and such circumstances these superhuman powers are not to be brought into action.

I will recapitulate the Laws before stated—

(1) Our Lord will not provide by miracle what could be provided by human endeavour or human foresight. He Himself, as far as we can see, never employs superhuman power or illumination to effect what could be arrived at by human effort.

(2) Our Lord will not use His special powers to provide for His personal wants or for those of His immediate followers.

(3) No miracle is to be worked merely for miracles' sake, apart from an end of benevolence or instruction.

(4) No miracle is to be worked to supplement human policy or force—as (for instance) those of Joshua were.

(5) No miracle is to be worked which should be overwhelming in point of awfulness so as to terrify men into acceptance, or which should be unanswerably certain, leaving no loophole for unbelief.

Before going into particulars about these Laws there is something to be said about the narrative of the Temptation itself, and the form in which it has come down to us.

The incident of the Temptation is recorded in all the Gospels except that of St John; but the account in St Mark's Gospel relates only that our Lord withdrew into the wilderness, and that He was there "forty days tempted of Satan." In the Gospels of St Matthew and St Luke we find, with some small variations to be noted presently, what is commonly known as the History of the Temptations of our Lord.

114 THE LAWS OF THE WORKING OF SIGNS.

The narratives, taken from the Revised Version, are as follows:

"Then was Jesus led up of the Spirit into the wilderness to be tempted of the devil. And when he had fasted forty days and forty nights, he afterward hungered. And the tempter came and said unto him, If thou art the Son of God, command that these stones become bread. But he answered and said, It is written, Man shall not live by bread alone, but by every word that proceedeth out of the mouth of God. Then the devil taketh him into the holy city; and he set him on the pinnacle of the temple, and saith unto him, If thou art the Son of God, cast thyself down: for it is written, He shall give his angels charge concerning thee: And on their hands they shall bear thee up, Lest haply thou dash thy foot against a stone. Jesus said unto him, Again it is written, Thou shalt not tempt the Lord thy God. Again, the devil taketh him unto an exceeding high mountain, and sheweth him all the kingdoms of the world, and the glory of them; and he said unto him, All these things will I give thee, if thou wilt fall down and worship me. Then saith Jesus unto him, Get thee hence, Satan: for it is written, Thou shalt worship the Lord thy God, and him only shalt thou serve. Then the devil leaveth him; and behold, angels came and ministered unto him[1]."

"And straightway the Spirit driveth him forth into the wilderness. And he was in the wilderness forty days tempted of Satan; and he was with the wild beasts; and the angels ministered unto him[2]."

[1] Matth. iv. 1—11. [2] Mark i. 12, 13.

"And Jesus, full of the Holy Spirit, returned from the Jordan, and was led by the Spirit in the wilderness during forty days, being tempted of the devil. And he did eat nothing in those days: and when they were completed, he hungered. And the devil said unto him, If thou art the Son of God, command this stone that it become bread. And Jesus answered unto him, It is written, Man shall not live by bread alone. And he led him up, and shewed him all the kingdoms of the world in a moment of time. And the devil said unto him, To thee will I give all this authority, and the glory of them: for it hath been delivered unto me; and to whomsoever I will I give it. If thou therefore wilt worship before me, it shall all be thine. And Jesus answered and said unto him, It is written, Thou shalt worship the Lord thy God, and him only shalt thou serve. And he led him to Jerusalem, and set him on the pinnacle of the temple, and said unto him, If thou art the Son of God, cast thyself down from hence: for it is written, He shall give his angels charge concerning thee, to guard thee: and, On their hands they shall bear thee up, Lest haply thou dash thy foot against a stone. And Jesus answering said unto him, It is said, Thou shalt not tempt the Lord thy God. And when the devil had completed every temptation, he departed from him for a season[1]."

[1] Luke iv. 1—13.

What we find in St Mark may have been generally known to our Lord's disciples from the earliest period of the ministry. But the account of the Temptations themselves, which we find in St Matthew and St Luke, can only have come from our Lord Himself. Assuming this to be the case, the passage before us is singular in two respects.

First, Because the Evangelists have here, and here only, altered the form of what our Lord delivered, and changed into a narration in the third person what must, in the first instance, have been expressed in the first.

Secondly, Because this is the only instance in which our Lord breaks through His reticence as to His own personal history on earth. Here and here only does He give us a glimpse of what had befallen Him or of what had passed within His breast.

St Matthew and St Luke differ as to the order of the second and third Temptations. I have adopted that given by St Luke. According to my view, our Lord in the one rejects the use of physical violence and in the other that of moral compulsion. It is more after our Lord's way to proceed from what is concrete to what is abstract, than in the reverse order.

I feel strengthened in this view by some of the characteristics of the Gospel of St Matthew, in the form in which it has come down to us. This Evangelist has always *the Kingdom* before his eyes. He would therefore be inclined to account the rejection of "all the kingdoms of the world and the glory of them" as the highest possible instance of the renunciation of self; and as he accounted it the most severe of the temptations he would naturally place it last. St Matthew moreover throughout his Gospel often puts together the discourses of our Lord according to their subject-matter, and not in the order in which they were spoken. He would therefore have no scruple about changing the order of the account of the Temptations which may have come before him as a detached document. On the other hand we do not know of any bias of St Luke which should lead him to prefer one order of events to another.

Another slight variation may be noticed. St Matthew tells us that He was "led up of the Spirit *to be tempted* of the devil[1]." The words imply that He was led up with a view to undergoing temptation. But in St Mark and St Luke we have "being tempted" without any intimation of purpose. Grave difficulties attach to the view that our Lord went into the desert with the set purpose of seeking and confronting temptation. Moreover it is of the essence of temptation that it should come on us unawares. If we know that endeavours are about to be made to persuade us to a particular course, we close our ears to all that pleads for it— being forewarned, we are forearmed; so that, as

[1] Matth. iv. 1.

regards these words, and indeed throughout the passage, I place more confidence in the version of St Luke than in that of St Matthew, or, to speak more accurately, that of his translator from Hebrew.

The words "Get thee hence," at the close of St Matthew's relation of the temptation on the mount, have been supposed to indicate the final banishment of the Tempter, and therefore to shew that this temptation came last. The force of the argument rests on our supposing, as no doubt the author of St Matthew's Gospel did, that the events here related formed three distinct visible scenes, occurring in close succession, towards the end of the forty days. Whereas I hold that we have here a representation of our Lord's inward conflicts, clothed by Him in a garb of outward imagery, that they might be the better understood. If this view be taken, the trials may have gone on simultaneously throughout the forty days, and may have been so far like our own inward troubles that one harassing perplexity may well have been most pressing at one moment and another at the next. But if these struggles are represented by visible occurrences, these occurrences must necessarily be related one after the other. The words "Get thee hence" might refer not necessarily to a final banishment, but only to the end of one assault. St Luke's version is reconcileable with the view that he understood our Lord to be speaking figuratively and personifying the voices that tempted him.

It may be asked, "At what period of His ministry did our Lord give the disciples the account of what passed in the desert?" We can only guess, but the guess is worth making. We do not know whether the account which we possess was contained in what critics call "the original document," on which the Gospels of St Matthew and St Mark are supposed to be based. Its omission by St Mark rather favours the supposition that it was not. It may have been, in the first instance, put down in writing by one who heard the recital from our Lord's lips, and may have come into the hands of the evangelists as a separate "parchment[1]." This document might contain no note of the time and place at which our Lord delivered the account—and, in the absence of information on this point, the compiler of the gospel might have made the alteration from the first person to the third, if it had not been made before, and have inserted the account in the place belonging to it in the order of events. I conjecture that the communication was made near the end of the ministry, possibly after the feast of the dedication[2], at the time when

"He went away again beyond Jordan into the place where John was at the first baptizing; and there he abode[3]."

[1] 2 Timothy iv. 13.   [2] Dec. 20, A.D. 29.   [3] John x. 40.

The place would recall what had happened after He had been "driven" from that spot by the Spirit into the wilderness about two years before.

Other considerations also lead me to this conjecture.

It is strange that no allusion is ever made to so important a record: and this would be far more strange if the knowledge had lain in the minds of the Apostles all through the period of our Lord's ministry, than if they had only obtained it when the close was at hand. Moreover, the absence of any account of the circumstances under which the relation was made inclines me to think that this must have taken place at a time of which our records are scanty; and there is no time in the sacred history of which the narrative is less full than the period at which I place the communication, viz., the early spring preceding the Passion of our Lord.

There is also this consideration of a different kind. In all education there are two elements, that which is communicated by the teacher ready made, and which the pupil has only to register, and that which the learner elicits by turning over in his mind the matter which gives food for thought. In our Lord's teaching of the disciples the proportion of the latter element to the former steadily increases from first to last. At first, sayings are given them to remember; latterly, they receive mysteries on which to meditate. In the Sermon on the Mount men are told plainly what it was desirable for them to know; afterwards, the teaching passes through parables and hard sayings up to the mysteries conveyed by the Last Supper. The lessons of the Temptation have the form of the later teaching of our Lord: they contain hard matters and only yield their fruit by being long laid to heart.

Not only would the lessons of the Temptation have been more intelligible to the Apostles towards the end of the ministry than at the beginning; but, turning as they do on the use of superhuman powers, they would suit the time when the Apostles were about to exercise similar powers themselves.

Now comes the great question of all : In what sense is the narrative to be taken?

Many writers accept it as literal history and suppose the Tempter to have appeared in bodily form and to have conveyed our Lord, also in the body, both to the mountain top and the pinnacle of the Temple. Others have regarded it as a vision; and intermediate views have been adopted by many.

On one point fortunately we may be pretty confident. The substance of the history came from our Lord. The most unfavourable critics allow this, from the extreme difficulty of referring it to any other source. It cannot have been introduced in order to make the Gospel fall in with Jewish notions of the Messiah, for there are no traditions that the Messiah should be tempted:

and if the passage had been devised by men, the drift of it would have been plainer, and the temptations would have been such as men would feel might have come upon themselves. We have many accounts, in the legends of the saints, of the sort of trials which present themselves to the imagination of human writers; and they differ totally from these.

I have let fall already a few words shewing in what way I regard the passage. I must now speak more fully on the subject.

It may be assumed that, in all our Lord's dealings with His disciples, His primary purpose was to do them good. He did not leave behind Him this reference to His sojourn in the wilderness and its momentous results, merely as materials for biographers. The trials which had beset Him would soon beset them also in doing the work He destined for them; before He left them He would therefore relate in what disguises the temptations had appeared and how they had been repelled. Behind the Apostles, who formed as it were the front rank of His audience, there stretched long files of hearers,—all those to whom His words have since come. At the end of this file we ourselves stand; and those among us who have special gifts, and are tempted to use them for selfish ends, or for putting a yoke, physical or mental, upon other men, may well take them to heart. My business however now is with the Apostles. It was likely that our Lord would give them some hint as to the principles on which superhuman power can be safely employed: and it was certain that this lesson would be put by Him in the form which would best convey it, and which would make the most lasting impression. The *form* then, as well as the matter of the lesson, must be worth studying closely.

One reason why this passage has such a powerful interest for men is that the history is a personal one. Our Lord riveted the most earnest attention of His hearers by speaking to them of Himself; and something of the same effect is felt by readers of the story now. We know how a teacher at once enchains the interest of his class when, leaving things abstract, or what he finds in books, he says, "Now I will tell you something that happened to me;" and we can understand the eagerness with which the Apostles would gather round our Lord, and can imagine how intently they would gaze upon Him, when He told them that He, like them, had been tempted, that He too had fought hard battles and that He would tell them what they were.

Another source of interest is that the story deals with inner struggles in a figurative way—the voices are personified and the action is localised.

That Satan should have appeared in a bodily form is, to my mind, opposed to the spirituality of all our Lord's teaching. Such an appearance presents endless difficulties, not only physical but moral. If our Lord knew the tempter to be Satan, He was as I have said forearmed; if He did not know him, this introduces other difficulties. He must at any rate have been surprised at meeting a specious sophist in the wilderness. Milton deals with the subject with great skill, from his point of view, in *Paradise Regained*. Certain points he leaves unexplained, and those I believe to be inexplicable. They are these. I cannot understand that our Lord should suffer Satan to transport Him to the mountain top, or to the pinnacle of the Temple, or that the Evil One should propose to Jesus to fall down and worship him.

I can however readily comprehend that our Lord should represent under this imagery and under these personifications what had passed within Himself. He could not indeed bring the lesson home to His hearers in any other way. To have represented mental emotions, to have spoken of the thoughts that had passed through His mind, would have been wholly unsuited to His hearers. We know how difficult it is to keep up an interest in a record of inward struggles and experiences. Men want something to present to their mind's eye, and they soon weary of following an account of what has been going on within a man's heart, void of outward incident. A recital of what had passed in our Lord's mind would have taken no hold of men's fancy and would soon have faded from their thoughts. But the figure of Satan would catch their eye, the appearance of contest would animate the hearers' interest; while the survey of the realms of the earth, and the dizzy station on the pinnacle of the Temple, would take possession of men's memories and minds.

The Apologue was to Orientals a favourite vehicle for conveying moral lessons; and we have a familiar instance in English Literature of the attraction of allegory. Would Bunyan's *Pilgrim's Progress* have possessed itself, as it has done, of the hearts of whole sections of the British race, if, shorn of its human characters and its scenery, it had only analysed and depicted the inward conflicts, the mental vicissitudes and religious difficulties of a sorely-tried Christian youth?

The use of the name Satan must be considered. This name, which means the enemy, occurs in the Old Testament, in the book of Job and elsewhere but not in the Pentateuch. The Jews we know had a dæmonology of their own. The gods of the heathen they regarded as devils, of whom the Sidonian deity Beelzebub was Prince. Our Lord never countenances these views. I believe that He uses the word Satan in a *generic* sense to personify evil spiritual influences exercised upon earth.

When the Apostles returned safe after being sent through the cities, our Lord regards this as an augury of their success in the great conflict and says that He "beheld Satan fallen as lightning

126 THE LAWS OF THE WORKING OF SIGNS.

from Heaven[1]." We have clearly impersonation here. He says also "If Satan hath risen up against himself and is divided[2]," a supposition which excludes the idea of an individual being, and agrees with the collective meaning I attribute to the term. When St Peter rebukes our Lord for declaring before His followers that He would be "rejected and killed and after three days rise again," our Lord says "Get thee behind me, Satan." St Peter, by saying of the suffering of which our Lord spake "this shall never be unto thee[3]," unwittingly had acted as the ally of those who would tempt our Lord from yielding implicitly to His Father's will, and our Lord therefore calls him Satan. On the whole then I lean to the view that the communication, or discourse of our Lord, which has been preserved in the form of the narrative of the Temptation, was delivered by Him in the form of an *apologue* or species of parable, in which our Lord, after Eastern fashion, introduced Satan as an embodiment of the powers of evil.

It must not be supposed that by giving up here the personality of the tempter we are making an abatement of what is superhuman in the Gospel, in order that, in virtue of having so done, we may hope to win this or that section of doubters over to our side—the whole question of evil remains a mystery, and in mystery there can be no degrees. It is of no use endeavouring to make infinity a trifle less infinite.

[1] Luke x. 18.   [2] Mark iii. 26.   [3] Matth. xvi. 22.

Whether the word Satan be here used collectively or personally is altogether a different question from the existence of intermediate intelligences, and is quite an open one even for the most orthodox.

Temptation to turn stones into loaves.

I now come to the Temptations themselves. As these trials were mental, we can only realise them by imagining what, consistently with our history, *may* have passed in our Lord's mind. What *actually did* so pass is of course beyond our knowledge altogether. We are however justified in supposing that, as our Lord was "tempted as man," the thoughts and feelings which actuated Him would be such as men might follow and more or less understand.

It would appear that when God lays a work on a man He gives him a general view of the end to be kept in sight, a vehement desire to accomplish it, and a forefeeling of the capacity so to do. But He does not shew him how he is to do it, He does not make the way clear so that he sees his course before him and marks its several stages. If a man were so guided he would not fulfil the conditions of human agency, there would be no room for his own will to act, he would have no responsibility. He would move along a pre-arranged path. God would, in effect, be doing all and he nothing, and so it would come to much the same thing as if the work were done once for all by God's *fiat*, independently of human action—and this, as we have already seen, is not God's way of governing the world.

When St Paul takes his last journey to Jerusalem, the Spirit, he tells us, "testifieth unto me in every city, saying that bonds and afflictions abide me." That he must go to Jerusalem he knew and to go he was resolved, but what course of conduct he was to adopt or what the result was to be he did not know at all; afterwards in like manner, he knew that he was to bear witness at Rome, but he had no directions as to what he was to do. It was left to him to act as seemed to him to be the best. This may give us a help towards understanding how it may have been with our Lord, when the mighty charge unto which He was born came home to His mind, and He felt, rising in Him, the wondrous powers given to aid Him in carrying it out.

Our Lord when driven by the Spirit into the wilderness would take no thought of food or shelter. The one thing He craved for was to be alone; He must have solitude, and the wilderness provided that.

When He reflected, He could hardly help asking Himself whether this light which had shone upon Him—this voice from Heaven,—were the resuscitation of His Diviner life or only something in His own eyes and ears? A sure test lay ready: when He had heard Himself hailed as the Son of God a conviction had risen in Him that God would give effect to His commands. He had only to try whether this was so and all doubts would be resolved. Perhaps the whisper came "Try this experiment in a *very small matter first.*" Who could think this apparent caution and prudence came from an ill quarter?

Spiritual evil always chooses a trifle, something from which it seems that no harm can possibly come, to win its victim to the first false step. Our Lord was hungry, and loaf-shaped stones were lying all about Him. Why not turn a few actually into the loaves they looked like? In so doing, how could He possibly be wrong?

However plausible the appeal of the Tempter, it was not entertained. We can conceive that a whole array of objections would arise; some may have been such as these—

This putting of God to trial by a test of my own choosing, that I may determine whether I will believe His words or not: this implying that I will admit His authority if He speaks in one way and not if He speaks in another—Is this befitting one called to a work like this?

Then came another point—He was hungry. As St Mark says nothing about the fasting it will be best not to assume that the fasting was part of our Lord's original purpose; but as, in the desert of

Judea, food could not be got without a journey of some miles, our Lord, whether designedly or not, had put Himself out of the immediate reach of food. Should He remedy this by using the mysterious power with which He felt He was invested? This power was given Him to forward God's Kingdom upon earth—should He use it for Himself?

Then the tempter might return to the assault. There are fluxes and refluxes in human feeling; we are always afraid that we have gone too far in one direction, or been too obstinate about our own point; it strikes us that perhaps we have made more of it than it was worth, and then we listen submissively to the other side.

Such a whisper as this may have come—" These powers are given you to enable you to set up God's Kingdom upon earth; for this you must win adherents. These adherents must be maintained. Your opponents are supported by the great ones of the earth; the God of Heaven has committed to you His powers for the support of yours. This little incident of the loaves only points the way to a much weightier matter; you *must* use your special powers to supply your own bodily wants in the coming contest,—why not begin with using them for this purpose now?"

Here we have arrived at the gravest point of the debate—Were these powers really to be used for His bodily wants or not? As the true conditions of His work rose before Him, the principles grew clearer; He was to deliver mankind as the Son of Man, He was to work as man, to suffer as man, that suffering men might always look to Him, saying "He was one of us." And how could this be, if His lot was so unlike theirs that He met His own wants by a word of command directly they arose? How could His followers own the duty of labouring for their daily bread, if stones at a word were turned into loaves for Him? How could He tell men not to think overmuch of the meat that perisheth, if He had used Divine powers to provide it for Himself as soon as He possessed them? If He were to be the stay of loving human hearts, He must say to men, "As you live, I live: of all your ills and troubles I claim my part."

Our Lord's answer points out a train of thought along which He may have passed, until at length He reached a firm resolve and reduced the Tempter to silence. It will not be irreverent to imagine what might, consistently with what we learn, have been its nature.

Man wants no reminding that he lives by *bread*. There is no fear of his not giving care enough to the needs of his body; but there is danger lest he should think of nothing but these needs, and starve his soul and become such that eternal life, without a body to care for, would only be a condition of aimless weariness. He resolved therefore to keep His powers apart for spiritual ends. He will work no miracle to shew that He *can* work a miracle, or to assure either Himself or others that He is the Son of God; neither will He use this power to provide what others win by toil, or to preserve Himself or His followers from the common ills of human life.

There are a few of our Lord's Signs which might, at first sight, look as if in them this principle were not observed. At the marriage of Cana in Galilee, the Sign is worked as an act of kindness to save the host from mortification arising from an accident.

I have mentioned, as regards the miracles of the loaves and fishes, that on both occasions the supply which our Lord's own company had with them was sufficient for their immediate wants. The crowds, however, had, by their rapt attention to our Lord, been detained away from their homes and their supplies, and, if they had had to go a distance to buy bread, they would have suffered from taking so long a journey fasting. The case was an exceptional emergency parallel to that of illness, and our Lord meets it by miraculous means.

The miraculous draughts of fishes benefited probably all who were partners in the vessel, but they were not wrought to meet any necessity on the part of our Lord. All night long they had taken nothing; this scarcity may have been part of the lesson of the miracle, and the great draught is only a bounteous compensation. This is a miracle of instruction, as I said in the last chapter: it tells men that a turn comes at the moment when they are about to give up, and that the faith which bears up long is rewarded. Moreover, to recur to what I said in the last chapter, St Peter had been told that he was to be henceforth a fisher of men; and when multitudes, both of Jews and Gentiles, were gathered into the Church in Jerusalem he must have thought of this as answering to the Sign.

The miracle of the stater in the fish's mouth also requires notice. It is not wrought to obtain the coin, but to keep before Peter's mind that he as well as his Master were the children and not the servants or tributaries of God.

From St Peter's answering without hesitation that his master would pay the didrachm, it is clear that there was no difficulty about producing the small sum. He does not speak to our Lord on the matter, but our Lord, directly he enters the house, asks him, "What thinkest thou, Simon? the kings of the earth, from whom do they receive toll or tribute? from their sons, or from strangers[1]?"

This miracle, as we said in the last chapter, is one of instruction. The payment according to the received view was the half-shekel that every Israelite had to pay for providing victims for the Temple service. It gave the idea of a tribute to God which stood in the way of the conception of perfect sonship. It implied that Israelites alone had part or lot in the worship of the living God. Our Lord

[1] Matth. xvii. 25.

would have St Peter regard God as the Father of mankind and not only as the Lord and ruler of Israel. The whole point of the lesson lies in the words "then are the children free." These words would be stamped on St Peter's mind by the finding the stater in the fish's mouth; and they would recur to him and bring their proper lesson with them when the right moment came. The circumstance is not in itself necessarily miraculous, but it was rendered so in this case by our Lord's foreseeing that the coin would be found in the first fish that came.

The Temptation on the Mount.

Next comes a scene in which the Spirit of the World is represented as pointing out all the glories of the empire of the inhabited earth, and offering it to our Lord on the strange condition that He should fall down and worship him. This represents, in plain and very forcible imagery, a spiritual temptation to which those who have laboured to regenerate mankind have fallen victims over and over again. Those who have most nearly attained universal conquest, Mahomet, Zengis, Timour, and many great political leaders as well, have begun with a genuine wish to alleviate the ills of mankind, of whom eventually they became a scourge.

I believe that what our Lord sets before us here is the temptation to aim at visible and comparatively immediate success, and to bring about our ideal by using the arts of worldly policy; which were to be supported in the case before us by superhuman power.

We can conceive a Tempter, such as the Satan of *Paradise Regained*, saying as he does,

"Great acts require great means of enterprise,"

and urging worldly counsels such as these:—"You seek to set up a perfect kingdom upon earth, to minimise evil by wise laws, and to make men love God and serve God out of love. You want success and you want it soon, in order that in your lifetime you may see your plans matured. For this, first of all, you must have at your back not merely disciples who shall listen and meditate, but men who can advance *a cause*. The uppermost feeling of the people among whom you have come is the desire to be free from Rome. They have drawn from the Scriptures a notion that a Messiah will soon come and restore the kingdom to Israel. With this view, be it right or wrong, you must fall in. You carry with you powers like those wielded by the prophets of old. Proclaim yourself such a Messiah as men expect. Strike to the ground the Roman eagles that are sent against you. Offer to all who fall on your side a paradise of palpable enjoyments such as they can understand. Shew yourself invulnerable, and be everywhere foremost in the fight. Your superhuman power will balance the enormous might of Rome. In order to win the empire of the world you must employ policy as well as arms. You must excite enthusiasm. You must fascinate crowds by eloquence and lead them to serve your purpose when they think that you are serving theirs. When you have secured the empire, you can inaugurate a golden reign and call on men to bless your Father who sent you to their aid."

If suggestions such as these had been made to our Lord by such a Tempter as Milton imagines, we can see from the reply in our narrative how they would have been met. This kingdom, our Lord would say, so gained might indeed be mine but assuredly it will not be God's; and my business is not to work for myself but for Him. It was this utter absence of self, in our Lord, which men could not comprehend; their common standards could not measure Him—they are bewildered by this, and all but the higher sort are put out of touch with Him.

The picture which our Lord leaves us of His struggle with the evil suggestions of His insidious foe teaches us many lessons, but the clearest of all are these—If we fight the world with its own weapons we soon put our hands out for using any others than those. If we seek what the world has to give we soon fall down and worship it, without having the least intention of doing anything of the kind. But besides giving a lesson for after ages, our Lord here indicates a particular resolve which shaped His action upon earth. It was this,—He would not employ His superhuman powers to force men to obey, or even to resist the violence which might be offered Him. He would not use them to assist in setting up the outward fabric of a Kingdom of God: and then, going a little further, He determines not to set up by His own hand any outward fabric of such a Kingdom at all. He was not to be an aspirant for worldly distinction—He was not to be the *leader of a cause*—He was not to be the founder of a school of philosophy or of any external form of religion at all. He came to do a *Work*, The Central Work of the History of mankind. He declared God, and declared Himself to be united to God, and that He would be with men for ever until the end of the world. But all that has to do with organisation, outward customs, effective sanctions, or the condensing of doctrines into the formulæ of creeds, belongs to the human side of religion, and men of different climes and ages must shape such matters for themselves. He came, as I have said, only to kindle the fire and to set a new force moving in the world. This Law,—that neither force nor worldly policy should be used to carry out the Work of God,—governs all our Lord's acts. It need hardly be said that there is no miracle of our Lord's recounted in the canonical Scriptures in which violence is either done or repelled. In the apocryphal Gospels we find endless legends of the retribution which our Lord brought on those who injured Him, especially in His boyish years.

Neither do we ever find that our Lord so displays His signs or shapes His conduct, as to win from the crowd material support for the work He is carrying on. It was never more important for Him to win over the enthusiasm of the people than when He taught in Jerusalem in the week of the Passover: but no public miracle at all is then performed. It must have seemed strange to the disciples that He did not confound Pilate on his judgment seat, or Herod on his throne, but *we* see that the whole meaning of His coming would have been lost if He had. The disciples however are not left at that time without some indication that His Divine power remained unimpaired—the withering of the fig-tree, and the foretelling to Peter that he should deny Him thrice, shewed them that Jesus was still the Lord. When the Lord in the hands of His enemies turned and looked upon Peter, how striking must have been the contrast between the Kingdoms of the earth and of God!

There is one occasion where our Lord is urged to act in violation of this principle. The sons of Zebedee ask whether they may not call down fire from Heaven on those who would not receive them. "But He turned and rebuked them[1]."

Again, if He had come down from the cross when challenged to do so, this principle would have

---
[1] Luke ix. 55.

THE LAWS OF THE WORKING OF SIGNS. 139

been broken through. Those who said "He saved others, Himself He cannot save[1]," uttered a truth deeper than they dreamed of: it was of the very essence of His mission that He should not use His powers for Himself.

In connexion with this it may be noted that when St Peter is delivered from the prison[2], and St Paul and Silas at Philippi, these deliverances are represented, not as being worked *by* St Peter or St Paul, but as being worked *for* them by the Divine power, without any doing of theirs.

The Temptation on the Pinnacle of the Temple.

When the temptation to employ open force was repelled, a more insidious one came in its stead. It was to use moral compulsion, and, by the public display of a resistless manifestation, to make doubt and opposition disappear.

Our Lord, as I believe, clothes this suggestion in imagery suited to His hearers: He represents Himself as borne to the pinnacle of the Temple and bidden to cast Himself down. Of this pinnacle an account is given by Dr Edersheim: he considers it to have overlooked the Court of the Priests. The following extracts are from his account:—

"In the next temptation Jesus stands on the watch-post which the white-robed priest has just quitted. In the Priests' Court below Him the morning sacrifice has been offered......Now let Him

---

[1] Mark xv. 31.   [2] Acts xii. 7, 8. Acts xvi. 26.

descend, Heaven-borne, into the midst of priests and people. What shouts of acclamation would greet His appearance! What homage of worship would be His[1]!"

This pinnacle, supposing my view to be correct, would offer a fitting scene for the story of this trial, not only as being a giddy height, but because also the spot was a public one, and a crowd of spectators would witness the display. If our Lord had only been tempted to assure Himself of His power by a miracle of adventurous rashness, any precipice would have served as well. The essential force of the temptation lay in the suggestion to prostrate men's minds, and to subjugate their wills, by performing before their eyes an appalling act, the superhuman nature of which could not possibly be gainsaid.

When we leave the external imagery, and come to the gist of the lesson, we find in it the truth which we have had before us over and over again[2]. A man's belief is not *his* belief and will not be effective for moulding his life unless his mind and his will have some part in the acceptance of it; and if his own endeavours were to be on a sudden superseded by Divine action, this would be inconsistent with that studious culture of man's distinctive freedom which runs through the conduct of the world. If will and reason are to be dumb-

---

[1] *The Life and Times of Jesus the Messiah.* Dr. Edersheim, 1. p. 304.
[2] See pp. 23, 24, and pp. 57, 58.

THE LAWS OF THE WORKING OF SIGNS.   141

founded by the interference of absolute power, why should men possess them or care to put them to use? As a fact, God *suggests* but does not *compel*, and our Lord's signs agree herewith. They emphasise His lessons, and witness for God to those who have eyes for Him—but men can reject the lesson, signs and all if they please.

Let us imagine the form the Tempter's arguments might take in the mouth of one like Milton's Satan: "You wish," he might suggest, "men to believe that your power comes from on high. Leave them no room for doubt. People about you look for a Sign from Heaven, such as Joshua worked in Ajalon, and Isaiah displayed in the days of Hezekiah. Beelzebub, they think, may work Signs on earth, but Heaven, they own, is God's domain, and what is written in the skies carries God's hand and seal. Shew men these Signs for which they ask, and display your wonders so as to strike men the most. Cures and works of mercy, witnessed by a few score people, create but little stir. Shew something that all Judea, or at least Jerusalem, can behold *at once;*—great emotions take strongest hold among men in a mass: display a comet or darken the sun; or, to begin with, stand on the pinnacle of the Temple—there is a tradition that there the Messiah should appear[1]—and in the presence of all the crowd hurl yourself into the Priests' Court below."

[1] Dr Edersheim.

To meet these thoughts suggested by the Tempter, there would rise in our Lord's mind a crowd of arguments: some of these I have already ventured to imagine. If our Lord had displayed a Sign of overwhelming effect, and bidden men deny it if they could, He would have paralysed intellectual growth in mankind. Men had been gifted with faculties fitting them to explore and to judge of spiritual things: if these were curtailed of room for exercise, they would languish like limbs disused. Should He bar investigation in one-half of reason's realm? Should He so appal mankind, as to enforce an involuntary acceptance of His claims? Would not this be putting fresh fetters on those whom He was come on earth to set free?

Some miracles of a stupendous character are worked by our Lord, no doubt: such are the Transfiguration and the raising of Jairus' daughter. But, marvellous as these two manifestations were, they were not worked for the mere wonder's sake; men were not brought together to see them. The wondrousness is an inevitable accompaniment of the declaration of God's Kingdom and the disclosing of His ways, but it is not the prime motive of the act. There is no display, no appearance of effort. Expectation is not awakened or the imagination aroused by the announcement of a coming prodigy. Neither were these great works wrought to win proselytes: the few who witness them are already convinced of their Master's Divine power; it is not so much a fuller assurance that they derive from them, as a deeper insight into the ways of God. To the three apostles who already best discerned God's ways, God's power is in these manifestations more fully displayed; no others behold it. Here as everywhere, it is to those who have that more is given.

This same Law governs the appearances of the risen Lord. He does not stand forth in triumph and confound disbelief. He had only to shew Himself in the temple and His enemies would have lain at His feet. But men were not to be convinced against their will: all our accounts agree that it was to His apostles only that our Lord appeared. St Peter says to Cornelius and his friends:

"Him God raised up the third day, and gave him to be made manifest, not to all the people, but unto witnesses that were chosen before of God, even to us, who did eat and drink with him after he rose from the dead[1]."

This limitation is very carefully maintained. Our Lord never appears *in His own form*, when there is any chance of His being beheld by others than disciples. In the garden, at the tomb, and on the way to Emmaus, He shews Himself to disciples in a strange shape and is only made known to them for a moment: He was not to be seen and recognised by any ordinary passer by. His resurrection was not to be a subject of popular rumour

[1] Acts x. 40, 41.

or one for the wonderment of the crowd. Some might say, with the man in the parable, "Nay, but if one go to them from the dead[1], they will repent," but our Lord is averse to sensational impressions: men had had the option of believing or not, and they had made their choice. When however the apostles are together in their upper chamber and the doors are shut, He appears in His accustomed form, with the print of the nails upon His hands and feet, for there was no need then for disguise.

The principle that room is to be left for man's will to act in determining his creed is observed not only in all the New Testament but throughout the spiritual history of mankind. Towards the close of the third chapter I have remarked on the analogy between an overwhelming manifestation, such as a Sign from Heaven, and a rigorous demonstration that Christ's revelation is of God. Men have at times cried out both for one and the other; but if what they demand had been given them, the higher knowledge would have been discontinuous, with uncertainty on one side of a line and absolute certainty on the other. There would have been rigid dykes, as of granite, crossing the field of spiritual thought, which would have baulked our progress.

The Laws which I have stated concerning Signs are steadily observed throughout the canonical Scriptures, although the writers of the books knew nothing of any such Laws. The

---
[1] Luke xvi. 30.

Apocryphal Gospels on the other hand violate these Laws at every turn. This opens out almost a new line of argument on internal evidence. Is not the coincidence strange, supposing that the writers allowed play to their fancies, that all the four Evangelists should have uniformly refrained from introducing any miracle worked merely for miracles' sake; or any one which served to minister to the bodily wants of the worker; or which was employed either to enforce submission or to punish hostility? Is it not also strange that neither in the Gospels nor the Acts have we any instance of any public display of power such as should awe the crowds into belief against their wills?

In this chapter I have considered the series of Temptations, with reference to their bearing on the miracles. I have tried to shew that they supply insight into our Lord's way of solving the problem of introducing the infinite element without causing the finite to disappear. But this is only a student view; and the lesson which the church has always drawn from them is of infinitely greater practical worth. The heads of this lesson are: that the great prizes of life presented themselves to Jesus as they do to us; that they glittered in His eyes as they do in ours; that they offered themselves to His grasp as they sometimes do to ours, and were deliberately renounced by Him as hollow, compared with the blessing of knowing and doing the will of God. Without this record, could we have conceived our Lord as being "Man of the substance of His mother born in the world"? Might we not have looked on Jesus Christ as only a manifestation of Deity, clad in outer human guise, but without human affections; visible indeed to men's eyes, but destitute of a pulse which beats in unison with theirs? This error would have lodged Christianity in mens' heads instead of in their hearts and would have destroyed its universality and force; and this error, the narrative of the Temptation—whether we regard it as apologue or fact —is alike effectual to dispel.

CHAPTER VI.

FROM THE TEMPTATION TO THE MINISTRY IN GALILEE.

Outset of the Work.

WE now come in sight of that part of our Lord's work which is the special subject of this book. We have been shewn something of what passed in His mind during the days in the desert; but we are not told what He intended to accomplish or by what practical steps He would proceed. We need not suppose that He came forth from the desert with His plan of action completely prepared. He may not have settled where He should lay the scene of His work or whom He should take for His helpers. All this would grow clear to Him as time went on. But though He may have been waiting for the guidance of inner voice and outward circumstance as to the way of executing His charge, yet that He had God's work to do and meant to do it is written unmistakeably in His air.

We are shown Him in St John's Gospel on His way to Galilee. A glimpse is given us across His path, and we see Him pass along with the assured tread of one whose part is taken and who knows whither His steps lead. On one point touching the form of His work He is already clear. He is not to come as a practical reformer or as a claimant of power; in these characters He would need active human aid, and the Spirit of the World would enter in: but though He is given functions beyond teaching, yet, in order to wear a garb familiar to the people, He will be in their eyes nothing more, at first, than "a *teacher* come from God[1];" His followers are to be purely *disciples* and not adherents of any other kind. His concern was not with political or social forms of order,—these must be different in different times and different lands. His province was to waken into activity the capacity for knowing God which was practically dormant in the mass of mankind. Before laying down any plan or organising any society, He passes some months in *exploring*, so to say, the tempers, and minds and capacities of the different classes of persons in Jerusalem and Galilee. He is in search of the fittest receptacles for the word. He looks into the hearts of the disciples of John, and of those who like Nicodemus were "scribes instructed into the kingdom of heaven." He turns His eye upon Samaritans and peasants of Galilee; and finally, as we know, decides to choose the quiet Lake shore for the cradle of the *Faith*. The peasants and fishers whose ways He knew—unsentimental, serviceable men—were taken as witnesses for the

[1] John iii. 2.

new revelation: they offered the new flasks wanted for the new wine.

A man who sets about regenerating society commonly begins by remodelling institutions; he trusts to good institutions to make men good: our Lord, as a Teacher, begins at the other end; He goes straight to the men themselves and tries to make *them* better; better men would bring about better ways of ordering their outward lives; but each generation must do this for itself. The success of His enterprise did not rest on its immediate acceptance; and so, He did not aim at drawing *numbers* round Him or at gaining influential proselytes or at consolidating a school or a sect. Christ's work was to go on for ever, and mankind would be redeemed equally, whether many followers or few attended Him while on earth.

It may be asked "Did our Lord from the first see all that lay before Him?" The conclusion from the facts of the history must be that, unless when it were specially summoned, His divine prescience remained in abeyance, and that He, as the Son of Man, was subject to those uncertainties as to the future which attend ordinary human action. He could not have worked together with men, as He did with the Apostles, if He had differed so essentially from them as to know perfectly every day what was going to happen on the next: he could not have experienced surprise; and surprise our Lord certainly shews at the dulness of the disciples in catching His meaning: "He *marvelled*" too at the unbelief of some districts. On occasion we know that He could search men's hearts; but they did not lie bare to His view. Neither can we suppose that, when He charged men not to publish their cures, He knew that He would be disobeyed; or that He chose Judas for an Apostle knowing that he would betray Him. The general drift of the purport of His coming, and His insight into it, grew clearer and clearer the nearer He came to the end; but we have no warrant for supposing that the details of all that would happen on the way lay before Him from the first.

He draws His disciples to Him at first with a cheerful hope: but towards the close of His career He has the air of one moving under a load; and once He gives utterance to what lies at His heart. The words in which He does this throw a light on the question of His purpose and His plan; they are spoken apparently to St Peter—

"I came to cast fire upon the earth; and what will I, if it is already kindled? But I have a baptism to be baptized with; and how am I straitened till it be accomplished![1]"

It needed one sent from God to kindle this fire, and to bring home to men the truth that His Spirit worked within them to will and to do; but when the kindling was once effected, the rest might be left to human effort. Men could feed the flame

[1] Luke xii. 49, 50.

and men could fan it; and so, following the law we have traced in operation so often, to men the flame was left, for them to feed and fan. "This being done," our Lord might say, "this for which I came,—why do I linger here? what more do I want?" and yet He might add "My whole work is *not* done: the crowning act remains. Men will never understand my love at all unless I die for them.". Until He was baptised with this baptism of suffering, He was like one straitened on every side by an imperious task which claims his every thought.

Our Lord's movements from the Temptation on to the Ministry in Galilee are made known to us by the Gospel of St John. Jesus appears on the banks of the Jordan, where John was still baptising his disciples; He mixes with the throng; the Baptist points Him out to two young men, one of whom, Andrew, brings his brother to visit Him; the other was probably the Evangelist himself. Afterwards our Lord Himself finds Philip, and Philip finds Nathanael, and the little party travel on foot to Cana of Galilee. No writer, who did not confine himself to facts about which he was certain, would have given so homely a story of the beginning of so mighty a matter.

The Gospel of St John is manifestly written by one who is in the position of a disciple; he sees everything from the disciple's point of view: what the *disciples* thought of things that happened seems to be always uppermost in his mind. He is not a writer composing a continuous biography of our Lord, but a disciple drawing lessons from particular scenes of his Master's life; and he no more thinks of considering *why* our Lord took the course He did, than he would consider why the seasons change. An historian might have looked for reasons why our Lord did not appear in public life in Jerusalem; but John does not look on the matter with an historian's eye.

I will here summarise the occasions on which the disciples are mentioned, in the period of the history embraced in this chapter. We first hear of them in the account of the wedding at Cana. The Evangelist relates that "He manifested forth His glory, *and His disciples believed on Him*[1]." Next we find the disciples spoken of, as if they stood in a kind of family relation to Him. "He went down to Capernaum, He, and His mother, and His brethren, and *His disciples*[2]." When we come to the account of the cleansing of the Temple, it is pointed out how that action struck the disciples. They talked it over among themselves; they recalled the verse in the Psalms, "The zeal of Thine house shall eat me up[3]," and thought they saw a Messianic prophecy fulfilled: we are told too that after our Lord's death they recalled His words about building the Temple in three days. We hear also that they were numerous: "*many* believed

[1] John ii. 11.   [2] John ii. 12.   [3] John ii. 17.

on His name, beholding the signs which He did[1]." Next comes a fact of great importance; it is that, though our Lord did not baptise adherents, yet that His disciples did so, and that finally more resorted to them than to the Baptist[2]. A few disciples attended our Lord in the journey through Samaria, and to them His first recorded discourse as a teacher is addressed: there is no further mention of them during the period embraced in this chapter. Such is the summary of the matter bearing on my subject; I proceed to discuss points of interest that arise out of it.

The advent of our Lord differed from that of other enlighteners of mankind in one very striking way. He had, in the Baptist, a special forerunner, who gave out, on all occasions, that the final cause of his own preaching was to prepare the way for one greater than himself. Events of national history, themselves part of that wide-spreading "Preparatio Evangelica" which, to my mind, underlies the history of the world, had raised a ferment in the minds of the inhabitants of Palestine. To this movement the Baptist gave a particular turn. He brought men to desire that the world should become better, and taught them that they must begin by becoming better themselves. Without this preparation, the germs of truth which our Lord scattered would more largely have failed to quicken: the Baptist had broken up the soil to

[1] John ii. 23.   [2] John iii. 22, iv. 2.

receive the seed; his preaching put the people in an attitude of expectancy, and an expectant condition is a receptive one. The Old Testament prophecies had worked to this same end; they had made expectancy congenial to the nation's mind. The Israelites were like spectators waiting to see a great king come with a procession: the sight of a forerunner sets the crowd astir, and such a forerunner John was. I have observed before, that in carrying out His own work our Lord is careful to use *preparation*. The disciples are sent "to every place where He Himself would come." Men were not to be repelled from the new movement by reason of its being strange to them. What this preparation did for the villages of Galilee the Baptist did on a grander scale for all Judæa.

We get but a glimpse of the nature of the relation between John and his disciples, and need only notice it briefly. Young men did not, like those who sat at the feet of a Rabbi, resort to him for definite instruction: the disciples of John did not look to be taught interpretations of the Law or of the Prophets, but they looked for a rule of life for themselves and a brighter future for their country or their race—they were ill-satisfied with the present and eagerly turned to one who represented both in aspect and in utterance the prophets of old. There was one feature in John's ministry, so distinctive that he drew his appellation

THE OUTSET OF THE WORK. 155

from it.—He caused his disciples to be baptised. The doctrines implied in the rite do not now concern me; to some it symbolised the cleansing from sin, to others the rising into a new life; but the practical effect of it was to make those who received it feel that they had, in a way, pledged their allegiance to John by receiving baptism at his hands: they had assumed a badge, and were bound by ties of personal loyalty to their master and to one another[1].

But John's disciples were not separated off from the outside mass by baptism alone. To the mind of his countrymen a religion was not a religion at all, unless it included a *regimen*, unless it parcelled out their days, according to hours of prayer and times of fasting. With such a distinctive rule John provided his followers. He taught them to pray[2], he accustomed them to voluntary fasts[3]; and on some points of ceremonial, such as purification, he may have had tenets of his own[4].

We will now trace the steps by which our Lord gathers disciples round Him. It is possible that even before our Lord left Galilee He had been the centre of a group of young men who looked up to Him, and the Galileans among John's dis-

---

[1] "I thank God that I baptized none of you save Crispus and Gaius; lest any man should say that ye were baptized into my name." 1 Cor. i. 14, 15. This, with the context, illustrates the notion of a personal tie established by baptism. St Paul is combating the charge of establishing a sect of his own.

[2] Luke xi. 1.   [3] Luke v. 33.   [4] John iii. 25.

ciples might therefore have heard of Him. It falls in also with this supposition, that our Lord seems to have been already acquainted with Philip of Bethsaida, and to have purposely sought him out. We read—"He *findeth* Philip, and saith unto him, Follow me[1]." Philip hastens to Nathanael[2], who came from Cana in Galilee, and tells him that the Messiah has been found in the person of "Jesus the son of Joseph, *the man from Nazareth*[3]." The words in italics *may* imply "of whom we have all heard;" for Cana was not more than six miles from Nazareth, and Bethsaida was in the same district. The Baptist, we know, regarded Him, when He came to be baptised, as his equal or superior in the favour of God.

Five of the Apostles—John, Andrew, Peter, Philip and Nathanael—were drawn to our Lord in the few days spent at Bethabara on His return from the desert; and probably all these went back with Him to Galilee. Among these five we find traces of a lasting tie. This is worth noting, because such a tie would naturally arise from comradeship in early years, and of this comradeship St John's Gospel speaks. These five had gone together from Galilee, in the zeal of their young days, to listen to the strange preacher in the desert of Judæa; they had lived together, faring alike, and baring their hearts each to the other in

---

[1] John i. 43.   [2] John i. 45; xxi. 2.
[3] τὸν ἀπὸ Ναζαρέτ. John i. 46.

the confidence of youth. We can understand that this would bind men fast together, and that St John writing his Gospel at the end of his life, with possibly St Andrew at his side, should have been mindful of all the circumstances in which these old friends took part, and have gladly taken occasion to mention their names[1].

Accordingly, we find mention made in the Gospel, without positive occasion, of these Apostles by name. We did not need to know that it was Andrew who said "There is a lad here who hath five barley-loaves and two small fishes[2]." The Synoptists[3] all relate the miracle of the feeding of the five thousand, but Andrew is named by St John alone: Philip, another of this little company, is close by; he is addressed by our Lord, and Andrew interposes. We find Philip and Andrew together at a later time.

---

[1] A fragment of a very ancient account of the Canon of the N. Test. has been preserved by Muratori. I will quote the translation of it from Professor Westcott's work. (Prof. Westcott, *Gospel of St John*, p. xxxv.) "The fourth Gospel [was written by] John, one of the disciples (*i.e.* Apostles). When his fellow-disciples and bishops urgently pressed (*cohortantibus*) him, he said, 'Fast with me [from] to-day, for three days, and let us tell one another any revelation which may be made to us, either for or against [the plan of writing] (*quid cuique fuerit revelatum alterutrum*)'. On the same night it was revealed to Andrew, one of the Apostles, that John should relate all in his own name, and that all should review [his writing]." If we accept this authority, John and Andrew were together in their age as they had been in their youth. Philip also was at Hierapolis not very far off.

[2] John vi. 8.

[3] i.e. the Evangelists Matthew, Mark, and Luke.

When the Greeks who came up and worshipped at the feast wished to see Jesus they applied to Philip[1]; then we have

"Philip cometh and telleth *Andrew:* Andrew cometh, and Philip, and they tell Jesus."

St John here seems almost to go out of his way to speak of Andrew.

Philip also, who scarcely appears in the Synoptical Gospels, is mentioned six times by St John; and he is found in company, now with Andrew, now with Nathanael, as if the ties of old companionship still held. The particulars we have of Philip are instructive. Our Lord, as we have seen, "found him," which I take to mean, not that He merely *lighted upon him*, but that He sought him. He thought him, therefore, a suitable companion for His coming journey to Jerusalem for the Passover. A point of fitness may have been that he knew Greek: his Greek name would not by itself go far to prove this; but, taking it along with the fact that when the Greeks come up to worship in Jerusalem they address themselves to Philip, it seems likely that he knew their language. Our Lord at the Passover would meet many Israelites who talked Greek more readily than Aramaic, and a Greek-speaking follower would be of service

[1] John xii. *vv.* 20—22.

to Him. Again when Philip says, "Lord, shew us the Father and it sufficeth us[1]," our Lord replies, Have I been *so long* with you and you have not known me? The words "so long" are particularly applicable to Philip, as he had been called a year before the twelve were formed into a body, and may have remained in constant attendance on our Lord when the other disciples quitted Him after the return through Samaria.

With Nathanael also there is much interest connected. He, in the last chapter of St John's Gospel, is called Nathanael of Cana of Galilee, and is named among others who are Apostles. He is identified, on good grounds, with the Bartholomew of the Synoptical Gospels[2]. We mark in Nathanael an aptitude for discerning spiritual greatness; but, with all this, he held stoutly to old prejudices in which he had been born and bred; and when Philip comes to him with his tidings, he breaks out with: "Can there any good thing come out of Nazareth?" There is no reason to suppose that Nazareth was held generally in bad estimation. Natives of Jerusalem would look down on all villages in Galilee without distinction, but Nathanael belonged not to Jerusalem but to Cana. Cana and Nazareth were a few miles apart, each being the chief town in its own district; and the local jealousy and ten-

---

[1] John xiv. 9.
[2] Bartholomew = son of Tolmai, so that Nathanael son of Tolmai or (as Dr Edersheim writes it) of Temalgon, would be the full name.

dency to mutual disparagement between neighbours, which is not unknown among ourselves, and was rife in those times, will account for Nathanael's words[1].

It was of no ill augury for his holding fast the Faith when he had found it, that he clung to the old traditionary feeling of his native town. He was not blinded by it; he is ready to "go and see." Here our Lord exercises His singular gift of introspection, "Behold," says He, "an Israelite indeed, in whom there is no guile."

"Nathanael saith unto him, Whence knowest thou me? Jesus answered and said unto him, Before Philip called thee, when thou wast under the fig-tree, I saw thee. Nathanael answered him, Rabbi, thou art the Son of God; thou art King of Israel[2]."

Probably Nathanael recalled what had passed in his mind when he had been under the fig-tree. Perhaps some mystery of existence had then

---

[1] Tacitus speaking of Lugdunum and Vienna on opposite sides of the Rhone, tells us that they regarded each other with the animosity which "serves as a link between those whom only a river separates" ("unde aemulatio et invidia et uno amne discretis connexum odium"). Tac. *Hist.* I. c. 65.

St Matthew speaks of that "which was spoken by the prophets, He shall be called a Nazarene." This prophecy, in the words given, is not found in our canonical books. The Evangelist is supposed to refer to Is. xi. 1. The Hebrew word for a Branch, there used, is *Natsar*.

[2] John i. 48, 49.

weighed upon his soul, and on coming to Christ he found "the thoughts of his heart revealed[1]."

In our Lord's reply to Nathanael we find His first recorded utterance as a Preacher of the Word; here He first speaks of Himself as the Son of Man, and here we have the first hint of the Law, "To him who hath shall be given," a law which has been several times before us and will be so again before long. Nathanael *had* something already; he was enough in earnest to drop his prejudices; a slight token had enabled him to see in our Lord "the Son of God, the King of Israel:" he is told that he shall see greater things than these. Jacob had dreamed of old[2] that there was a ladder between earth and heaven, by which God's angels went and came; such a ladder Christ was, and he, the Israelite in whom there was no guile, should see "the angels of God ascending and descending upon the Son of Man[3]."

So far I have followed the Gospel of St John. The Synoptists afford corroborative matter to shew that the little company, which had met at Bethabara, continued to hang together.

(1) In St Mark's[4] list of the Apostles—the names "and Andrew, and Philip, and Bartholomew" come together in the enumeration. If we were asked for the names of a society of twelve men whom we knew—they would occur by the twos and threes

---

[1] Luke ii. 35. [2] Genesis xxviii. 12.
[3] John i. 51.   [4] Mark iii. 17—19.

who were most together. St Peter, whom we may regard here as St Mark's informant, gives the names as they came to mind. He recalls journeys in the hill country, when the disciples had walked in scattered groups, three or four together. In one of these little knots Andrew, Philip, and Bartholomew may commonly have been found.

(2) From the way in which St Matthew's[1] list is given we may infer something of greater interest still. St Matthew gives the names of the Apostles *in pairs:* Simon and Andrew, James and John, Philip and Bartholomew, Thomas and Matthew— and so on. Immediately after the list of names we have the sending forth of the Apostles to the cities of Israel. I believe that the Apostles went on this mission in the pairs which are above-named. Why else should the names be coupled together? The Evangelist had in his eye the party as they had stood listening to their Master's words, with their staves in their hands, ready to start. He recollects their separating—two going one way, and two another,—and therefore, two by two, he puts them down in his list[2]. It is curious that though St Matthew *couples* the names, yet he does not say,

---

[1] Matth. x. 2—6.

[2] If a party of young men were in the habit of separating for excursions and going two by two, and one of the party were afterwards asked for a list of the company; it would help his memory to recall them, pair by pair. The Evangelist is going to tell us of our Lord's directions to the twelve about their mission. It then strikes him that he must record their names.

as St Mark and St Luke do, that the Apostles were sent *two and two* together. The coupling in St Matthew is a kind of coincidence with that express direction which is preserved by St Mark and St Luke.

Not only, then, is there probable evidence to shew that, out of the little body of the earliest disciples, three clung together; but also that two of them—Philip and Bartholomew—formed one of the pairs that went forth declaring to the villages of Galilee that the Kingdom of God was at hand. At all events the Synoptists testify to a special intimacy between two disciples; and circumstances, which are disclosed by St John alone, shew how this intimacy naturally arose. Thus we have, what is always worth noting, a corroboration by the Synoptists of the narrative of the fourth Evangelist.

To return to the history in the Gospel of St John. Our Lord sets out on His return to Galilee, and may have been Nathanael's guest at Cana for the night preceding the wedding. It does not fall within my scope to say more about the miracle than has been said already. The statement important for my purpose is, that our Lord manifested His glory, "and *His disciples* believed on Him[1]." The fact that a new teacher worked wonders and drew disciples round him made a stir in the district; and this may throw light upon the passage which follows.

[1] John ii. 11.

"After this he went down to Capernaum, he, and his mother, and his brethren, and *his* disciples: and there they abode not many days[1]."

This event leads to no consequences in the history. It would only have been mentioned by one who, having the sequence of occurrences in his head, detailed them all. Still, there must have been some motive for this removal of the whole family to Capernaum. I will hazard a conjecture, which if correct will help to explain the following text which occurs later on:

"And after the two days he went forth from thence into Galilee. For Jesus himself testified, that a prophet hath no honour in his own country. So when he came into Galilee, the Galilæans received him, having seen all the things that he did in Jerusalem at the feast: for they also went unto the feast[2]."

Why does the Evangelist say that our Lord was Himself an instance of the rejection of a prophet in his own country, at the very time when he is about to say that the Galileans *did* receive Him because they had seen what He did at the feast? There must have been some previous occasion on which He had *not* been received. I believe that the last quoted passage, fully expressed, might run thus: "He went forth from thence into Galilee *but not to Nazareth*, for Jesus Himself testified that a prophet hath no honour in his own country," and *therefore* He passed by Nazareth and went on to

[1] John ii. 12. [2] John iv. 43—45.

Cana, a few miles further north. Now, at what time could our Lord have experienced this ill reception? I find no occasion on which such disparagement of His claims can have been shewn, excepting in the short interval between the miracle at Cana and this withdrawal of the whole family to Capernaum. I would therefore conjecture that on leaving Cana, after the miracle, our Lord had returned with His mother to Nazareth, and that the inhabitants had then in some way shown ill-will[1]. He probably brought with Him some disciples belonging to Cana—a place of which they were jealous—hailing Him as Rabbi, and proclaiming Him their Master. The people of Nazareth resented this assumption of superiority on the part of a townsman whom they had known from His birth. The whole family are involved in the unpopularity, and remove to Capernaum, to wait the time for going up to the Passover.

Though St John makes no mention, in its proper place, of the animosity of the people of Nazareth, yet the recollection of it remains in his mind; so that, when he says that our Lord went *into Galilee* on His return from Samaria, this seems to him noticeable, as though it were strange He should go where He had been ill received before; and he tells us why He is well received on this occasion; namely, because some had brought back word of His vigorous action in cleansing the

[1] The tone of His discourse delivered there, after His visit to Jerusalem, falls in with this view.

Temple. Our Lord does not go to Nazareth, but again makes His stay at Cana.

To return to this short stay at Capernaum. The point I am most concerned with is, that it is here that the disciples are first mentioned as attached to our Lord in His movements; they form, as it were, part of His family. If our Lord had already met with opposition, as I have conjectured, this would have helped to bind the little company closer together. We hear of no preaching or working of Signs during the short stay at Capernaum. We are not positively told that the disciples went with our Lord to Jerusalem[1]; but I imagine that the five of whom we have read went up to the Passover, though some may have returned to Galilee soon after the feast[2].

The narrative of the cleansing of the Temple shews how burning was our Lord's indignation at practices that degraded men's notions of God.

---

[1] It must be recollected that there is no mention in St John's Gospel of any disciple *by name*, after the first chapter, until we come to the sixth.

[2] It may be asked, How were the disciples maintained during several weeks at Jerusalem? Though not of the poorest class they could not have lived long without labour. John may have been spared because James remained to help his father in his work. But if Peter and Andrew had both stayed at Jerusalem through all the early summer, it is hard to see how they, and Peter's wife, could have been supported. I should conjecture therefore that if Peter went to Jerusalem to the first passover, he only made a brief stay. There were, at this time, apparently no contributions such as we hear of afterwards (Luke viii. 3).

Personal attacks He bore with meekness, "when He was reviled He reviled not again, when He suffered He threatened not[1];" but He gives free vent to a godly wrath when He finds men driving a traffic in holy things.

A personal characteristic of our Lord, shewn again and again, comes for the first time before us here: He carried authority in His air, an authority that needed no assertion, but to which men bowed. The owners of the oxen yield without resistance to the determination He shews. It is only the Hierarchy who ask, "What sign shewest thou unto us, seeing that thou doest these things[2]?" I need not say that on demand He will work no Sign at all: this is His invariable rule.

St John says nothing of the nature of the miracles wrought by our Lord at this time; we only hear that they induced people "to believe in His name[3]." They may have been chiefly miracles of introspection, like the recognition of Peter, the seeing of Nathanael under the fig-tree, and the divining of His mother's meaning when she said "they have no wine;" for St John assiduously keeps before his hearers this insight of our Lord into men's minds. In particular he says, in reference to the disciples who gathered round Him in Judæa,

"But Jesus did not trust himself unto them, for that he knew all men, and because he needed not that any one should bear witness concerning man: for he himself knew what was in man[4]."

[1] 1 Peter ii. 23.   [2] John ii. 16.   [3] John ii. 23.   [4] John ii. 24, 25.

When our Lord drove out the money-changers and those who sold doves, people thronged to Him in Jerusalem, thinking that the leader whom they sought had come. But these were not disciples after His own heart, not such as should receive the kingdom of God as little children. These were men who had both notions and a purpose of their own; men who would follow Him as long as He went *their* way; and who, when He did not, would "go back and walk no more with Him[1]." The relation of our Lord to these early Judæan disciples was very different from that in which He stood, either to the five who had gone with Him from Bethabara to Cana and Capernaum, or to those who afterwards thronged to His preaching of the Kingdom of Heaven. To these Judæan disciples our Lord as far as we know delivers no lessons and issues no directions; we do not hear that they were especially chosen for witnesses of the Signs in Jerusalem, or that they formed an organised body in any way. It seems rather as if a body of men ranged themselves round our Lord and, from their admiration for Him, took the name of His disciples, but did not hold themselves to be under orders, and came and went as they pleased.

Our Lord had not yet begun His real Ministry; He was probing the capacities and natures both of individual men and of different classes in the community, with a view to testing their fitness for taking part in His great work.

[1] John vi. 66.

Something inclined Him, we may suppose, to take Galilee for the cradle of the new movement; and the circumstance that those who first adhered were all Galilæans pointed along the same way. It would appear to be a method of Divine guidance, to speak by a whisper within, and, at the same time, so to order circumstances without, that one should fall in with the other: sometimes this coincidence will be perceived and will strike the beholder with a kind of awe, and sometimes it will operate on him without his being aware.

There was much that made Galilee suitable: its position was at once central and retired, and its inhabitants were, according to Josephus, sturdy and independent, and, of course, free from the pedantry of Rabbinical schools. Jerusalem however claimed a trial from our Lord. He desired to know what was passing there in the minds of those who were seeking truth. It was possible that a cradle for the infant church might be found among the followers of the Baptist, or among Scribes like Nicodemus. Our Lord gauges the fitness of both these bodies of men. We know what conclusion settled itself in His mind during those early days: He must not put new wine into old bottles. The enlightened party among those in authority were more after the type of Erasmus than of Luther, they lacked force: they had been trained to pick their way through difficulties of interpretation, but not to grasp great principles, still less to *act;* and though they divined that there was a truth dawning from afar, yet their feeling for it was not so much a passion as a taste.

After the discourse with Nicodemus the Evangelist returns to narration, and tells us of a visit of our Lord and His disciples to the district where the Baptist was carrying on his work. It may have been that he meant to represent our Lord as turning from Nicodemus to John's disciples; as if, when He found the former unequal to the need, He would try how the latter might serve. The words are

"After these things came Jesus and his disciples into the land of Judæa; and there he tarried with them, and baptized. And John also was baptizing in Ænon near to Salim, because there was much water there: and they came, and were baptized[1]."

It is not said that our Lord actually went to the spot where John was; but the narrative favours the view that the two companies were not far from one another. We are told that followers were drawn in large numbers to our Lord and that His disciples baptised them. This adoption of the rite which, though not unknown before, had been brought into special prominence by the Baptist, excited jealousy in John's disciples—

"And they came unto John, and said to him, Rabbi, he that was with thee beyond Jordan, to whom thou hast borne witness, behold, the same baptizeth, and all men come to him[2]."

[1] John iii. 22, 23.   [2] John iii. 26.

One reason of the anxiety of the disciples to baptise may possibly have been this; they saw how that outward rite supplied John's disciples with a badge that marked them out and made one body of them; they were all bound together to the same master by having received baptism at his hands,—bound together not merely by holding the same opinions and honouring the same man, but by something that had been *done*, by a work wrought upon *them*. Some might interpret this "outward and visible sign" in one way and some in another, but all could see the value of such a sign or symbol for giving coherence and permanency to their new community.

In the fourth chapter we find that the Pharisees at Jerusalem,—they who constituted the religious world of the place,—had come to the knowledge that the resort to Jesus was greater than that to St John—

"When therefore the Lord knew how that the Pharisees had heard that Jesus was making and baptizing more disciples than John (although Jesus himself baptized not, but his disciples), he left Judæa and departed again into Galilee[1]."

I make out St John's meaning to be, that our Lord quitted Judæa because He found Himself thrust into apparent rivalry with John the Baptist. The Judæan disciples wanted a sect of their own; and the Pharisees regarded our Lord's following as

[1] John iv. 1, 2.

an offshoot from the movement of John, an offshoot which was likely to out-top the parent tree.

It seems to me that our Lord was taking a survey of the different religious sections in Judæa and examining their fitness to furnish helpers for His work. Scholars who like Nicodemus were quick to ask "How can these things be?" were not of the right order for setting a great movement afoot. If men were fully possessed with the momentous nature of God's spiritual working in the world, the idea of this as a *fact* would take up all their minds leaving no room for the question of *mode*. If Nicodemus had been capable of seeing how sublime was the future presented to him, he would never have expected to understand *how* it could come to pass. Next our Lord tried the disciples of John; these may have been too full of the spirit of partizanship, and too much taken up with questions of purifying and the like, to be fit foster parents for the new Faith. Whatsoever were the cause, in neither of these classes did our Lord find a cradle for the faith. He required men plastic and receptive, capable of devoted self-surrender and possessed of self-transforming and expanding powers. These did not grow freely in the social climate of Judæa; our Lord's thoughts then, we may suppose, went back to His own people and His own country, and He preached the Kingdom first in Galilee.

Our Lord's leaving Judæa was precipitated by

the rivalry which was threatening between His adherents and those of John; more especially as that rivalry was taking the form of a competition in point of numbers. For the spirit which this would engender was to our Lord abhorrent in the extreme. When sect strives with sect, and they would decide the contest for superiority *by counting heads*, they are both in a way to fall down and worship the Spirit of the world.

Our Lord was not founding or setting up a form of religion to which He personally would convert mankind; but He and His work were part of the subject-matter of all religion—the relations of God to man. The apostles are never encouraged to exult in the number of their converts. Even when they were sent through the cities, on what we might regard as a missionary errand, they are not directed to win men over by strong entreaty—they are not then bidden, as men afterwards were by St Paul, to "be instant in season and out of season[1];" they are only to proclaim the Kingdom of God: those who have ears to hear will hear, and the rest will go their way.

Any competition with John the Baptist was above all to be shunned. Our Lord and the Baptist were bound together by early ties. Jesus had sought and received Baptism at his hand, and we always see a delicate and unswerving fidelity in His behaviour towards him. It might be that He was

[1] 2 Tim. iv. 2.

to increase and John was to decrease, but it should not be by any action of His that that change of relative position should be brought about. The Gospel itself, then, discloses grounds for our Lord's sudden departure into Galilee. Thus early, among the hearers of our Lord and the Baptist, appeared an insidious tendency to form parties, a tendency which broke out disastrously in later times; when some said, "I am of Paul" and others "I am of Apollos[1]."

There is no valid reason for supposing that our Lord left Judæa from fear of persecution. The Pharisees may have been in commotion when they heard that Jesus baptised more disciples than John; and there may have been some stir in sacerdotal circles at Jerusalem, but there is no appearance of violence having been threatened. Neither do I connect our Lord's journey with the captivity of the Baptist. I believe that John was not thrown into prison till three or four months after this journey through Samaria; but supposing that the imprisonment had already taken place and it had seemed likely that Herod's jealousy of John would extend to Jesus, our Lord would not have left Judæa, which was not under Herod's jurisdiction, and have gone into Galilee which was so.

At any rate our Lord quits Judæa and the Judæan disciples, or all but a few of them, and travels back to Galilee with a little company who

[1] 1 Cor. i. 12.

were bound to Him, and who tended Him, it would seem, with affectionate solicitude[1].

It does not come into my plan to discuss the discourses of our Lord except so far as they bear on the training of the apostles, and so I pass by the discourse with the woman of Samaria, as I have done that with Nicodemus. I believe that only three or four disciples attended our Lord on His journey: if they had been numerous, they would not *all* have left Him, wearied and alone at the fountain. But in visiting a strange town in Samaria, it might be unwise to enter with a smaller party than three or four; so that if the disciples numbered no more than this, we can account for our Lord being left by Himself.

This journey through Samaria has an important bearing on my subject. Here, for the first time, we have a conversation of our Lord with His disciples; and, what is more, we get a glimpse of an office in store for them, of a work that is to give a meaning to their lives. The disciples of the Baptist had been learners and listeners only; but our Lord's disciples were not to be mere passive recipients of teaching. They were to be taught by doing as well as by hearing; they were to take part with Him in the great work that was to be wrought in the world. They were not servants—"for the servant knoweth

[1] John iv. 31. They press Him to take bodily support about which they thought Him careless. This must be an eye-witness's account.

not what his lord doeth[1]," but they were friends joining in the common cause. We may wonder why no earlier converse of our Lord with His disciples is preserved. Possibly, before this, there were in the company some of those to whom He "did not commit Himself[2]." While these were present, our Lord may have maintained a reserve, and said nothing bearing on His work which it was important for the Evangelist to record. But, when our Lord set out through the semi-hostile country of Samaria in the midst of the early summer heat, those only followed who were in earnest, and on whom He could rely.

I pass on at once to that address to the disciples to which I have alluded. Our Lord had been cheered by the Samaritan woman's openness to the truth. On leaving the well He comes on a scene, than which few are more gladdening—a great expanse of corn growing luxuriantly, swaying with the wind and glistening in the sun. We mark that He was always keenly alive to external impression, and in all He saw espied matter that fitted what He taught. Our Lord is struck by the sight, He sees in it something that answers to His thoughts, and which seems to convey a promise which rejoices His soul—not for Himself but for His disciples. The discourse is as follows:

"Say not ye, There are yet four months, and *then* cometh the harvest? behold, I say unto you, Lift up your

---

[1] John xv. 15. [2] John ii. 24.

eyes, and look on the fields, that they are white already unto harvest. He that reapeth receiveth wages, and gathereth fruit unto life eternal; that he that soweth and he that reapeth may rejoice together. For herein is the saying true, One soweth, and another reapeth. I sent you to reap that whereon ye have not laboured: others have laboured, and ye are entered into their labour[1]."

The work before the disciples is only to reap: others had ploughed and sown. Prophets and teachers, and also rulers and judges, all who had helped to bring the Israelites into the condition of being ripe for better things—these past teachers of men, as well as all the impersonal workings of the unseen hand which had smoothed the way— all these answered to the ploughers and sowers of the crop which the apostles were now to reap. This "Præparatio Evangelica," so often before us, had been the combined result of many sorts of action, and into the fruits of this labour the disciples were now to enter. They, along with all those who had sowed and tended, should one day rejoice together, when the grain was garnered in heaven, and when those accounted worthy of the Resurrection to Eternal Life should enter on their reward.

Gleams of gladness in our Lord's career come rarely, and His joy is always for others' sake. It is not for Himself, not even for the cause that He rejoices—that cause would surely triumph in its own time—but His joy is, that He beholds a successful

---

[1] John iv. 35—38. See Chronological Appendix.

and glorious career opening before His fellow-labourers, the few friends at His side. On the return of the seventy recorded by St Luke, this same joy for His disciples' sake is especially spoken of.

"In that same hour he rejoiced in the Holy Spirit, and said, I thank thee, O Father, Lord of heaven and earth, that thou didst hide these things from the wise and understanding, and didst reveal them unto babes: yea, Father; for so it was well-pleasing in thy sight. All things have been delivered unto me of my Father: and no one knoweth who the Son is, save the Father; and who the Father is, save the Son, and he to whomsoever the Son willeth to reveal *him*[1]."

It would seem that such happiness as our Lord found on earth came from marking the affectionate fidelity of the Apostles and their growth in favour with God. "Ye are they," says He to them, "who have continued with me in my temptations[2]" and He speaks of the "joy in heaven" and again of the "joy in the presence of the angels of God," "over one sinner that repenteth[3];" every one who turned to Him with a single heart brought Him gladness. This joyousness, we may believe, spread a gleam over the life of our Lord and of His disciples, until when near the end the shadow came. The disciples were always slow to understand His hints of coming sorrow; they could not conceive that the spiritual triumph was to be emphasised by being contrasted with bodily

[1] Luke x. 21, 22. [2] Luke xxii. 28. [3] Luke xv. 10.

suffering; and He had no more the heart to break the whole sad truth to them, than He had to waken the sleepers at Gethsemane. Circumstances would teach the apostles all the truth in time, but even His plain words on the last journey[1] do not seem to have been taken literally.

For reasons given in the chronological appendix I place the return of our Lord through Samaria early in May A.D. 28.

Between the return through Samaria and the journey up to 'the feast of the Jews[2],' some months have to be accounted for. St John relates but a single incident, the cure of the nobleman's son at Capernaum, as belonging to this time; but I would also place here the preaching in the synagogues in Galilee mentioned by St Luke. His words are—

"And Jesus returned in the power of the Spirit into Galilee: and a fame went out concerning him through all the region round about. And he taught in their synagogues, being glorified of all[3]."

This is parallel with St John's statement, before discussed, "The Galilæans received Him, having seen all the things that He did at Jerusalem at the feast[4]."

I also refer to this period the preaching in the synagogue at Nazareth. The tone of this discourse as I have already observed (pp. 164, 165) tallies with the notion before advanced of a previous ill

[1] Mark x. 33, 34. [2] John v. 1. [3] Luke iv. 14, 15. [4] John iv. 45.

reception of our Lord at Nazareth. There is no mention of our Lord's mother or brethren, they had left Nazareth (John ii. 12) and we do not hear of their return. At other places in Galilee, our Lord had been received with enthusiasm, but at Nazareth petty jealousies prevailed. He does not, in this sermon, speak like one returning with renown to a warm welcome in his own town. He has an air of expecting opposition, as if He had met with it before. He condemns the narrow localising spirit of His hearers, and goes so far as to impugn the exclusive claim of the people of Israel to be the recipients of the favour of God.

It is to be remarked that no mention is made of *disciples* being in attendance upon our Lord, from the time of His reaching Galilee by way of Samaria to that of His presenting Himself to the four Apostles by the Lake shore—that is, as I take it, from May to October A.D. 28[1]. The little company that came through Samaria probably broke up on reaching Galilee. They had their bread to earn and for the most part went back to their callings; while our Lord during the summer of A.D. 28 was preaching in various synagogues, and went, almost

---

[1] If a body of disciples had accompanied our Lord to Nazareth, they would probably have offered some opposition to the Nazarenes. The absence of all mention of disciples in St Luke, chap. iv. gives reason for supposing that the visit to Nazareth here recorded is not the same with that related in St Matthew and St Mark; for the disciples were then present. See Mark vi. 1—6, Matth. xiii. 53.

unattended, to Jerusalem. The absence of His followers would account for the scantiness of our information as to this period.

I suppose that the feast spoken of in St John's Gospel (chap. v. 1), took place early in the autumn of the same year A.D. 28. It was, I conceive, about the close of this feast that the Baptist was thrown into prison; upon this, our Lord returned into Galilee, and His official ministry began[1].

We cannot suppose Him to have been quite alone at this feast at Jerusalem, because some one must have been there to report what took place. I do not think that John was with our Lord at the feast, because, if he had been so, he could only have been absent from Him a few days before our Lord rejoined him on the Lake shore, and the incidents of this call give the impression that the separation had been of much greater length. I incline to think that our Lord was attended by Philip, who alone, at that time, had received the

[1] I incline to the old view which identified this feast with the feast of Tabernacles; the time suits well with my chronological scheme. This was "*the* feast" of the Jews, it caused great stir. Now Josephus tells us, that Herod put John in prison because men came to him in crowds. This was more likely to happen when men were set free from their work by the holiday than at other times. It is true that in ch. vii. 2, John calls the feast of tabernacles by name. But he is there writing his own account, while here he is only recasting, as I believe, what he has received from an eye-witness. This may account for the difference of expression. Some MSS. but not the weightiest, read "*the* feast," in John v. 1. If this were received it would go far to settle the point.

182   THE OUTSET OF THE WORK.

order "Follow Me[1]." If John drew some of his information from Philip, this will help to account for his frequent mention of him[2].

It was on our Lord's visit to this feast that He first incurred the active enmity of the Scribes. It followed from His miracle at the pool of Bethesda, which took place on the Sabbath day. Since the cure was wrought by a word there was no breach of the law; but "the Jews" (by which word St John indicates the hierarchy) were shocked that He should tell the man to carry his bed on the Sabbath day.

"The man went away, and told the Jews that it was Jesus which had made him whole. And for this cause did the Jews persecute Jesus, because he did these things on the sabbath. But Jesus answered them, My Father worketh even until now, and I work. For this cause therefore the Jews sought the more to kill him, because he not only brake the sabbath, but also called God his own Father, making himself equal with God[3]."

The hostility of the Scribes, we see, is very deadly. The Pharisees are often scandalised at infractions of their sabbath notions, but they do not seek our Lord's death as the Scribes do. The latter were probably Sadducees, tinged with

[1] John i. 43.
[2] The historical part of John Chap. 5, vv. 1—18 has the air of an account condensed from materials furnished by another. We are told that Philip was bishop of Hierapolis in Phrygia. He may therefore have kept up communication with John at Ephesus.
[3] John v. 15—18.

western philosophy, and they were actuated by other motives beside zeal for the Law.

For one thing, they were in reality made uneasy by our Lord's assertion that a living God was working among them and close by. Ministers of state who have possessed themselves of sovereign power are startled and infuriated if their nominal monarch personally asserts his power: and, something in the same way, a priesthood occupied in promulgating ecclesiastical laws and carrying on the externals of worship were frightened at the announcement that God, instead of leaving matters for them to manage, had Himself come to reign and rule upon the earth.

But what was more effective than even spiritual awe was their personal alarm. The dread which one of their body afterwards expressed—" The Romans will come and take away both our place and our nation[1]"—was always over their heads. They were a sacerdotal oligarchy trembling for their existence. The people hated the Romans, and the Scribes were bound to stand well with both: an outbreak might bring to an end whatever ecclesiastical independence they still possessed. The priesthood saw something in our Lord which might lead the people to take Him and make Him a king.

The reply, "My Father worketh hitherto and I work[2]," is characteristic of our Lord's way. He does not meet the charge by contesting the inter-

---

[1] John xi. 48. [2] John v. 17.

pretation of the Law. He ignores all quibbles of legality and goes to the root of the matter. It is by the working of God that the world is maintained. His Father worketh hitherto, on Sabbath days and all, and He, the Son, follows in His Father's ways. The same test of Sonship—that the child takes after the Father—is applied in the Sermon on the mount[1].

I must notice another verse of this discourse,

"I am come in my Father's name, and ye receive me not: if another shall come in his own name, him ye will receive[2]."

Our Lord here lays bare the reason why so few would follow Him. He touches the very centre of the matter. To kindle enthusiasm among a mass of men, you must have a person or a name. A cause is best embodied in an actual claimant standing before men's eyes; but failing this they will often rally to a *name* that they know. Our Lord used only His Father's name; this did not move their human sympathies for "The Father" had no personality for them. It was reserved for the Apostles to draw men over to the Faith, and they were given the advantage which Jesus was content to forego. They could put forward a personal claimant for the loyalty of men: they had Christ's story to tell and Christ's name for a watchword and they won men for the kingdom of

---

[1] Matth. v. 45.   [2] John v. 43.

God by gaining their homage for the Son of Man.

The temporary separation of the Apostles from our Lord during the summer of A.D. 28 may have answered higher ends than merely enabling them to earn their livelihood. It gave them time to think over the events of the last six months.

It is a feature of our Lord's way in His course of teaching, not to suffer one set of ideas or influences to be disturbed before they have had time to take root. After a period of stress, or when new impressions had been stamped on the minds of his disciples, He provides for them an interval of calm. When the disciples return exulting from their mission through the cities, He says, "Come ye yourselves apart into a desert place, and rest a while." When crowds thronged them and courted them for access to their Master, He carried them away, that the impressions He wanted to preserve might not be effaced in the turmoil. It may have been in pursuance of this treatment that, after the resurrection, they were sent for a time into Galilee, there to wait and to watch.

All teachers know that the time of rest that follows a period in which new matter has been taken into the mind is precious for good mental growth: conceptions then become more clear and complete, and effect a sure lodgement in the mind: but this, like many processes in education, helps to widen the distance between the weak and the strong. For it is only with the more thoughtful that this half unconscious brain-process goes on; the active minded mature their acquirements during rest, while the unthinking let them fade away. It argued well, in consequence, for Peter and Andrew and John, that Christ's influence had lost nothing through (as I believe) weeks of separation, but that as soon as they were called they sprang to their feet at once,—"they straightway left the nets and followed Him[1]."

Reverence for great men whom we have known, and the power of appreciating them, grow during absence. We may have been living so familiarly with one far above the common standard, that we may almost lose thought of his greatness; the little matters of common life, which come before us every day, take more than their share of notice; and, as regards these, great men and smaller ones must be much alike. But when we are away from our guide, our recollections turn to what is distinctive of him—to the points in which he contrasts with everyday men: what he had in common with such disappears, and our mental portrait preserves what is characteristic, and gives us the individual more forcibly than our nearer view had done. We often first become aware of the true proportions of greatness, when we look back on it from a little way off. Out of a range of mountains, all, when seen from the valley, appearing much of a height, one is found to vastly out-top the rest when we mount the opposite hill-side.

Matth. iv. 20.

We may suppose that some process like this was going on in the minds of Peter and Andrew and James and John during that summer spent in their fishers' work by the Sea of Galilee. Our Lord's image would, all the more, be kept alive in their minds because when they chanced to meet their talk would be of Him; and their Master's form would seem to rise before them when they sat beside one another, with their boats drawn up on the beach. We need not suppose that they saw into their Master's plans, far less into His nature; we do not know that they had heard *from Him* about the Kingdom of Heaven which the Baptist had told them was at hand; but the foundation for Faith was being laid in a capacity for intense personal devotion. First they learnt to love the Master whom they saw by their side; next, by thinking of Him while He was away, they learned how much they loved Him, and became aware that their affection for Him had in it something different from the common affections they knew. Shortly, as we shall presently see, a sense of shelter and of fostering protection mingled with this love, and grew into a trust, first in the Master who was with them, and afterwards in the Lord in Heaven. It is hardly too much to say that the germ of the new quality, which was to order the world afresh, was planted in men's hearts by the side of the Sea of Galilee in that summer of A.D. 28, and that then Faith—Faith as our Lord speaks of it— dawned upon the world.

CHAPTER VII.

THE PREACHING TO THE MULTITUDES.

IT was, as I believe, soon after that "feast of the Jews" lately mentioned (pp. 180 and 181 note), that the news of the apprehension of the Baptist by Herod reached our Lord at Jerusalem. At once He enters on His own Great Work[1] and

---

[1] I place this advent of our Lord into Galilee at the end of September A.D. 28, but the evidence is insufficient for a positive opinion. My reasons for supposing that John was not imprisoned till after this feast are as follows. The Synoptists say that after John's imprisonment our Lord came into Galilee preaching the Kingdom. Now when He returned through Samaria He did *not* begin to preach the Kingdom, and therefore the advent of Mark i. 14 refers to some other occasion; I believe to a subsequent one. In St John's Gospel chaps. iv. and v. we hear nothing of "the Kingdom" and no disciples are mentioned as attending our Lord. I think therefore that the events related in these chapters occurred before the advent into Galilee; this is one argument for placing this visit to the feast, where I do. Moreover it is hard to find another place for it. The Synoptical narrative is fairly continuous from the advent (Mark i. 14) up to the journey to the Feast of Tabernacles, and there is in it no mention either of a visit to Jerusalem, which must have occupied several days, or of our Lord's quitting His disciples. All proceeds consistently if we suppose, as I have done, that John was put in prison at the time of this feast or

goes straight into Galilee, preaching on the way that the Kingdom of God is come. The reasons for His holding back, came to an end together with the liberty of John. We lose now the guidance of St John, and we pass to the more continuous transcript of events which the Synoptists give.

Up to this time of His advent into Galilee our Lord was in part, as I have said, exploring the condition and the tempers of the people in quest of the fittest cradle for the Faith. It may possibly have been that our Lord in His visit to Jerusalem was giving the Holy City a last trial; but I see no ground to suppose that our Lord ever seriously contemplated any course different from that which He actually took. In any case, this outbreak of

soon after. But there is one difficulty about this. Our Lord says of the Baptist John v. 35, "He *was* the lamp that burneth and shineth, and you were willing for a season to rejoice in his light." The use of the imperfect tense is supposed to show that John was in prison when this was said, but surely if it is to be pressed rigorously it would mean that he was *dead:* for he received his disciples in prison and could give counsel and direction to those without. He did not cease to shine for *them*. I take these words to mean that he was no longer a light to the Priests and Levites. They had gone to him when he was preaching in the wilderness of Judæa, Matth. iii. 5, and afterwards they had sent to him in Bethany beyond Jordan: he was now in the territory of Herod, and there he was out of sight, and with the Priests and Levites he was out of mind. They could not make him a partisan or an ally and they had given him up. If John was in prison at this time, his imprisonment must have been a recent event, and we should expect our Lord to allude to it when He speaks of him.

hostility on the part of the scribes settled the matter: for the kind of mental growth which our Lord wished to bring about in the disciples could not go on in the midst of party warfare.

Young men on the watch for attack are not in a state for fertilizing "seed thoughts" or for turning over hard matters in their minds, and care for the state of the recipient characterizes the teaching of Christ. Men are to take heed *how* they hear, as well as what they hear, and are to reach full growth and shape, not from outward moulding but by living process from within. Our Lord's eye is never off His pupils, and yet visible direction hardly ever appears; He sways them by an insensible touch. A great truth is brought to light by an incident of wonder, a pregnant word is let drop, a hard parable is delivered now and then; but between whiles the disciples are left to dwell on their own thoughts, as their fishing boat sails along, or as they follow their Master among the northern hills. Our Lord is ever bent on making men thoughtful and on calling out in each the inner life which is proper to the man, and for this, tranquillity, or at least frequent opportunity for quiet communing with their own thoughts, was absolutely required.

The antagonism at Jerusalem might have stopped short of violence and yet the wrangling spirit of the place might have had a very evil effect on the disciples. It was above all essential that they should have a single hearted love of truth;

and this can hardly grow up when party is ranged against party and each tries to set the views and statements of the other in the most damaging light, and to dispose his own propositions in polemical order with a strategic view. As soon therefore as the hostility of the scribes was displayed, it became clear that the schooling of the Apostles must be brought about elsewhere than in Judæa. But apart from this, Jerusalem was, for other reasons easy to perceive, ill-suited for the purpose. It was too Academical; the place was full of Rabbis, round whose feet a circle of pupils sat. Each school adopted its master's *dicta* with the undiscriminating loyalty of youth; and the scholars of other teachers, by steadily taking it for granted that Jesus of Nazareth was a teacher like the Rabbis they knew, would have half persuaded His followers that there was something in common between Him and the Doctors who expounded the Law.

The Rabbis gave their scholars something to show for their lessons—expositions of the Law and systematic doctrine—and their pupils would have said to the disciples, "Our master gives us this or that; what does your master give you?" This would have set them looking for what was intentionally withheld. Our Lord did not fill them with opinions or directions to be remembered, but He made them what He wanted them to be.

To understand how wisely things were ordered, we must give a glance to what would have been the result of the most obvious and apparently "the most natural" course. Our Lord's brethren recommended that He should go and show Himself and teach at Jerusalem. I have shown the ill effects this would have had on the training of the disciples; I will now say a word on the way in which it would have affected the Church. If Jerusalem had been the seat of teaching, the disciples there, instead of numbering "a hundred and twenty," would have been a large body. Possibly they might have offered armed resistance to the apprehension of our Lord; and the whole moral of the action would have been lost if they had. But passing this by, if a large body of disciples dwelling at Jerusalem had claimed our Lord as peculiarly their own, the universality of His work would have been obscured. The Church at Jerusalem might have dwelt more on His being their particular Founder and Bishop than on His being the Redeemer of the World.

Again, How would it have been with the authority of the Twelve? Those who had sat at His feet and listened, just as the Apostles had done, might have hesitated when He was gone to acknowledge the Twelve as the *founders* of the Church; for the Church, they would have said, began with themselves. More than this, practical evils would have come about; for these original disciples, regarding themselves as the depositaries of tradition, would have recalled every practice of their Lord,—for instance the way in which He had given thanks at meat, or ordered service in prayer, as well as His practice as to the Sabbath and fasting,—these would have been passed down as Divinely sanctioned, and the externals of religion would have been stereotyped as thoroughly as though they had been a new Ceremonial Law, like that from which He desired to release mankind. Moreover the body of believers who had personally known our Lord, would have constituted a kind of ecclesiastical aristocracy; and distinctions —respect of persons—would have been introduced from the first. What actually happened was far more consistent with the general tenour of Christ's plan so far as we can make it out. The few original disciples at Jerusalem were lost in the crowd who were added to the Church after the day of Pentecost, and the Apostles ruled with unquestioned authority from the first.

Galilee we have seen, as a retired spot with an honest-hearted people, was admirably fitted for the scene of the ministry; but yet it could not be "that a prophet should perish out of Jerusalem," and it was imperative that there the end should come. The Holy City was also fitted, in a very peculiar manner, to be the centre from which the new movement was to radiate forth. The Lord's death, the Supreme Event in the history of mankind, was not to take place in a corner. The circumstances of it could not be too notorious or too widely vouched. It was to be made known in East and West to the Hebrew, the Greek, the Roman and to all mankind. Now Jerusalem, both geographically, and as the point to which the Jews of the dispersion bent watchful eyes from many lands, was wondrously adapted to be a centre of diffusion. It was in a very remarkable way a "city set upon a hill." It stood accessible to three continents, at the centre of gravity of the known world, and it was on the watershed of two civilizations: the Aryan and Semitic races and languages and the different modes of thinking which go along with the languages were brought together there.

Moreover, owing to the dispersion of the Jews and their custom of visiting Jerusalem at the great feasts when they possibly could, "devout men from every nation under Heaven" were drawn together there from time to time, and a common interest in what concerned "Israel" was spread over the globe. The agency of these festivals connected Jerusalem, as by electric threads, with every great city in the inhabited world, and the Israelites who were settled in every large town of the empire afterwards provided nests for the new Faith.

The Apostles, as was natural, after the Resurrection went back to Galilee. It can only have been owing to directions they must have received, that they *all* returned to Jerusalem for the Ascension. Our Lord then enjoined them to remain and from thence to propagate the Faith. This injunction

THE PREACHING TO THE MULTITUDES. 195

explains their abandonment of their homes and callings, which is hard to account for otherwise.

I now proceed with the history. During this chapter I shall for the most part follow St Mark, who relates the events nearly in the order in which I believe they happened. After a brief notice of John and of the temptation he proceeds thus:

"Now after that John was delivered up, Jesus came into Galilee, preaching the gospel of God, and saying, The time is fulfilled, and the kingdom of God is at hand: repent ye, and believe in the gospel[1]."

The Evangelist does not say that our Lord came from Judæa, but He could have come from nowhere else. It would seem that our Lord on arriving in Galilee went at once to the Lake shore and called the two pair of fisher brethren to His side.

"And passing along by the sea of Galilee, he saw Simon and Andrew brother of Simon casting a net in the sea: for they were fishers. And Jesus said unto them, Come ye after me, and I will make you to become fishers of men. And straightway they left the nets, and followed him. And going on a little farther, he saw James the *son* of Zebedee, and John his brother, who also were in the boat mending the nets. And straightway he called them: and they left their father Zebedee in the boat with the hired servants, and went after him[2]."

This passage would offer an opening for criticism, if it were not for the light thrown on it by St

[1] Mark i. 14, 15. [2] Mark i. 16—20.

John's Gospel, by help of which an apparent difficulty is turned into a coincidence.

If we did not possess the Gospel of St John, the story of the call of the Apostles would stand thus, It would appear that our Lord came down to the Sea of Galilee, and said to two fishermen—whom, for all we should know to the contrary, He had never seen before,—"Come ye after me, and I will make you to become fishers of men." These would seem startling words to hear from a stranger, but the brothers, without asking further, and without one consulting the other, at once left their work and followed our Lord.

This would be unlikely, but not passing belief; men are mastered in a moment, by personal influence, now and then; but still the preponderance of probabilities is against the truth of the story. The Evangelist however goes on to relate that our Lord passes on along the Lake side, and within a few hundred yards comes upon another pair of brothers, also fishermen; he addresses them nearly in the same terms and they also leave their nets and follow Him. Now this repetition, the critic would say, savours in itself of the Eastern legend. But, what is far more than this, the combination of the two improbabilities produces an improbability of a far higher order[1].

---

[1] For instance, if the separate probability of each of two events is $\frac{1}{10}$, that of the joint event is $\frac{1}{10} \times \frac{1}{10}$ or $\frac{1}{100}$, or there are ninety-nine chances to one against it.

The information gained from the Gospel of St John clears the difficulty away. We may learn from this, how a word or two of fresh information might, in like manner, clear away other discrepancies which are stumbling-blocks to learners now.

There we find, that these fisher brethren were old disciples of our Lord. It is consistent with the Gospel to suppose that during the summer they had been at their work, nursing the memory of their Master all the time. They now hear that He has come preaching the Kingdom of God in their own land. They are waiting for Him and expecting His call. The two pair of brethren stood in the same relation to Him, consequently they were treated in the same way, and the result was naturally the same. This unhesitating compliance on the part of the brethren, which seems so strange, points to a previous acquaintance with our Lord; of this acquaintance St John's Gospel speaks, and so St Mark strengthens St John just as St John does St Mark.

In the Gospels of St Matthew and St Mark, which we suppose to be both based on a primitive document, the story is told without the slightest idea of obviating objection or mistrust. The writers never appear to contemplate readers to whom the fact that Simon and the rest had, before this, been associated with our Lord should be unknown. They took it for granted that this was too notorious to call for mention.

But we have another Evangelist, St Luke, a more practised writer, whose design was to present his account in a coherent form. He did not possess the Gospel of St John and possibly did not know the particulars of the earlier call of Simon and Andrew and John. It may well have been that he was himself somewhat startled at the abruptness of our Lord's call to the Apostles, and at their unhesitating compliance with it, as related in the primitive document, and felt that it required to be accounted for: consequently, having the account of the miraculous draught of fishes among the materials he speaks of—an account not contained in the Gospels of St Matthew and St Mark—he finds in this Sign an explanation of the prompt adherence of the pairs of brethren, and he combines the two events.

We should gather from him that the Apostles were struck by the miraculous draught of fishes, and that the Lord thereupon invited them to follow and become "fishers of men," but I think it most likely that the call took place as St Matthew and St Mark relate. The circumstantial minuteness of the details in these two Gospels, and the naturalness of the picture—two brothers are engaged in casting, and the other pair in mending their nets—convinces me that this relation comes originally from one who saw for himself. This draught of fishes may have taken place some days after the call of the brethren. For we need not suppose, that, before the Twelve were chosen, those who were called abandoned the craft by which they lived, although they probably resorted to their Master day by day.

The early miracles were mostly wrought in the sight of the multitude; they seem meant to show that the Kingdom of God was come; but this miracle of the draught of fishes was performed when few but disciples were by. It was a miracle of instruction, it lent great impressiveness to great lessons; it emphasized in a way never to be forgotten the call to become "fishers of men," and it gave good augury of success. The thought of this draught must have come back to Peter at many a juncture in his life, a notable one being the morrow of the Feast of Pentecost, when "there were added unto them in that day about 3000 souls[1]."

The Apostles may have learned another lesson from this miracle. All night they had toiled and taken nothing, yet they had not given up in despair but had worked on hard; the morning brought success beyond all hope. Men, waiting long for the yield of their labour, have found encouragement in calling this to mind. Simon, though thinking there is little hope of taking fish, nevertheless obeys at once. He frankly tells his Master his view of a matter about which he might be supposed to know best, and leaves Him to judge, but he does immediately as his Master bids. Our Lord does not *promise* him success; He only tells him to try once more; and thereupon without a word, wearied and out of heart as he may be supposed to have been by a night of bootless labour, he does what

[1] Acts ii. 41.

he is told. It is enough for Simon to know that his Master wishes him to "Put out into the deep and let down his nets for a draught[1]." His cheerful compliance shews a happy disposition and a loyal nature; for if there had been a grain of peevishness or selfishness in him, it would have been likely to be uppermost then.

In the last chapter, we saw our Lord exploring the characters of classes of men. His eye is now turned on individuals; He is peering down into His disciples' hearts, taking them unawares, when their every day selves lie uppermost, putting them, by chance as it were, through some little exercise which shall reveal some tendency or some hidden quality; and to our Lord this incident brought the secret heart of Simon into the light of day.

It shewed that he was altogether free from that kind of stubbornness which is born of self-regard, and that he did not attach a sanctity to an opinion or a resolve, merely because it was his. He learnt from this miracle that it was best to trust to Christ. He might say to himself, "I never felt more convinced that we should take nothing by letting down the nets, than I did on that morning on the lake, but I let them down and found I was wrong." A memorable act is not done with, educationally, when it is over. The recollection of it is an attendant monitor always pointing the same way; and so this miracle may have done much towards ac-

[1] Luke v. 4.

THE PREACHING TO THE MULTITUDES. 201

customing Peter to look to the Lord's prompting, and to be ready at His word to give up that about which he felt most sure. It may well have helped him to that openness of mind, which stood the Church in good stead, years after at Joppa, when the envoys of Cornelius were knocking at Peter's door.

This miracle has been called a miracle of coincidence, meaning that the marvel lay in the passing of the shoal at the moment when the net was cast; it might not be a miracle at all, because the chances against its being a natural phenomenon, though enormous, are not absolutely infinite. It is not one which would appal ordinary beholders: the boatmen, we may suppose, thought chiefly of securing the fish. Our Lord is now testing the capacity of men for discerning God, and He therefore performs miracles of a less striking order first; these impress those only who have their eyes open for the manifestation of what is spiritual; and those who are found to possess this "vision and faculty Divine" are afterwards shewn "greater things than these."

Simon had no doubt seen our Lord work cures, but this mastery of our Lord over the creation comes more home to him than His power over disease, and his feelings break forth. It is characteristic of him, that what is in him *must come out* at once; whether it be an objection that occurs to him, or a motion of indignation or of elation, or of the panic to which Orientals are subject—out it must come; this is the point in which the identity of his character is most visibly preserved in all our narratives. Here he is mastered by the emotions of the moment and must give them outward show; and along with his gush of feeling comes the sense of his unworthiness, the impression of his being wholly unequal to the duty and position thrust upon him; an impression not uncommon with men in such junctures; though biographies abundantly show that those who feel it most very often acquit themselves admirably when the trial comes. Touched by this, Simon throws himself at his Master's feet and says, "Depart from me, for I am a sinful man, O Lord[1]."

We go back now to the course of the narrative in St Mark's Gospel, and there we find that the first thing which struck the hearers of our Lord was the *authority* with which He spoke.

"And they were astonished at his teaching: for he taught them as having authority, and not as the scribes[2]."

We saw in the last chapter, that men bowed to the authority in the air of our Lord when He purged the Temple of Jerusalem: this authority now passed into His words, and it swayed the hearts of men. It is the special instinct of a crowd that it quickly discerns those whom it must hear, and

[1] Luke v. 8.   [2] Mark i. 22.

this multitude saw that our Lord had something to tell them and that, not of tradition, but out of His own very self. Here was a genuine authority coming of nature or of God, by the side of which the stated legal authority of the officiating scribes paled away out of sight.

In what ways was it, we may ask, that this authority of Christ shone out now, and took such hold of men? First of all, I would answer, He brought to the birth, within men, thoughts which were lying in embryo in their own hearts. This, which was also Socrates' way, I have spoken of in the Introductory Chapter and once or twice since. Our Lord wakened within men the perception of truths which they seemed to have once known and forgotten; especially that God was the Father, not only of Israel as a nation, but of every particular man in it. The common people had been told by the learned that they were not worth God's notice, and when Christ asserted the dignity of each individual soul they said to themselves "we always thought it must be so; and so it is." The beatitudes in like manner commended themselves to men's hearts; they felt that if there was a God in the world, it ought to be as our Lord said it was.

Secondly, our Lord not only *told* men that they were the children of God, that they should strive after their Father's likeness, and that they might approach nearer and nearer to being perfect as He is perfect: but, what was more than this, in every word He spake,—whether of teaching, or reproof, or expostulation, or in His passing words to those who received His mercies—He *treated* them as God's children. Man, as man, has in His eyes a right to respect. Anger we find with our Lord often, as also surprise at slowness of heart, indignation at hypocrisy and at the Rabbinical evasions of the Law; but never in our Lord's words or looks do we find personal disdain. Towards no human being does He shew contempt. The scribe would have trodden the rabble out of existence; but there is no such thing as rabble in our Lord's eyes. The master, in the parable, asks concerning the tree, which is unproductively exhausting the soil, why cumbers it the ground; but it is not to be rooted up, till all has been tried. There it stands, and mere existence gives it claims, for all that exists is the Father's. This notion, that every thing belonged to God, and was therefore to be reverently regarded, lay very deep in the hearts of the children of Israel, even the poorest in Galilee; and when the Lord brought it to light, men listened to Him with breathless respect.

Thirdly. If a scribe spoke to the people, he bethought himself of topics within their comprehension: he had a double self; one he showed to them and one he kept for his equals: he was afraid of talking over his hearers' heads, so he took them on the side of what he supposed they might understand, of their interests, for example, and spoke of the advantages of good repute, or, at the highest, of the blessings which God brought on His servants in this life and hereafter, and of the ill fate which awaited offenders. All this implied, "We who speak to you, of course, have for ourselves higher principles and purer motives than those we have named, but these are quite good enough for you." Now there is nothing that men, young or old, so surely detect, as whether a man serves them with the same thoughts that he gives to himself and his friends.

The people, moreover, are always grateful for being supposed capable of higher sentiments than mere hope of gain and fear of loss, and for the appreciation shewn in taking them on higher ground; they seldom fail the speaker who boldly addresses their consciences; they are eager to justify his trust in them: "He has treated us as men," they say, "and men he shall find we are." Above all they feel the compliment of being not flattered, but supposed reasonable enough to hear the truth about themselves and shewn their failings; and we feel sure that men went away from the Sermon on the Mount confident of Christ's respect and regard for them, without His telling them of it in so many words. He talks to them quite naturally of *their* Father who is also *His* Father, just as men speak of any common tie: and this took hold of their hearts.

Fourthly. We find in the earlier portions of the Sermon on the Mount, which best represent this preaching to the multitude[1], that our Lord assumes a certain positive authority, by putting His own commands in contrast with the written Law.

It had probably been given out by our Lord's opponents that He had come to destroy the Law, and our Lord in this Sermon declares that He is not come to destroy but to fulfil.

We shall see the point most clearly, if we understand the word "fulfil," to mean, "carry out into its full completeness." For our Lord does not *destroy* the Law but he *supersedes* it by bringing God's ways to light, and merging in this light the previous partial revelations, of which the Mosaic Law was one. A mathematician supersedes the practical rules which the pupil at first employs for solving particular cases of a problem, by giving a complete and general solution of the whole subject. This may illustrate the way in which our Lord merges the particular case of human conduct in a wider rule embracing human dispositions, and which regards, not only what men *do*, but also what they *are*, and what they will *become*.

To take another point. Slavery to the letter of a written Law hampered moral and spiritual growth; it led men to regard authority as the sole test of truth; it tended to prevent their thinking for

---

[1] By comparing the Sermon on the Mount with the parallel passages in St Luke we find that much of it must have been spoken after the call of the Apostles: this applies particularly to the latter half of the discourse.

themselves as our Lord desired them to do. No word of our Lord countenances the idea of verbal inspiration. He treats the provisions of the Levitical Law as subject to criticism, He never attributes them·to God, but either to Moses or those of old time, and after quoting them in His sermon and elsewhere He commonly adds, "But *I* say unto you" and then delivers His own precept—embracing that of Moses no doubt—but so widely overstepping it, that it would seem to the people to amount to a repeal. A teaching which claimed authority coordinate with that of Moses might well startle the multitude by its contrast with that of the scribes.

It may be asked—" Why, if our Lord desired to free men's minds, did He not declare how far and in what sense their sacred books contained the word of God." We answer, "He would have caused utter bewilderment if He had entered on such a matter at all." The truth may be gathered by observing His practice. He never states abstract principles, but He acts as He deems fit and leaves us to infer His views by marking what He does. He never contests the rules about the Sabbath, but He observes them only in His own way. He does not tell the Jews that their Law is not traced by the finger of God, but He amends and criticizes its provisions as though they were of man.

Let us suppose, for a moment—not of course that He had cried down the Law like one who exulted in finding a flaw—but that He had attempted to put into men's heads views about it which their minds had not yet shaped themselves to receive; that He had told them, for instance, that laws must be fitted to human needs, and that as these needs vary, laws must vary too, and cannot be the subject of an ordinance unchanging and Divine. Could He, by such explanations, have given His auditors any true view of Divine rule? Would not the Galileans have cried out, "That if the tables of the Law were not graven by God's finger they were nothing at all?" Nothing, in our Lord's wisdom, strikes me more than His moderation with regard to error. What seems false to one man's mind may be true to that of another. When men, as soon as they spy out an error, cry, "Root it up," our Lord seems to answer, "Along with the tares some wheat needs must go." Men are complex beings; and much that is best in them is so intertwined with habits and association that we cannot sweep away long-standing notions and outward symbols and ceremonies without destroying also what is of the essence. Take away from an Italian woman her belief in the Virgin, or from a Scotch peasant that in the sacred obligation of the Sabbath, and a great deal of what is best in them will go too.

Our Lord's way of proceeding is always positive, never merely negative. He leaves the Law, but He sows seed which will grow up and displace the spirit of blind subservience to it: just as some particular species in the herbage of a land is often ousted when a more robust one is brought in. The Apostles had, up to the end, many wrong notions, and we may wonder why our Lord did not set them right; but it would have shaken the whole fabric of their belief if He had so done; and the sure teaching of circumstances would, as He knew, dissipate the errors in time.

So far we have dealt chiefly with the *matter* of our Lord's teaching of the multitudes, but something must be said about its *form*. One striking point in our Lord's practice in contrast with that of the scribes, is this. He cites no authorities, all comes from Himself; there is hardly a text of Scripture in the fifth chapter of St Matthew, except those which are quoted in order to be extended or gainsaid. The scribes depended on their learning, they overwhelmed men with quotations, they laid text by text, and built up their conclusions upon an array of authorities. Now a preacher, or a teacher of any kind, is sure to lose hold of his audience when he goes away from himself and gives other people's opinions instead of his own. They look to him for guidance; and when he says, "This is one man's view and that is another's," and not, "This is *mine*," then they turn from the trumpet of uncertain sound. The multitude suppose that in all questions there is a right and a wrong—just as there is a right and a wrong answer to a sum—and they do not want to know what one authority says or the other, but what they are to accept.

Again, rightly to apprehend the form of this discourse, we must bear in mind that it is not a written collection of precepts,—though St Matthew may have appended some delivered at a later time—and that still less is it a Code of Laws. It is an oral address to a crowd of villagers gathered on the top of the fell. We mark in it the natural rhetoric of earnest speech: the first necessity is always to win men to listen, and thus the speaker at the opening strikes His most impressive chords.

Words of blessing fell on the ears of those who were used only to hear of their shortcomings and to be treated as outcasts; and when their attention was caught by the unusual sound and they listened to hear who it was who were blessed, they found it was not the strong and the wealthy and the high spirited—those whom they regarded as having the good things of existence while they themselves had the bad—but the blessed are the poor in spirit, and this Kingdom of Heaven, newly proclaimed, belonged to them. The attention caught by the opening is kept alive by the unexpected nature of the matter.

Again, our Lord is at pains so to put what He says that it may not be taken for a fresh body of injunctions added to the Law; for the people were already, as He said, overburdened with such injunctions. He puts therefore what He has to say into such strong forms, and, by way of example, takes such extreme cases, that it is plain that He is illustrating a principle and not laying down a literal rule.

We have

"Ye have heard that it was said, An eye for an eye, and a tooth for a tooth: but I say unto you, Resist not him that is evil: but whosoever smiteth thee on thy right cheek, turn to him the other also. And if any man would go to law with thee, and take away thy coat, let him have thy cloke also. And whosoever shall compel thee to go one mile, go with him twain[1]."

He Himself, before the High Priest, does not submit to wrong, without asking in remonstrance "Why smitest thou me?" and the most literal minded of our Lord's hearers would not have felt bound to offer his cloke to one who had stolen his coat. The language shews by its very strength that it is figurative.

Indeed, a code of Law can hardly be delivered in an address to a multitude. If it is to meet all cases it must be complex, and to the hearer wearisome. If our Lord had delivered a treatise telling men what they were to do in the ordinary occasions of life, the precepts must have been so encumbered by qualifications that all impressiveness would have been lost. If to the saying "Give to him that asketh of thee" our Lord had appended all the obvious exceptions—such as the cases in which what is asked for would be hurtful—

[1] Matt. v. 38—41.

the whole force of the passage would have been frittered away. As long as a preacher delivers broad truths, put forcibly, his audience are ready to hear; but as soon as he begins to qualify his statements and to make exceptions, his hold over his hearers is gone, and they think he is unsaying what he said.

Our Lord wished to leave *seed thoughts* lying in men's minds. He knew that His words would have to be carried in men's memories for a long while before being written down. They must therefore be clad in the form in which they would last longest and be easiest to carry. He therefore embodied what He wished to have remembered in terse sayings, illustrated by cases which are familiar but extreme. The hearer could carry these sentences away, and would ponder on them all the more, because in their literal sense they are startling and impracticable as rules of conduct. I can conceive no style better fitted for the purpose which I believe to have been dominant with our Lord, than that employed in the Sermon on the Mount.

It seems to me to be part of the strange adaptation of circumstances to the needs of the Faith, that what was most vital and most universal was uttered in the Hebrew tongue. This was the language of the comparative infancy of the world; and there is in the genius of it much—especially its ready lending itself to the form of balanced sentences—which takes hold of the hearts of un-

THE PREACHING TO THE MULTITUDES. 213

tutored men. Such men store their wisdom in saws and proverbs; and in like manner the wisdom of the Hebrew is dropped in separate pearls, which can easily be treasured up. When the time came for touching cultured minds, and connected argument was required, Greek forms of thought and speech were needed. Saul was then converted; and Greek became the language of the Word.

Nothing in our Lord's ministry impresses me more than the extraordinary sobriety of the whole movement. We hear nothing of religious transport or ecstatic devotion. People listen in awe to our Lord's preaching as to a communication made from above. They never dare to applaud. He is too much above them for that. Many have since come crying "Lord, Lord," in different accents, at different times; we have heard of "revivals" among great multitudes, carried headlong by wild excitement, and of religious delirium reaching to the borders of mania. All this is in the strongest contrast with the ways of teaching of our Lord.

True human freedom was with Him a sacred thing; what man was made for was that he might be a free spiritual being; and a man is not free when he is fascinated by fervid oratory and becomes the blind tool of another, or when he is intoxicated by religious fanaticism and is no longer master of his own mind. Any agencies, therefore, which would impair the health and freedom of a man's will Christ refused to employ. They belonged to that Spirit of the World whose alliance He had refused. One cause of this sobriety of the great movement may be found in the elevation and tone of authority which has just been spoken of as characterizing our Lord. He seemed to move in a plane parallel indeed to that of men, but a little above it. For a speaker to kindle men's passions he must be possessed by the notions and feelings of the time: he and his hearers must have common objects of desire, or a common jealousy of those who possess what they themselves want, they must therefore wear the stamp of a passing and particular phase of mankind. Now it was the distinctive peculiarity of our Lord's Personality that it belongs not more to one time or class than to another. The Son of Man represents Humanity in the abstract, and no party has ever been able to claim Him as their own.

In the course of the winter of A.D. 28—29, Levi, in the vernacular of Galilee called also Matthew, a toll-taker on the borders of the lake, is summoned to follow our Lord. He justified our Lord's choice in a signal manner, for "he forsook all, and rose up and followed Him."

There must have been in this man "a soul of goodness" of rare efficacy in resisting influences to ill. His position must have offered temptation to exaction. This was corrupting, but the steady and persistent effect of feeling himself despised must have been more so even than this. He was hated not only as the tax-gatherer, but also as having accepted the service of the foreign oppressors of the land. However justly the publican might have striven to act, it would be taken for granted that he was endeavouring to fleece those who came into his hands; and a man soon becomes what people about him will have it that he is.

Now and then, however, in all positions, we come across natures which run counter to the influences around them, or which by a happy chemistry decompose the evil and turn its elements to good. Everything in the publican's calling fostered the love of gain; and to be able to save enough to give it up and live down ill report was his only hope. But Matthew breaks with his means of subsistence totally and at once. At one word of our Lord he throws all away without a moment's thought, and joins the little band of followers which was being drawn into closer attendance on our Lord. This man surely had "salt in himself."

St Matthew has left us his Gospel. We learn from this which way his thoughts lean, and we see that he was not of that type of mind most commonly associated with the idea of the Apostle of a new creed. He was probably not very young and his views were formed and fixed: his national sympathy was intense. God was to him, first of all, the God of Israel, and he regarded our Lord as the Messiah, after the type which Jewish hopes and fancies had fashioned for themselves. In all that occurred he saw the reproduction of what was narrated in the old books; and the burden "Now this was done that the Scripture might be fulfilled" runs through all his writings.

Here then, some might say, we have a man chosen as a witness and promulgator of a faith which is to be universal, yet this man's sympathies flow only along one narrow channel, and he is wedded to old ways of reading the mind of God. He was however a guileless, God-fearing, high-hearted man; and it could not but strengthen the cause to have among the Apostles one who could enter into the minds of those who looked for the consolation of Israel in the old Hebrew way. The first function of the Apostles,—one on which I shall soon speak pretty fully—was that they were to bear *witness* of Christ. This was set forth in that which, so to say, was their charter of incorporation. "Ye shall be my witnesses both in Jerusalem and in all Judæa and Samaria and unto the uttermost parts of the earth[1]." Now the more varied the characters of the witnesses the stronger would be the case when they agreed.

Our Lord, then, will have, among His immediate followers, minds of every sort. He does not pick out those only who are most after His own heart, nor does he mould men into one fashion, so that they should think on all points alike. We cannot have freedom among human beings without diver-

[1] Acts i, 8,

sity. St Matthew, we perhaps say, had old world views; but it may have been just because of these, that he was the most fit Apostle for the Eastern world. There would be crowds of men whom he would understand and who would understand him, but whose minds would have been closed to the utterances of Paul. The vineyard to which Christ called his labourers was the whole world; it contained vines of every stock growing on every soil. It was well then, that there should be labourers bred in various schools of husbandry, and that each should work in the fashion in which he felt he could do it best.

Another point to be noted about the call of St Matthew is this: The choice of a publican was a practical proof to the other disciples, as it is to the Church for ever, that Christ is in no way a respecter of persons. The two pairs of brethren who followed our Lord may have been startled at the call of Matthew, for they no doubt looked on publicans as their countrymen did; and this act of our Lord's taught them, more forcibly than any words could have done, that with Him outward circumstance went for nothing and the inward man was all in all. In this call of Matthew the spirit of universality which belongs to the Christian Church is folded up like the embryo in the seed. Our Lord makes no comment on this call; nor do we hear of any murmurs from the disciples, who had by this time learned that our Lord was wiser than they, as Peter had found when he let down the net,

Shortly before the call of St Matthew a miracle occurred, the cure of the sick of the palsy, when our Lord's renown was at its height—a miracle at the performance of which "there were Pharisees and doctors of the law sitting by, which were come out of every village of Galilee and Judæa and Jerusalem[1]." The presence of these strangers bears on what follows.

Hitherto we have read of no contest or conflict in Capernaum; but these Pharisees conceived misgivings about the movement they had come to see. This hostility was very different from that of the Sadducees in Jerusalem, who, regarding the movement as an insane delusion likely to bring things about their ears, set themselves remorselessly to root it out. But the Pharisees do not seem at first to have borne our Lord any personal hatred, but only to have been uneasy about the new teaching which went too far for them, and did not follow the course which they had expected.

The Pharisees, nevertheless, were now on the watch for occasion to find fault. This is not an occupation which brings out the amiable side of men's natures; and they became still more soured by finding nothing on which to hang a charge; so that at last they even leagued with the Herodians, their natural opponents, against our Lord. The most popular of all accusations, and one for which

[1] Luke v. 17.

it was easy to find ground, was a breach of the traditional rules for keeping the Sabbath.

The Sabbath was an inestimable Law. It was maintained by Divine sanction at a time when a Law could not be upheld by any other means: it debarred men from "doing what they would with their own" on one day out of seven, so far as regarded the labour of themselves or of their children, their servants, their ox or their ass. It secured for the race this portion of time against the greed of gain: but all this was done *for men*, although the Jews had come to look on it as something done *by men for God*, and in so doing they made God a taskmaster like the gods of the pagans. Moreover the Sabbath kept alive in each Israelite his self-respect as one of God's people; however sordid his calling, he put away every seventh day his squalor and his toil and resumed the dignity of Abraham's son. The Sabbath question was the chosen battle-ground of those who reduced all virtues to that literal unquestioning obedience to authoritative records, which was so damaging to moral and spiritual life. Men thought that God's favour was won or His wrath incurred in virtue of acts—such as the keeping within or the overstepping the limit of the journey allowed on the Sabbath-day—which in themselves had no moral significance at all.

Here again we see how our Lord deals with views falling short of the truth. The moral creed of His countrymen was imperfect; it unduly exalted and obtruded formal duties, but it was all that they had; their whole life and that of their nation was moulded by it; instincts fostered by it had become hereditary, and to break it ruthlessly down would have been to lay waste men's souls.

In the instance before us our Lord introduces a freer practice; and trusts to this to give birth in time to more intelligent notions about the Sabbath day.

One passage in the history I purposely passed by. I thought that I might have to write of it at such a length as to break the continuity of the narrative, and I therefore kept it for the close of the chapter. The passage in question, which I subjoin, immediately follows the account of the entertainment of our Lord in Matthew's house.

"Then come to him the disciples of John, saying, Why do we and the Pharisees fast oft, but thy disciples fast not? And Jesus said unto them, Can the sons of the bride-chamber mourn, as long as the bridegroom is with them? but the days will come, when the bridegroom shall be taken away from them, and then will they fast. And no man putteth a piece of undressed cloth upon an old garment; for that which should fill it up taketh from the garment, and a worse rent is made. Neither do *men* put new wine into old wine-skins: else the skins burst, and the wine is spilled, and the skins perish: but they put new wine into fresh wine-skins, and both are preserved[1]."

[1] Matth. ix. 14—17. I here adopt St Matthew's version in preference to that of St Mark ii. 16—22. St Matthew was not likely to

The Pharisees practised fasting on the second and fifth days of the week: the same practice was probably followed by the disciples of John; and if we suppose that Matthew made this feast on one of the fasting days, this would bring the contrast between the ways of John and of Jesus more sharply out.

Before examining the charge and the reply, a word must be said on the absence of all distinctive religious observances in the practice of our Lord and His disciples.

The Baptist, we know, enjoined stated fasts and taught his people to pray, and above all enforced the initiatory rite from which he drew his name. At a later period our Lord's disciples beg to be taught to pray, "as John also taught his disciples[1]."

In those days people looked to a religion to order the externals of a man's life; hours of prayer portioned out his day; and so, even the disciples appear to have felt that with them there was something lacking, and that they were at a disadvantage compared with John's disciples because they were not, through conformity to a special rule, formed into a body and marked with a badge.

forget any circumstance of his call, least of all the words then used by our Lord; and the quotation "I will have mercy and not sacrifice" which he alone relates, is exactly in our Lord's manner. The passage printed above differs also from St Mark's version in this, that in the latter the *disciples of the Pharisees* put the question together with John's disciples. Some disciples of John may have belonged to the Pharisees as their religious party.

[1] Luke xi. 1.

It is easy to find reasons why our Lord should have avoided doing what John did. If He had enjoined any system of religious observance, this would have limited the spread of His Kingdom, and have laid on observances in general more stress than He desired. One Law or one ritual would not suit all nations, or all times; for forms must vary with men's modes of life, and if our Lord had introduced a form of worship He would have *particularised* that which, of its very essence, was meant to be universal. John came as a prophet and forerunner, and he set on foot a sect, which was held together and long kept alive by usages of its own; but the very observances which gave it vitality as a sect prevented its ever becoming anything more than a sect. Our Lord is not founding a sect at all; He is not a missionary making converts. He comes on earth to proclaim that God loves men, and to open a way by which men should "come to the Father." He leaves behind Him men suited to direct a religious movement, but He organises none himself. Whether He drew many round Him or few, His great work for the world would equally be completed on the Cross. He never baptised, never instituted rites, laws or fasts, or stated services of prayer; it is not till He leaves the earth that He enjoins the sacraments of His Church. It was to be left to men to put all into shape, for *the outer form belongs to man;* and, if He had Himself adopted any particular practice in any of the matters above named, men might imagine that this was binding for evermore and had a virtue in itself.

We come now to our Lord's plain and practical answer to the particular questions of the Pharisees which have led to these remarks. Fasting comes by nature when a man is sad, and it is in consequence the natural token of sadness: when a man is very sad, for the loss of relations or the like, he loses all inclination for food. But every outward sign that can be displayed at will is liable to abuse, and so men sometimes fasted when they were not really sad, but when it was decorous to appear so. Moreover a kind of merit came to be attached to fasting as betokening sorrow for transgressions; and at last it came to be regarded as a sort of self-punishment which it was thought the Almighty would accept in lieu of inflicting punishment Himself. Our Lord does not decry stated fasts or any other Jewish practices, they had their uses and they would last their times; only He points men to the underlying truth which was at the bottom of the ordinance.

When our Lord spoke, the children of the bridechamber the companions of the bridegroom's youth, were still with Him, but He and they would soon have to part. Sorrow must needs come upon them for the following reason, if for no other, that man's education cannot be perfect without it. Then indeed would they fast, not because it was enjoined, not of any stated precept, but because they were bereaved of their Lord.

Our Lord now turns to a metaphor, it was a familiar one. The lesson it seems to carry is this: our Lord will not meddle with the old form of things, He will not patch up the old tenement in order that the new spirit may make shift to dwell in it. Change with Him is never mechanical, always organic; it comes, not by alteration in construction, but always purely of growth. He is propagating spiritual truth in the souls of men; the time is not yet ripe for rites and ordinances and hours of worship. But the days would come when the truth would need a garb—it would have to struggle amongst human institutions, and it must then have outer expression just as other institutions have. This expression men must give, and Christ was careful that, when the time came for this to be done, the right men should be in their place to do it.

He takes a second metaphor to set forth the second part of His work: He will have new flasks for the new wine. This new doctrine was not committed either to the disciples of John or even to scribes enlightened about the kingdom of heaven, but to those who, having no preconceptions, received it as children do their parents' words. This new wine would go on working and would want room to expand. Peter we know expanded with it; but men whose minds had stiffened into shape under existing systems were like old flasks of skin, so harsh and dry that they would sooner crack than stretch; they were neither plastic nor elastic, and our Lord wanted vessels that should be both the one and the other. These new flasks were now soon to be chosen; and when this was done the work would enter on a new phase.

Up to the time of the call of the Apostles, our Lord's most conspicuous concern is for the multitudes. After that call, the Apostles occupy the foreground, and the whole manner of teaching is rather suddenly changed. It is no longer adapted to a congregation of peasants; parables take the place of plain speech, and instead of everything being done *for* the learner as before, much is left to be done *by* him for himself. We mark another change also in the manner. Hitherto there has been no *haste*, all has proceeded in the most leisurely way; but soon danger will begin to threaten and time to press, and act to follow act in close succession.

Following the subject of my book, I have been careful to mark how our Lord from the very first had an eye for characters of the sort He wanted and how He shaped them, with an unseen hand; but I must not have it supposed, because we see little lasting outcome from the preaching to the multitude, that therefore it was unimportant compared with the training of the Apostles. We must not suppose that Christ taught and healed chiefly that the Apostles might listen and learn.

226 THE PREACHING TO THE MULTITUDES

We can discern two kinds of good wrought by our Lord. In preaching to the multitude he was, then and there, bringing God's light into the souls of men. In choosing and fashioning the disciples, He was providing for the future of His Church. The work which the Apostles should set on foot would spread over the earth and affect all future times, while our Lord could Himself touch but a single generation in a single spot. Those, however, who heard Him, carried to their homes a memory to last their lives; among them His Personality survived. If, afterwards, troubled questions arose about Him they would put them by, feeling that they had drunk at the source before the stream had got sullied on its way.

When our Lord came into villages where He was known, people crowded to him from all sides, and the new delight of communion with God—the assurance that the whisper which told them that God cared for them was a true voice—beamed from the hearers' faces and gladdened the Master's soul.

It was during this active ministry of our Lord, that the choice of the Apostles was made and the foundations of their education were laid. The differences in their minds and characters would be brought into prominence by the greater intensity of the lives they afterwards led; new capacities would peep out among those who, beholding the intense earnestness of our Lord, learned to be in earnest themselves. No defined line was as yet drawn between the multitude and the disciples. Those who were of the multitude one day, and chose to follow, might count as disciples on the morrow. Our Lord never wholly loses sight either of the multitude or of the disciples; but, while the former were His first care in the period embraced in this chapter, the disciples, and especially the apostles, will be so in that which will come before us in the next[1].

[1] St Mark distinguishes between these two objects of our Lord's care, the multitude and the disciples. When our Lord after His journey to the North is passing through Galilee we read that "He passed through Galilee, and would not that any man should know it, for he taught His *disciples*." Mark ix. 31. And soon after, when he is beyond Jordan, we have "and *multitudes* came together unto him again; and, as he was wont, he taught *them* again." Mark x. 1.

CHAPTER VIII.

THE CHOOSING OF THE APOSTLES.

IN treating of the calling of the Apostles, we encounter the questions, "What led our Lord to surround Himself with a constituted body of this kind?" and, "In virtue of what qualities were its members chosen?" I am led to conclude that our Lord presaged that which actually came about, and provided for future needs which he foresaw; so precisely do the measures he takes meet what subsequent occasions required. The choice of the agents, moreover, is singularly happy with respect to the extraordinary part which was put into their hands; and it must be noted that this part was one which Jesus alone, and, if He had only been what some of His biographers represent, not even He could have contemplated: while for the parts, which, from the obvious prospects of the case it was likely they would have to play, they were not calculated at all. The apostles were not suited to advance a social or a political cause or to spread doctrinal views; but they were specially fitted, as I shall shew, to gain credence for facts which they could declare had passed before their eyes.

Before choosing the Apostles our Lord spent the night alone on the mountain in prayer; on one other occasion only did He do the same[1]. If we regard only the duties expressly laid upon the Twelve at their call[2], and the immediate services expected from them, our Lord's concern about them may seem more intense than the circumstances explain. But if we regard them as the heirs of His work, as those by whom the fire kindled by Him on earth was to be kept alive and spread, then our Lord's keen anxiety about them is accounted for. He looked to an early death, and when this death came it would depend on their constancy to carry the cause through the moment of dismay; and it would depend on the trust they commanded among men, whether it should be believed or not, that He had risen in triumph from the dead.

If we should find that the Apostles were, as a body, specially qualified to fulfil particular functions, and that these very functions it fell afterwards to them to discharge; then, surely, it is not unreasonable to suppose that our Lord, in choosing the Twelve, was guided by His foreknowledge of the situation in which they would be placed, and of the particular kind of work which they would be wanted to perform.

It will be shewn that the Apostles were qualified

---

[1] viz. after the miracle of the feeding of the five thousand. Matth. xiv. 23.

[2] viz., "that they might be with him and that he might send them forth to preach and to have authority to cast out devils." Mark iii. 14, 15.

to be trustworthy witnesses of fact? If the course of events had been such that there had been no fact to witness, this capacity of theirs would have found no sphere; it would have been provided and never employed; but, as it was, the transcendent Fact that Christ died and rose again took place before their eyes.

The knowledge of this Fact was to be the most precious possession of the human race. How then was it to be preserved and transmitted? A fact only subsists for a future time in the relation of witnesses. So the greatest care is taken to provide for this Fact witnesses who would command belief. Some hearers will soonest trust one kind of witness and some another; witnesses therefore of different kinds are provided, that every man might be likely to find one in whom he could confide: but all these witnesses have this in common—they are all convinced of the reality of what they relate, and are not men to be easily carried away by their fancy or their feelings. If the religion had depended on the promulgating of theological doctrines which needed subtle expositors, then the Apostles would not have been the right men for the work; but being founded as it was upon the facts of Christ's life and death, what was wanted was, that credible witnesses should be present when these facts occurred and should remain to tell the tale. This want was supplied with a completeness which to my mind testifies of design.

THE CHOOSING OF THE APOSTLES.

To proceed with the history. During this winter of A.D. 28—29, our Lord, keeping Capernaum for his place of abode, made excursions to the neighbouring towns, preaching as he went, and shewing by His miraculous cures that the Divine power was working through His hands.

After the call of the fishermen on the Lakeside, He was constantly accompanied by His disciples, and from that time forth the education of His followers was always in His mind. This education went on like the quiet processes of nature; the subjects of it never felt that they were being educated at all, but those who were of the right natures slowly changed in the direction of what He would have them be. He did not make them all copies after one pattern. That which was native to the man, and which marked him off from all other men, was lovingly preserved. He intensified in each man his proper life, which grew with all the greater vigour through being let to follow its own bent. As yet we hear of no lessons given to the disciples *by themselves*, they only shared what was said to the crowd: this may have been as much as they could then receive, and possibly their greatest profit came from what was not given in the way of lessons at all, from words dropt in daily intercourse and from watching their master's doings in the thousand little occurrences of their wayfaring daily life.

It is worth noting that during all this time of

their earliest spiritual education all was prosperity. From the autumn, in which, as I believe, our Lord called the fisher brethren, to the springtime which we have now reached in the narrative, His renown had steadily grown. Wherever He went, men were grateful for His coming, and drew close to hear; all seemed eager to press into the kingdom of Heaven, and to clutch at it as at treasure trove[1]. First from the neighbouring towns, then from Judæa and Samaria, and, at the time when this chapter opens, even from Idumea and Tyre and Sidon, men came to listen to one who was said to have the words of Eternal life.

Those who took their early impressions of Christ's service from those days, would retain a glowing recollection of it all their lives long. Their minds would be strung to hopeful confidence. When persecution came they would regard it as something permitted by their Master for reasons into which they did not inquire: the allegiance of mankind belonged, they would say, to their Master of right; He might for a moment waive his claim, but He could always resume it when He chose.

Our Lord sets a high value on the personal trust and devotion of his disciples, both for its own sake and because it was the bud which was to

---

[1] βιασταὶ ἁρπάζουσιν αὐτήν, Matth. xi. 12. "ἅρπαγμα especially with such verbs as ἡγεῖσθαι etc. is employed to denote 'a highly prized possession, an unexpected gain'." Bishop Lightfoot's *Philippians*, p. 111. Compare Ps. cxix. 162. "I am as glad of thy word as one that findeth great spoils."

THE CHOOSING OF THE APOSTLES. 233

blossom into the new and transforming quality of Faith: this was forwarded in its early growth by the sunshine of success. The general who would win the young soldier's heart must lead him to glory in his first campaign; he will cling to him through all disasters after his heart is won.

I take up the narrative at the beginning of the third chapter of St Mark's Gospel.

"And the Pharisees went out, and straightway with the Herodians took counsel against him, how they might destroy him. And Jesus with his disciples withdrew to the sea: and a great multitude from Galilee followed: and from Judæa[1]."

The Evangelists seldom speak of our Lord's motives, but here the collocation indicates that it was this confederacy of Pharisees and Herodians which caused our Lord to leave Capernaum. The Herodians were more formidable than the Pharisees. The latter would only set the law in motion, but the former did not scruple to employ violence; and the Macedonian guards of the Tetrarch were at Tiberias within call. Our Lord never, until His time was come, exposed Himself unnecessarily to danger; and at this particular moment His freedom and safety were of vital importance. All that He had done would, humanly speaking, be lost or have to be done over again if He were cast into prison or slain: the pressure of

[1] Mark iii. 6, 7.

this danger may have hastened the appointment of the Twelve. The body of disciples following our Lord had as yet no corporate life of its own; it was only held together by gravitation to Him and would fall to pieces if He were taken away; at this juncture then, there was no time to be lost in giving the body organic life. As soon as the Twelve received their commission this body became possessed of a vital centre, and the continuous existence of the Church was secured, even though its Master should be removed from earth.

This plot of the Pharisees was probably known but to few—people when they take counsel together do not publish their design on the house-tops— and the absence of excitement among the crowd favours the view that the danger of the prophet of Nazareth was not suspected by them. Whatever may have been His motive, our Lord left Capernaum, together with His followers, and took, it seems, the road along the sea shore towards the north.

Some words of our Lord, belonging probably to this place, are recorded by St Matthew.

"But when he saw the multitudes, he was moved with compassion for them, because they were distressed and scattered, as sheep not having a shepherd. Then saith he unto his disciples, The harvest truly is plenteous, but the labourers are few. Pray ye therefore the Lord of the harvest, that he send forth labourers into his harvest[1]."

[1] Matth. ix. 36—38.

St Matthew probably found in this need of labourers a sufficient reason for the call of the Apostles. More hands were wanted for ministering to the multitude, and it was desirable that some should be set apart for the work. But our Lord's great earnestness in the matter points, as I have just said[1], to something more than this, as though this calling of the Twelve was of vital concern for the great work that was being done for the world.

It would only have bewildered the disciples if our Lord had explained to them the meaning and motive of the commissioning of the Twelve. They could not be told that Christ's Kingdom on earth was being vested in the Twelve as an undying body in order that it might not be shattered by His death. They could not yet be told of the coming Resurrection, or that they were being trained to bear witness of Christ's spiritual presence with His own. Our Lord's talk with His disciples was primarily suited to their wants and to their minds, and not to those of the people of after times: we must not therefore expect to find in it answers to the questions we want to put. But we have one advantage which the disciples had not; they, as actors in the drama, were taken up with their parts for the moment, while we contemplate it as spectators from beginning to end; and even if we cannot quite follow the action, yet we can make out enough of sequence to see that this action forms a whole:

we mark the drift of the earlier incidents when we see the goal for which all was making, and our Lord's purposes are sometimes made more apparent by the course of His acts than by His words.

Without pretending to enter into our Lord's mind, we cannot help imagining the considerations which the situation must have inspired. The danger to the cause from allowing it to hang upon a single life was becoming more pressing day by day. Though our Lord in passing through the country, had kindled men's hearts as He went along, yet He had left no working agency behind. There was no rallying point, no minister, no constituted body in any district or town. It may be asked, "Why did not our Lord do as St Paul did?" Why did He not "ordain elders in every city," and establish His religion territorially step by step, just as an advancing army occupies the ground it has won? This is part of the wider question, "Why did not our Lord found a Church Himself?" to which an answer has been given before. His business was to "kindle the fire" and only to kindle it. What has been said of ritual (p. 222) applies to Church government as well. Church polities, like forms of secular government, were to be formed by men of each age for themselves; and to lay down a system, for which a Divine authority would inevitably be claimed, would bar all human intervention in matters ecclesiastical, and hamper men's minds in ways that I have glanced at before. If a system of Christian communities had been spread over Galilee by our Lord as it was spread over Asia Minor by St Paul, the forms of ecclesiastical government so sanctioned, and all that related to outer worship would have been regarded as a part of revealed truth. A visible Church framed by our Lord would have afforded a model, from any line in the construction of which it would have been a heresy to swerve. Men would not only have consecrated the principles of its polity but they would have seized on the visible constitution and points of practice and have battled for these to the death. We should have had an institution, Divinely authorised, and which therefore could not in the smallest particular be changed, imposed on races inheriting different temperaments, and one ecclesiastical rule would have been fixed for all time.

In all matters of procedure the one question asked would have been, "What was the practice of the Lord?" Church polity would have depended wholly on conclusions drawn from antiquarian study and, what would have been worse than all, people having outgrown the institutions regarded as Divine would have lulled their consciences by being studiously regardful of the form after the meaning had disappeared, and they would have stretched the formulæ to make them fit the times. In doing this they would have played fast and loose with their honesty of mind. Moreover it seems to me an incongruity that the Redeemer of the World should also be the founder of a local Church; the disproportion is so vast between the two terms.

A way was perfected in that night of prayer upon the hills, whereby an organic life was imparted to the little community without setting up a Church, from the pattern of which no deviation could be allowed. The Twelve formed a centre round which the disciples might cluster, and this rudiment of organisation was enough for the time. Christ gave only such a germ of external polity as the immediate need required. The commissioning of the Twelve imposed no particular form of rule; but it taught the lesson that organisation and order and the distribution of duty were essential in things spiritual as well as in things temporal, and that it was well for the children of light to be as "wise in their generation" as the children of the world.

When a danger or perplexity offers itself to men, they seek counsel one of another, but our Lord takes counsel of the Father alone, there is with Him no hesitancy, no balancing of this course against that. In this case, when the morning comes His resolve is distinct, and it is forthwith carried out. The constitution and proper functions of the body that He should create, as well as the persons who were to be the first members, all were determined on.

We read:

THE CHOOSING OF THE APOSTLES. 239

"He went out into the mountain to pray; and he continued all night in prayer to God[1];"

again, we have

"He goeth up into the mountain, and calleth unto him whom he himself would: and they went unto him. And he appointed twelve, that they might be with him, and that he might send them forth to preach, and to have authority to cast out devils[1]."

This is all we are told of the planting of that germ, of which the upgrowth is the Church of Christ. The organisation thus introduced was just enough to make of the disciples one body. Henceforth they could speak of themselves as "we;" but as yet, they were only pupils, chosen to be about their master's person, intrusted with special powers for the good of those among whom they ministered, but with no authority over the rest of the disciples.

The hour to which our Lord had looked forward, the time "when the bridegroom should be taken away," arrived at last, and our Lord's timely measures in finding the right men and training them in the right way proved of signal service then. When the critical moment came the men proper for the work were found upon the spot. When our Lord at Gethsemane, declining all superhuman aid, resigned Himself into His captors' hands, consternation and bewilderment for a moment overcame the Twelve—"they all left Him,

[1] Luke vi. 12.   [2] Mark iii. 13, 14.

and fled[2]." The recollection of this moment's failure may have been of service to them in after days; it may have made them more lenient to the lapses of others, and, like the "thorn in the flesh" given to St Paul, might prevent their being "exalted overmuch." The situation in which the Apostles found themselves called out the qualities desired. As soon as their Master had suffered there came upon them the sense of responsibility, and they rose to the circumstances as men with depth of character do. The cause did not die down even for a moment, it was kept alive in that upper chamber where the eleven met. To them, from the first, the other disciples looked for direction, and to them they brought their news. The women never doubted about where they were to go with the news that the sepulchre was empty, and late in the Resurrection Day the disciples from Emmaus proceeded straight to the upper chamber, knowing that the eleven would be there.

Hardly had the two who returned from Emmaus told their tale, when

"He himself stood in the midst of them, and saith unto them, Peace *be* unto you[3]."

The eleven had taken the helm quietly, as a matter of course, when the ship seemed to be disabled. They had been faithful in a little and straightway they are called unto much, they are

---

[2] Mark xiv. 50.   [3] Luke xxiv. 36.

THE CHOOSING OF THE APOSTLES. 241

chosen for witnesses of the Supreme Event in the history of Man, of the Resurrection of our Lord and Saviour Jesus Christ.

It is this character of witnesses which distinguishes the Apostles from all other depositaries of a Master's cause. This was the charge that governed the disposition of their lives. Other men might organise churches and set forth the teaching of the Lord, but in the character of appointed witnesses of the Resurrection they stood alone. Before the Resurrection they are told

"And ye also bear witness, because ye have been with me from the beginning[1],"

and afterwards it is as witnesses that they are singled out by our Lord, "And ye shall be my witnesses both in Jerusalem and in all Judæa and Samaria, and unto the uttermost parts of the earth[2]." In this distinctive light too they regard themselves. When a successor to Judas has to be appointed, St Peter says, "of these must one become a witness with us of his resurrection[3]" and Peter and all the Apostles say, before the Sanhedrin, "We are witnesses of these things." Peter again, speaking to the brethren from Joppa calls the Apostles "witnesses chosen before of God[4]."

I find in the Twelve a special fitness for the particular work which it fell to them to perform.

---

[1] John xv. 27.   [2] Acts i. 8.   [3] Acts i. 22.
[4] Acts x. 41.   For other instances see Luke xxiv. 48; Acts ii. 32; iii. 15; xiii. 31.

They brought to the attestation of the Resurrection the concurring evidence of eleven eyewitnesses, simple, truthloving, matter-of-fact men, of different types of mind.

The unanimity of the eleven, both as to their testimony and as to their adoption of a particular course of conduct has been less dwelt on by Apologists than I should have expected. If one or two could have been gained over by the Scribes to dissent from the account of the rest, the moral force of the evidence would have been lost. The chances against the agreement of the entire body in an illusion or a misrepresentation are enormous. But an event so transcendent as to wipe out of the minds of the witnesses everything else—"all trivial, fond records" would efface small subjective differences by the overwhelming force of the objective impression; and the occurrence of such an event would account for that perfect agreement in action among men who had not uniformly agreed before, which is among the many striking phenomena which the book of the Acts of the Apostles discloses to our own view.

The chosen witnesses have exactly the qualities which a judge would point out to a jury, as grounds for giving particular weight to their evidence on questions of fact coming within their view. I must say something more on this point.

Nothing carries more weight with a jury than the impression that the witness has an intense belief in the truth of what he says. Such an impression the Apostles conveyed; the possibility that they should themselves doubt in the slightest about any fact to which they speak never occurs to their mind; all through the Acts and the Epistles the atmosphere is one of certainty, settled and serene. The Apostles had not been always so assured; we find them in the Gospels impatient for clearer statements and more decisive signs: " Now speakest thou plainly and speakest no parable" they regard as high praise. But after the Resurrection all this is changed, they are then quite certain of the fact that Christ is Divine, and they have given up trying to understand the ways and forms in which the Divine power might show itself. They had probably, once thought, like Naaman, that it must operate something after the fashion which absolute power uses upon earth. They have got past this when we meet with them in the Acts.

I have spoken of the difference of character among the Apostles for this reason. That eleven men, and a *particular* eleven, should all have agreed in an account of what they said they had seen, when by so doing they gained none of the objects of human desire, is hard to explain unless we suppose that they were convinced of the truth of their report. If, however, these men had but one mind among them, either because one or two master spirits controlled the rest, or because they had been so carefully drilled into uniformity that they could not help judging alike, then the value of this unanimity would disappear, for the eleven would become, virtually, only one or two. Now that the Apostles were men of independent minds is clear from what we hear of their disputings by the way, and from the offence taken at James and John when they ask for seats on the right and left at their Master's side; and, indeed, the Gospel portraiture of all the Apostles leaves on us the impression that they were of different types of character and had personalities that were strongly marked.

Certainly St Peter had a turn of mind which was specially his own. He arrived at steadfast conviction not by reasoning from step to step—this was a mental process rarely practised by Galilean fishers—but by inward intuition, after his own strong Hebrew sort. When an impulse seized on him it must have its way, and when his heart was full of a matter he must pour it out.

Of Matthew what I said (p. 215) may stand in place of a notice here. His Gospel shews us from what side he looked on the work then being set afoot.

James and John the "Sons of Thunder" may be set down as representing energy and vehemence. They were not likely to follow a lead, or to fall in with a fantasy started by anyone else. Our notices of Thomas and Philip and Bartholomew, remind us of sketches, in which a few spirited pen-strokes present a figure which we can fancy we have seen.

Though Thomas so loved our Lord that he was the first to propose to go with Him to Jerusalem that "they might die with Him[1]," yet he will not take it on hearsay that Christ is risen. He knew how dearly the disciples longed to have their Master back, and he mistrusted their report because he feared that their impression might come of their strong desire. His doubts however like those of Nathanael, are those of an investigator, not of an assailant; like him he is "without guile" and is glad to accept the offer "Come and see." Of Philip I have often spoken. His words, "Shew us the Father and it sufficeth us" lay his mind bare before us.

These three men last named were all inclined to be incredulous, they were matter of fact persons, looking without rather than within, and such are the most trustworthy witnesses to external fact. Of one Apostle, Simon, it is true we learn that he had been a "zealot," that is, that he had once belonged to a band of men fired with fanatical devotion. But, when we hear of him, he had caught sight of a different kind of Divine Kingdom from any that he had thought of bringing about, and he was by degrees learning that "the wrath of man worketh not the righteousness of God[2]." Not one of these men had sufficient imagination—sufficient creative faculty—to embody his longings, even if he had such, in a vision so unexampled as that

---

[1] John xi. 16.   [2] James i. 20.

we have. That some of the eleven should have had one illusive fancy and some another would not have been improbable, but that all should have had the same would have been inordinately so. As a matter of fact the portraiture of the risen Lord given in our different memoirs is a conception singularly consistent, and one which the writers could not have drawn except from concurring traditions or personal knowledge of the facts.

There was one Apostle who did not witness the resurrection—Judas Iscariot. With all that has been written about him, the problems of his call and of the purpose of his treason remain unsolved. If, as many suppose, Judas came from some place in Judæa, Kerioth by name, he was, among the Apostles, the only one who was not a Galilæan. It is possible that he may have been one of those who attached themselves to our Lord at Jerusalem before His active ministry began. Our Lord did not "trust Himself[1]" with these as a body but one or two may have gone with Him through Samaria into Galilee. Judas may have been of a mind less simply receptive than the rest of the twelve. Perhaps he had aims for Israel, perhaps also for himself, the patriotic element may sometimes have been uppermost and sometimes the selfish one, and perhaps he wanted to hasten the Divine scheme and help it forward in His own way.

His presence among the disciples shews that

[1] John ii. 24.

our Lord did not confine his choice to those who were of one type, and that a man who had in him great possibilities, attracted his sympathy, although these possibilities might be turned to evil, and the things meant for his good might become an occasion of falling.

But while each individual of the Apostolic body had a specific character of his own, yet beneath this lay a generic condition common to them all. They all belonged to the lower middle class, living by labour but above want; they were able to read and write and some could probably talk Greek with the neighbouring Hellenists in the country to the north. The Apostles were plain and homely in their minds and in their talk. In what they heard they saw little beyond the meaning that lay on the surface of the words. This literal mindedness does not belong to one Apostle or two, but characterizes them all, and it appears in St John's Gospel as frequently as in the other three. The Evangelists relate these displays of simplicity without ever dreaming that they throw thereby any disparagement on the Apostles: such they expected them to be, and such they note that they were.

When men have the wants of the day full in view every morning of their lives, and must supply these wants by the labour of their hands, their thoughts naturally take a practical turn. Now this we note as a signal trait in the behaviour of the Apostles and it is exactly what would characterize men brought up as they had been. They always look first to what under the circumstances has to be *done*; like seafaring men, they are prompt in resource. When the five thousand stay till nightfall on the mountain side far from any place where food could be got, the thought of the Apostles is, " How are they to be fed ?" They take it on them to advise that the crowd be sent away while there was still daylight enough for them to reach the villages. In the little daily business of common life they act as if matters of service fell within their own sphere and on them they had a right to speak. I have already spoken of their pressing our Lord to take food on the journey through Samaria. Again, when the three Apostles are with our Lord on the Mount of Transfiguration, Peter evidently supposes that they have entered a new and heavenly country where they are to stay, and his first thought is to be of service. People, he supposes, will want abiding places in the new country as well as in the old land they had left, so he proposes to build huts as if they had been camping in the hills. An Alpine guide would have spoken much in the same way. These little distinctive characteristics are carefully preserved, and the instinctive thought of the attendant Apostles for their Master in their little acts of personal service is true to nature in a rare and delicate way.

Such men are good witnesses for they have eyes for everything. I contend then, first that the

Apostles were singularly adapted for affording the testimony required, and next, that, if men were especially picked out on account of their qualifications as witnesses, then our Lord must have had in view some great event for which witnesses were required. In the selection of these plain men to found the church we light upon the first hint of the distinctive feature of the Christian revelation mentioned above, viz. that it was to be centred, not in *notions* but in a stupendous Fact (p. 230).

When the gospel had to be preached to Greeks who sought after a methodical system, and the need came for doctrine, the work was given to St Paul. But twelve St Pauls as witnesses to fact would not have carried as much weight as the Apostles did, for though the most truthful of men, yet the world of his own thoughts was nearly as present to him as the world without, and it was not always perfectly clear when he was speaking of one and when of the other. The minds of the Apostles, on the other hand, were quite limpid; they received all "as little children," registering truly what came from without, and declaring it just as their five senses set it before them.

I have said (*l.c.*) that the Apostles were not the men whom the Founder of a policy or a school would have chosen to win men over to his views. Our Lord does not choose his successors for their power of attracting crowds. He does not teach them to argue or to preach. They prevailed by what they were and what they did, more than by what they said. They had not the art of kindling enthusiasm and leading captive the minds of men. They do not possess the magic which masters the will. Their success comes of what they had to say, not of the way in which they said it. They were indeed to be the promulgators of the religion which was to grow up around the person of Christ, they were to "teach all nations[1]," but they are not to dominate men and bear them down by impetuous oratory. This is too near akin to delusion and tyranny for teachers of the freemen whom "the truth makes free." Nor were they to rate their success by the multitude of those they baptized. The truths revealed in Christ's life and death were given to the world to be part of its possessions through all time, and whether they were generally accepted a little sooner or a little later was of small account.

It may be remarked here what a small part in the Divine economy, the gift of eloquence plays. Moses had no utterance, the speech of Paul was contemptible, and the Apostles can, indeed, say what needs saying, but have not the gift, so infinitely valued by the Greek, of leading men captive by persuasive words.

But though to have been witnesses of the Resurrection was the great glory of the Apostles, yet they were something more than witnesses; they were also the first guardians and propagators of

[1] Matt. xxviii. 19.

the Faith that transformed the world. They were the depositories of the leaven which gradually set up its working through the minds of men.

For this other function of their office they were also singularly qualified in various external ways.

The social position of the Apostles was advantageous for the promulgating of a Faith which was to become universal. They belonged to the stratum in which the Centre of Gravity of Humanity lay. The small land owners and handicraftsmen in Galilee were in contact with people in different stations of life; they could talk with the rich and they could feel with the poor; they were on the border land between the learned and the ignorant, and had just enough knowledge to be able to get more when they wanted it. There was one truth, essential and vital to a Faith which was to exalt and dignify all mankind, which in the class from which the Apostles came was found growing with especial vigour as on its native soil. This truth was the surpassing value of a man as man,—the sanctity which clothes a human being who is made in the image of God. The sense of this truth is much keener among the poor than among the rich; it is the poor who are most scandalised if a human being is treated like a brute. The rich have wealth, dignities and the like, on which their thoughts rest with satisfaction. But when the poor man takes account of his condition he finds but one item on the credit side, and he makes the most of it: it is that "He too is a Man." The upper class in Palestine had little mind for anything wider than a philosophical or political sect, and they treated the poor as if they had no souls. Christianity therefore could not have made its cradle with them, and the lowest class had little intelligence and no power of combination and would have been at once trodden under foot. Unless the Church had taken root in the lower middle class, it could hardly have spread as it did. That its earliest promulgators belonged to this class I will not suppose to have been a matter of mere chance.

To proceed with the course of events. Our Lord having called to Him "whom He Himself would" and chosen the twelve, assigns to them their name. They are "Apostles," men sent forth to preach. But it was not till the risen Christ appeared to the eleven in that upper chamber and said, "Peace be unto you; as my Father hath sent me even so send I you," that they saw all that was meant by this name; viz. that Christ was the Apostle of His Father and that they were the Apostles of Christ.

Our Lord on coming down with the Twelve from the mountain found a great gathering of people waiting for Him on a spot of level ground.

St Luke's account is this.

"And he came down with them, and stood on a level place, and a great multitude of his disciples, and a great number of the people from all Judæa and Jerusalem, and the sea coast of Tyre and Sidon, which came to hear

THE CHOOSING OF THE APOSTLES. 253

him, and to be healed of their diseases; and they that were troubled with unclean spirits were healed. And all the multitude sought to touch him: for power came forth from him, and healed them all[1]."

The address to the newly chosen Apostles which follows this passage in St Luke's gospel has been incorporated by St Matthew with the Sermon on the Mount. The portions belonging to it may there be recognised by the absence both of allusions to the Law and of the opposed phrases, "It was said to those of old time" and "But I say unto you," phrases which point the contrast which forms the main theme of the earlier address.

The multitudes who awaited our Lord "in the level place" were made up of Apostles, disciples, and people "who came to hear him and be healed." In some passages of this discourse our Lord had the disciples, and in others the rest of the people, particularly in view.

It was to the disciples that He turned when He began to speak.

"And he lifted up his eyes on his disciples, and said, Blessed are ye poor: for yours is the kingdom of God[2]."

The four beatitudes are, to my mind, expressly addressed to those who are about to take service on Christ's side. It was only to a disciple that our Lord could say that He would be hated, and cut

[1] Luke vi. 17—19.
[2] Luke vi. 20.

off and vilified "for the son of man's sake," and it was only disciples, and disciples too who were active in spreading the word, who could be brought into comparison with prophets either true or false. The interpretation also of these beatitudes depends on the fact that our Lord is speaking to the disciples. Blessing did not belong to the poor as an appanage of their poverty but because they were His disciples and theirs was the Kingdom of God; it was easier for the poor than the rich to enter this Kingdom, and then their earthly poverty brought out by contrast the greatness of their spiritual wealth. There is this difference between the lessons taught here and those delivered in the Sermon on the Mount; here all is personal while there it is general. Here, our Lord is speaking to His disciples and says, "for *yours* is the Kingdom of Heaven," and "*ye* shall be filled." In the Sermon on the Mount the corresponding pronouns are *theirs* and *they*.

A special lesson is conveyed to the Twelve in the last of these beatitudes.

"Blessed are ye, when men shall hate you, and when they shall separate you from their company, and reproach you, and cast out your name as evil, for the Son of man's sake. Rejoice in that day, and leap for joy: for behold, your reward is great in heaven: for in the same manner did their fathers unto the prophets[1]."

Although the enthusiastic reception of their

[1] Luke vi. 22, 23.

THE CHOOSING OF THE APOSTLES. 255

Master must have cheered the Apostles and set them forward in good heart, yet they were not to think that they were called to share in a triumph that was already won. They were not to be over-elated by this passing favour of men. The danger was, lest they should be too sanguine and be carried away by the fascination of popular goodwill. Well might they be lifted up. Their Master had just entrusted them with superhuman powers, and multitudes had come from miles around and had waited for them all night at the foot of the hills. So, in the midst of the flush of success, our Lord tells them that the criterion of their being true soldiers of God is their winning, not the world's praise but its hate. There is in the world an enmity to God as God. There are many who will readily enough acknowledge a Deity so long as He is not real and actual and is not brought too near; they find in the abstract idea a serviceable support for their social institutions; but from the notion of a living God close by them they shrink in dismay, and along with their terror goes hate.

Parallel with these beatitudes run the denunciations of woe.

"But woe unto you that are rich! for ye have received your consolation. Woe unto you, ye that are full now! for ye shall hunger. Woe unto you, ye that laugh now! for ye shall mourn and weep. Woe unto you, when all men shall speak well of you! for in the same manner did their fathers to the false prophets[1]."

[1] Luke vi. 24—26.

These denunciations are not found in the Sermon on the Mount. That discourse was addressed to people mostly of the same class and in the same posture of mind. When our Lord first spoke to the crowds on the hillside people had not begun to take sides; but, at the period of the history now before us, they had already clustered into parties; some had declared for the word and some against it, while many remained indifferent or in doubt, and to these several parties our Lord speaks in turn.

I think that when our Lord began to utter "Woe," he turned to the men of station and substance in whom curiosity was mixed with considerations of prudence. They are not denounced for being rich any more than the poor are blessed for being poor; but their calamity is this, that in riches they find enough consolation to prevent their striving heartily after anything better. They do not "hunger and thirst after righteousness," they do not "seek a country;" they do not steadily seek anything; but, if they feel for a moment uneasy, they clutch their possessions and say, "At any rate I have thus much comfort secure here." This it was which made it next to impossible for them to enter the kingdom of God, and our Lord cries unto them, "Woe."

In the last denunciation our Lord comes back to the disciples again. The ills that men's hatred brought with it were patent enough, but men's favour was an insidious snare; for it might lead

THE CHOOSING OF THE APOSTLES.

them unawares to love "the praise of men more than the praise of God." The more kindly the young preacher is received, the more distressing it is to him to incur dislike; and consequently the greater is the temptation to soften down Christ's sternness and to meet the world halfway. Our Lord warns his new helpers by the example of those who in old times had prophesied smooth things, and had gone the way of the world while the world had made believe it was going theirs.

The beatitudes and warnings of woe form the prelude, and when this was over our Lord may be supposed to have lifted up his eyes from those who stood nearest—probably the Apostles and most notable persons—and to have addressed the whole multitude; for, His words, "But I say unto you which hear[1]," I take to imply, "*all* you which hear." The twelve verses which follow form a sermon of general application of which "Love your enemies" is taken as the text.

On this sermon being ended we read

"And he spake also a parable unto them, Can the blind guide the blind? shall they not both fall into a pit? The disciple is not above his master: but every one when he is perfected shall be as his master[2]."

This parable is addressed to the newly appointed Twelve. It bears on the temptations of young teachers. They are in danger of being elated

[1] Luke vi. 27. [2] Luke vi. 39, 40.

at finding themselves teachers when they had so lately been learners; they might lean to correction, and might incline to be over busy in giving directions and in finding fault; they might persuade themselves too that they thought only of the learners' good, when in reality there was, mixed with this, a good spice of the love of exercising superiority. They are told that if they are to act as guides they must see their own way first; the light within them must not be darkness.

The last verse of the last quotation, refers, not to Christ and *His* disciples—there is no suggestion that these should reach *His* perfection—but to the disciples and *their* scholars. The especial point of the verse is the responsibility laid upon the teacher, by the pupils taking him as their ideal. The pupils of the disciples would copy the disciples themselves, and they could not excel their pattern. The learner could not be above his master, what is cast in a mould cannot be better shaped than the mould itself; but the perfected work that is turned out exactly represents the mould. The disciples therefore must watch against every defect, for their pupils would copy them faults and all.

The text has another application besides this, the pupil when perfected would stand on a level with his master; the latter had no indefeasible superiority. When they had lighted the lamps of others the light of the rest would be as bright as their own. If they were to glory it should be, not in their superiority to their pupils, but in their pupils having become as good as themselves. They were not to be like those teachers who keep back from their prentices some special secret of their art.

Next comes the verse, "For there is no good tree that bringeth forth corrupt fruit[1]." This applies both to those who teach and to those who learn. If the master's scholars mostly turn out ill it may be inferred that he is a bad master; and if the master be self-seeking at bottom, whatever disguise he may put on, the evil will come to light: selfishness always generates counter-selfishness, and false pretension detected in one case may lead a young man into general mistrust.

In another view of the verse, the behaviour of the man is the fruit and his nature is the tree. This fruit is not without value in itself, but is of more value still as an evidence of the condition of the tree. This falls in with the constant burden of Christ's teaching, "God looks to what you *are* as well as to what you *do*, and part of the importance of what you do comes from its shewing what you are, or from its helping by way of practice to confirm you in your ways whether good or bad."

In the last four verses of the address our Lord again speaks to the whole company of hearers. He takes one of His familiar topics, viz., that good is not only to be admired, it must also be done. This is expressed by the illustration of the

[1] Luke vi. 43, also Matth. vii. 17 where the converse is added.

house on the rock and that on the earth. Many who followed Him counted themselves His disciples because they carried away his commands in their heads and talked about them. He tells them that they can only get firm hold of them by putting them into practice. There were many hearers who would put our Lord's precepts away somewhere in their memory, and be satisfied with possessing right and beautiful thoughts without carrying them into practice, keeping them like curios in a drawer. These were like men building on the earth, who do only just what the moment requires. But the habit formed by steady obedience effects a structural change in the man's own mind. This is a lasting possession—it has taken time and pains to acquire, but it is storm proof like the house upon the rock.

When speaking of the Sermon on the Mount, I touched on the form in which our Lord delivers what He says. The remarks there made apply to the discourse before us and, in addition, it may be said, that this address is admirably adapted to be carried away by the hearers as a whole. It is strongly marked by its characteristic style, so that an addition or alteration by another hand would strike even an unpractised ear, as not having the true ring. There are four beatitudes and four denunciations, corresponding each to each; this numerical symmetry assists recollection. Then comes the sermon, made up of sayings so short and terse that the most unlettered may carry the whole away; and finally all ends with a parable, which is so well suited to the popular mind that it is now perhaps the best known of all pieces of Bible imagery. Those who like may trace in this a certain prevision, a designed fashioning of the garb of the word to suit it for that oral transmission on which, at one period, its preservation would depend.

When our Lord had finished His discourse He returned to Capernaum.

"And he cometh into a house. And the multitude cometh together again, so that they could not so much as eat bread. And when his friends heard it, they went out to lay hold on him: for they said, He is beside himself[1]."

There were occasions in our Lord's life in which the Divine nature seemed to glow through the human receptacle. It was so when He came down from the Mount of Transfiguration, so too, when he went forward, apart from the rest, at the outset of His final journey to Jerusalem; and so I believe it was when He came back to Capernaum bringing with Him the Twelve whom He had chosen to form the nucleus of His everlasting Church. Something in His air seems to have amazed His friends, "they said he is beside himself."

The Scribes, marking the temper of the crowd, thought it wise to drop their schemes of violence, but they set afoot the notion that He was possessed

[1] Mark iii. 20, 21.

by the Prince of the Devils and ruled the spirits of evil in his name. Our Lord made no long stay at Capernaum, but took the Twelve with Him on a journey to the cities in Galilee that they might see how He preached and taught, and, what was more, that they might learn to put complete trust in His wise guidance and sheltering love. This was the first practical lesson they collectively received.

It was in the interval between the calling of the Twelve and the despatching of them, two and two, on their missions, or possibly while they were gone, that the messengers sent by the Baptist came up with our Lord and His party.

As the next chapter will be taken up with the lessons belonging to this mission of the Twelve, I shall deal with this incident in this chapter, although, chronologically, it might fall in the next. It is related by St Matthew as follows:

"Now when John heard in the prison the works of the Christ, he sent by his disciples, and said unto him, Art thou he that cometh, or look we for another? And Jesus answered and said unto them, Go your way and tell John the things which ye do hear and see: the blind receive their sight, and the lame walk, the lepers are cleansed, and the deaf hear, and the dead are raised up, and the poor have good tidings preached to them. And blessed is he, whosoever shall find none occasion of stumbling in me[1]."

[1] Matt. xi. 2—6. See also Luke vii. 18—23.

The question asked by the Baptist shews us his condition of mind. A voice in his heart had told the Baptist that he was born to be the forerunner of one mightier than himself, and the sign at the Baptism had shewn him who that Person was. He had recognised in Him "the Lamb of God who was to take away the sins of the world," the Son in whom the Father was well pleased. This conveys the impression that John regarded our Lord as the Jewish Messiah, but the Baptist's notions about the Messiah may have been vague, like those which the people and even the Scribes entertained; although he was a prophet and more than a prophet, he would not know more than other people, except on matters directly revealed to him. The Divine light is indeed a "lantern to a man's path," but it is a lantern that throws its light only in the direction in which he who carries it has to go. I believe that John sent to our Lord because he was bewildered by what he heard. That the Messiah should preach and heal was agreeable to what he had expected: but, "Was this to be all?" Was He going to restore the kingdom Himself, or was another to come and take up that portion of the work?

Our Lord, it would appear, wished to give John as nearly as might be the same advantages as His disciples had. The emissaries are accordingly made witnesses of the Signs. They are told to relate what they saw and He adds the significant words, "And blessed is he whosoever shall find none occasion of stumbling in me[1]." Our Lord could not say that He was the Messiah without letting loose all the divers erroneous imaginations which hovered round the name. Our Lord, after His fashion, gives the Baptist a suggestive hint, leaving it to him whether he should follow out the clue rightly or not. As soon as John's messengers, who for a while had witnessed the works that He did, had turned back home, our Lord addressed himself to the company who were with him, people, disciples and all, and spoke to them of John. This discourse contained lessons of tolerance which helped to widen the disciples' minds, and I shall therefore discuss it at some length. It has a bearing extending beyond those to whom it was addressed.

I shall take St Luke's version of this discourse because in that of St Matthew it is, I think, mixed with matter spoken on other occasions.

It is our Lord's way to point the drift of a whole discourse by a pregnant sentence at the end, in which the expositor finds the key to the whole. Such a saying we have here, in the closing words,

"And wisdom is[2] justified of all her children[3]."

The meaning of the passage turns on the sense given to the word "justified." It is employed, near the beginning of the discourse, in the same sense which it has here at the end, and this helps us to

[1] Luke vii. 23.   [2] Marginal rendering, *was*.   [3] Luke vii. 35.

understand its particular meaning in this place. I refer to the passage:

"And all the people when they heard, and the publicans, *justified* God, being baptized with the baptism of John. But the Pharisees and the lawyers rejected for themselves the counsel of God, being not baptized of him[1]."

The word "justified" is used in this passage in the sense it has when we say "my son has justified all my outlay," or "the event justified all my precautions."

The publicans by accepting the baptism of John shewed that God's good offices in their behalf were not thrown away, that they had not been regarded with excessive hopefulness or a too indulgent eye; but the Scribes and Pharisees frustrated God's good purpose in their behalf. So far as they were concerned his measures were of no effect. They would have none of them. The fact was, that, though they talked about God, they were in fact Godblind, and when asked to follow His teachers they found special reasons for declining in each particular case. John renewed an ideal which had passed out of sight; he appeared in the ascetic garb of the prophets of old; his strict life and his outspoken words disturbed their consciences and they put him aside by the readiest of expedients, they declared that he was mad. Then came our Lord declaring Himself the Son of Man, living as other men did,

[1] Luke vii. 29, 30.

and consecrating thereby the ordinary course and usages of human life. In His case also the Scribes had an objection to make. A messenger from God, they thought, would come upon the earth in a different way from other men, and all his doings would be of an exceptional kind: whereas Christ lived to all appearance just as they did themselves. In the same way that courtiers surround a prince by a wall of etiquette in order to elevate him and hold him apart from the people, so would the Scribes have encompassed God's messenger with hallowed observances. They were not likely to understand that the closer Jesus kept to the ordinary and universal ways of men which were of natural growth, the more He was at home in the Kingdom of His Father who had made the world and ordered the ways of men.

Christ goes to the root of both these objections. He takes an image drawn from what was always under their eyes. He supposes a crowd of children playing in the market place, while others are sitting somewhat sullenly by. They play at a wedding, and they pretend to pipe and dance, but those who sit by will not stir; and then they change to a funeral, and imitate the wailing of the relatives and of the train of hired mourners, but those whom they wish to gain for playmates will not have this either; *they do not want to play at all.* The people would learn from this image as much as was within their comprehension. They could see that when the Pharisees objected on opposite grounds to two courses, their aversion was really not to either course but to that to which both courses tended. But the last verse, "wisdom is justified of *all* her children," goes beyond what the people would see at the time; and, indeed, as St Matthew in his version omits the important word *all*, it looks as if he had himself missed the full sense.

The text conveys a lesson of ample tolerance which even in these days, all minds are not stretched wide enough to receive. The point is this. God has children of more types than one, and all these, in their own different ways, justify God's thought for them by taking advantage of His help. The ways of Jesus and the ways of John differ widely, but men may reach God coming round by either way. Some may gain access to the Kingdom through John and others by Jesus; but all who *are* God's will get there by some way or other. If the Scribes and Pharisees were winnowed away by this trial it was because the germs of a Divine nature within them had been suffered to perish. They were God's children no longer, and God's ways for His children would not succeed with them.

That wisdom is justified of all her children, is a truth carrying to different generations the precise lesson of tolerance it needs. It was not long before the Apostles themselves had occasion to call this very lesson to mind. An exclusive spirit, and the desire to have their privileges all to themselves led them to forbid a man who followed not with them to cast out devils in their Master's name. They are very gently set right. Our Lord is never hard upon errors arising from mistaken notions; he gently checks them at the time and takes early occasion, by a parable, or some lesson of circumstance, to suggest the proper counter view.

But though the Apostles might profit by this apophthegm, yet it was aimed directly at the Scribes who held that in all questions there must be one right view, all others being wrong; so that toleration of anything that deviated from the accepted view, implied indifference to truth. But it is only "truth absolute" which is *one and exclusive* and this, in spiritual matters, can only be attained by an unmistakeable *dictum* of revelation. In a geometrical investigation, we have an infallible logic dealing with definite notions; we therefore get one precise result, and all that differ from this are worthless. But in matters spiritual an element of infinity must be present; notions enter which cannot be defined; men may use the same words in stating their views, but whether these words convey the same conceptions to them all, no one can possibly say. In things spiritual, therefore, no one answer completely excludes all other answers because we never get a perfect solution at all; we only get approximations. In like manner there are insoluble problems in Mathematical Physics to which we can only get answers approximately correct. These being points in a circle round the unattainable centre may be infinite in number.

These hard sayings shew that Christ, when he spoke, looked beyond his hearers into infinite space and saw there "other sheep who were not of this fold[1]." He must also have felt sure that these words of His would be preserved for after times; for certainly, it was not merely for Galilean hearers that our Lord uttered pregnant words like those I have just discussed[2]. The candle was not lighted to be put in a cupboard. The hard sayings of our Lord as well as many of His passing words, which called forth no notice at the time, are to me part of the witness, everywhere peeping out, of our Lord's prospective view in what He said and did. He must have had in view persons or bodies of men, who would find, some in one of these utterances and some in another, what answered to a want or a question rising in their hearts; and, as a fact, men have in every age lighted on words of our Lord which seemed to be a revelation directed to their own case, the key to the special riddle which vexed their souls. There are herbs and simples growing on the earth, which men for ages have passed carelessly by, but some new form of malady has one day appeared, and in the disregarded plant has the needful help been found.

[1] John x. 16. [2] p. 265.

CHAPTER IX.

THE SCHOOLING OF THE APOSTLES. THE MISSION TO THE CITIES.

THE point we have now reached in the history is marked by a signal change as well in the form of our Lord's teaching as in the outer tenour of His life. His discourses are no longer a string of positive precepts, but they consist largely of parables, commonly closing with a moral put into a striking, not to say a paradoxical, form. His way of life is altered also, it is no longer that of a resident of Capernaum, but that of a wayfarer undertaking considerable journeys, accompanied by the Twelve who had left all to follow Him. Outward circumstances, such as danger from the side of Herod, may have had influence in bringing this latter change about, but all things fell together to further the kind of education desired for the Twelve. This change from a stationary life to a wandering one was conducive to the growth of certain qualities valuable for the founders of a Church. These qualities we find conspicuously displayed by the Apostles in the Acts, and we may ask whether they had not acquired them in this course of practical education, and also whether our Lord did not frame this course with a view to its educational effects, and the fitting of the Apostles for their work. Was it of pure accident that all this came about?

We can also, although with less positiveness, draw some inferences from the courses which our Lord avoided taking as well as from those which He took. When we are disposed to wonder why our Lord did not take some particular step, it is a good plan to consider what would have come about if He had done so. We shall often find that the proposed course would have had an ultimate effect, very different from that immediate and obvious one which had at first occurred to us. So, by examining the educational consequences which would have resulted from certain courses that were *not* taken we shall, I think, learn something about what to avoid in education ourselves. Although the education of the Apostles is a purpose ever in our Lord's view, yet it is only now and then that we are plainly told that something was said or done for the Apostles' sakes. This silence as to the effect which is aimed at is, in education, often a necessity. If a pupil is told by his master that he is put through certain studies, not that he may learn the subject, but that he may perfect himself in certain mental motions and improve his capacities, he is apt to be made self-conscious and coxcombical or else, feeling satisfied that his mind and capacities are very well as they are, he gives small attention to what he is told.

From the very first we have seen indications that our Lord was divining the natures of men, selecting them with a forecast to their coming work, and fitting them to receive and promulgate His revelation of God. But this inner purpose, which, until the Twelve are called, has lain underground, now crops out on the surface and forces itself into view; and we feel bound to ask of every subsequent incident in the sacred History, "How was the Apostles' character influenced by this?"

I have spoken of the "Schooling of the Apostles" for want of a better phrase, but the mental changes wrought in the disciples by their Master's company constitute a very different sort of schooling from what commonly goes by the name. They receive no doctrinal instruction in dogmatic form, they obtain nothing which they can display, they are shewn no new system for dealing with the problems of life, nor are they given fresh views about the Messiah. Those who come asking "What they are to do?" are always told that they already know, or should know, this very well of themselves. Among the great Teachers of the world there is hardly one, whose chosen pupils have received so few tenets in a formulated shape as those of Christ; and yet the Apostles at the time of the Ascension have undergone a transformation, compared with what they were when our Lord first found them, greater than was ever wrought in men in the same time before.

One special function was assigned to the Apostles which sets them apart from all other men. In them was engendered a new quality belonging to spiritual life; they were the trustees of mankind for a new capacity; they were the depositaries of the faculty for realising "the assurance of things hoped for, the proving of things not seen[1]." In them Faith, which elsewhere existed only in the germ, was brought to perfection and bore fruit, and scattered seed. Their progress in this quality proceeds by certain steps; these are roughly indicated in the first chapter of this book (pp. 8, 9), but I will name them here again.

First of all, the men who were chosen for the work had a more than usual power of savouring the things of God. They are brought under the influence of One whom they regard as the Messiah but about whom something of mystery hangs. They conceive for him a passionate loyalty, and an affection, of which that inspired by the highest human natures will only serve to give a bare idea; they are with him day by day; they look on his Signs and Wonders, but it seems to them so

[1] Heb. xi. 1.

natural that a Man like Him should work wonders, that they scarcely marvel at them. Inward evil, selfish thoughts and all, disappear when He is by. Again, they are educated to feel that in His company they are safe against outward dangers. This growing confidence[1] was tried and found wanting when they were with their Master on the Lake and the storm arose; the lesson had to be studied a little longer. As soon as it was fully learned they were advanced another stage; the Apostles, in the great practical lesson which is the leading matter of this chapter, were taught that Christ's power reached beyond His presence, that it could even be delegated to them, and that His shelter could be spread over them, though He might be far away. They are sent forth without purse and scrip that they may the better feel that they are in Christ's hand and need give no thought to petty daily cares. The same lesson is afterwards given to the Seventy disciples. The Crucifixion brought about an education of a very different kind, that of affliction and trial; but the Apostles do not, at once, wholly lose their Master, He is withdrawn from them by degrees. After the Resurrection though He no longer lives on the earth a common life with men, yet His disciples feel that He is not absolutely gone; He seems to be still close by, and they may at any moment see His loved and honoured form and hear the words

[1] Mark iv. 35—40.

THE MISSION TO THE CITIES.

"Peace be unto you." The stranger who joins them on the road may prove to be He; they may catch sight of the Lord's features as He vanishes away. Then comes the last stage of separation when He is completely lost to eye and ear, and Spiritual Communion only is maintained. Most carefully and by wisely ordered degrees had they been brought to apprehend this Spiritual Communion, and they were actuated by the inner sense of His presence during all the rest of their lives. This it was, this realization of our Lord's words "Lo, I am always with you unto the end of the world," which rendered—and still is rendering —the Christian Church a body living and organic, and not a mere exponent or depository of doctrines, and of traditions about the Lord.

Christ is the Divine core of the true life of Humanity, and He, when one set of views are outgrown, may whisper to the "company of God's faithful people," and there may be disclosed to them another aspect of that truth absolute which men in the body cannot completely discern or receive.

Soon after the call of the Apostles the fixed residence of our Lord at Capernaum was broken up. Very little consideration will be wanted to see that it was serviceable, with a view to the education of the Apostles, that it should be so.

Up to this time the fisher brethren had gone on working for their livelihood more or less, but now their Master saw that He should be but a short time with them and He would have them all to Himself. Of labour, both bodily and mental, the Apostles should indeed have enough, but so long as they were with their Master—so long as the bridegroom was with them—all this labour must tend to the single object unto which they were to consecrate their lives. We can readily see that so long as Christ was on earth it was their one duty to follow and to hear; they should be engrossed by the sole duty of attending Him and were not to be distracted by sordid cares or by having to labour for their daily bread. They were to learn that the work to which they were called was of a sublime order, and that the business of common life was as nothing by its side. After this time the Apostolic party were supported from their own savings or from the contributions of their friends, or of others interested in the "words of eternal life." The following passage belongs to this time:

"And it came to pass soon afterwards, that he went about through cities and villages, preaching and bringing the good tidings of the kingdom of God, and with him the twelve, and certain women which had been healed of evil spirits and infirmities, Mary that was called Magdalene, from whom seven devils had gone out, and Joanna the wife of Chuza Herod's steward, and Susanna, and many others, which ministered unto them of their substance[1]."

[1] Luke viii. 1—3.

But as soon as they ceased to labour for their daily bread, they were kept continuously and actively engaged in their Master's service; for they were not to be exposed to the dangers attending the lack of settled occupation. Thus we find that as soon as they ceased to earn their livelihood they were occupied incessantly, journeying in attendance on our Lord. This matter may be approached at either of its two ends. It may have been our Lord's first care that the Apostles should be freed from secular labour, and the journeys may have been secondary to this purpose; or the journeyings may have been of primary importance, and the Twelve would then necessarily abandon their callings, and have to be supported out of some common fund. In both cases the educational effect was the same.

If the Twelve after being freed from earning their livelihood had remained in Capernaum, there must have been some part of the day when they were not in actual attendance on their Master; they would have to meet the reproach of idleness, and they might lose some self-respect by feeling that they were eating others' bread; or, in their spare time they might fall into those polemical discussions from which our Lord safeguards them with especial care.

All these evils were obviated by the course which was actually taken. Our Lord left his fixed home at Capernaum, and He and the Twelve

THE SCHOOLING OF THE APOSTLES.

adopted a wandering life. These journeys taken in company supplied a need which in all education is a foremost one, that of discipline. They were given duties to perform. When men travel together, faring hardly on rough mountain ways, bound to start together and to keep up each with the rest, whether disposed to do so or not, they soon come to set inclination on one side and to learn what obligation means. There is no kind of companionship which binds men in a closer and heartier fellowship than this journeying together. Thus the Schooling of the Twelve went on, without their guessing it, as they went with their Master, sometimes on foot over the hills, sometimes rowing the boat on the Lake, sometimes providing for His reception in the cities, or marshalling hearers to listen to the word; and sometimes, when multitudes had to be fed, arranging them, plot by plot, so that they might be reached by those who distributed the food[1].

This work afforded the very training required. Nothing is more remarkable in the Apostles than their unbroken mental health. The histories of religious communities are full of instances of ecstacies and hysterical delusions; but never do we find among our Lord's followers anything approaching to a spiritual craze. Such crazes are commonly the growth of solitude, and no Apostle

[1] Mark vi. 39, 40.

while the new ideas are working in him is suffered to be long alone. This health of theirs came in great measure from their being constantly employed about matters of which their hearts were full. The training of the Apostles fulfils all the conditions for sound spiritual health; the Twelve lead lives of out-door labour, with constant change of scene, with varied interests, with occupations to engage their minds; some had the provisioning to see to[1], some the contributions, some were sent on in advance to secure lodging[2], and some wrought works of healing in their Master's name. All this was conducive to their becoming self helpful, fertile in practical resource, as well as earnestly devoted to their Master, confident both of His power and of that delegated to themselves. Their way of life brought them also into acquaintance with the various dispositions and ways of men: all of this was essential for their work.

At the same time this regular occupation, though sufficient to prevent any evil spirit finding in them a corner "empty, swept and garnished," yet was not absorbing or exhausting, it left their minds and wills free play; they could fall into groups as they chose, they could talk freely on the way, they could debate on the meaning of a parable, or on the nature and time of coming of the Kingdom of Heaven.

[1] Possibly Philip had this charge, see page 306.
[2] Luke ix. 51, 52.

After, what seems to have been a short mission journey, with the Twelve, into the villages of Gennesareth, which served to initiate them into their new life and to teach them confidence in their Master, our Lord came back to the Lake coast where a great crowd assembled, whom He addressed from a boat upon the Lake near the shore.

The crowd that gathered there heard a teaching new to the world both in matter and in form; men who had listened to the Sermon on the Mount might scarcely believe that the speaker was the same; hitherto the lessons to the multitude had placed before them truths of life, moral and spiritual, put in such a way as to require no effort of the learner to be fully understood; the right or wrong about some matter, with which they had daily to deal, had been set before them in a light in which they had never seen it before. But what they heard now was not apopthegm, not precept, but, on the face of it, only a simple tale. "This" they would say "is all well, but how is it like the Kingdom of God?" Whether much more might not be learnt, even from these plain lessons, by turning them over a second time in the mind, was a question which only a few asked, and of these few the greater part were probably already among the disciples of Jesus. They were no longer given instruction in a condition ready for use, but only material from which they should extract it for themselves; and to do this they must both use their wits and have hearts alive to God. I shall speak, further on, of the principle on which our Lord acted in withdrawing from the mass the opportunities they had had before. He states it himself, in words I have many times cited, "to those who have shall be given"; words which we have not done with yet, but which it would draw me from my point to discuss now.

It was apparently for the sake of the Apostles that this form of teaching is introduced. One of the services it rendered is obvious, it set the hearers thinking. A new form of intellectual exercise was laid before the listeners, something was proposed which they had to solve for themselves; they are given the solution in two cases, and they are provided with other examples on which they are to try their own skill. Beside the stimulus thus given to intellectual activity by the new kind of teaching, it kept before the eyes of the students those lofty conceptions of Divine agency in the world which preachers of the Kingdom of Heaven would require. Personal trust in our Lord's words, cooperating with some intuition of their own, had made them feel sure that God's Kingdom had come. Now they were told that they might know something of its ways; they are set to ponder on them, but the direction their thoughts are to follow is marked out; they are not left to rove hither and thither in their own imaginations, they are not suffered to pass disjointedly from notion to notion as in a dream; the puzzle of the parable arrests their attention, and the thread which the circumstance of it supplies serves as a clue confining their thoughts to move along a certain path. Here again, as we have observed so often, a selective action comes in, for it is the more active intellects that are most drawn towards a puzzle. They find in it something that their minds may work upon and this is what they seek; while the sluggish desire nothing of the kind, but turn aside from anything they cannot at once understand.

Again, if the Apostles solved a parable for themselves and thereby arrived at a new aspect of some Divine truth, this fresh knowledge would be much more their own, and have a far greater effect in forming their minds, than if the solution had come from their Master. A problem solved by the pupil himself does him more good than a dozen of which he reads the solutions in a book. The parable suggested certain parallels between things outward and things spiritual in the world, and, without conceiving anything so abstract as an analogy between these two orders of things, the Twelve may have caught a glimpse of the truth, that a workmanship betokening the same hand runs through all provinces of the universe.

When the disciples had thus been filled with new thoughts and new ideas, our Lord withdrew them from turmoil that the ideas might germinate undisturbed, we read

"And on that day, when even was come, he saith unto them, Let us go over unto the other side[1]."

An incident in this little voyage served as a test of the condition of that Faith, the growth of which in the Apostles' hearts was being, I believe, watched anxiously by our Lord.

"And there ariseth a great storm of wind, and the waves beat into the boat, insomuch that the boat was now filling. And he himself was in the stern, asleep on the cushion: and they awake him, and say unto him, Master, carest thou not that we perish? And he awoke, and rebuked the wind, and said unto the sea, Peace, be still. And the wind ceased, and there was a great calm. And he said unto them, Why are ye fearful? have ye not yet faith[2]."

This *yet* is emphatic. This was a miracle of instruction, and it served also as a test of how far the Apostles were fit for the high lesson in store for them, that namely of trusting in the Lord's protection when they were out of His sight. Their behaviour shewed that they had not as yet fully mastered the easier one of trusting in Him when He was by.

First let us notice a trait of nature in the recital which shews the hand of an eye-witness. The

[1] Mark iv. 35.
[2] Mark iv. 37—40.

words "Master, carest thou not that we perish" exactly express the irritation of alarm, which turns against those who remain undisturbed. No fabricator would in those days have hit on this trait; and a compiler from tradition, unless he had felt constrained by his authority, might have preferred to pass it by.

It is not quite clear from the account whether the disciples hoped for superhuman help from our Lord or not. The works of His which had most gained notice had been cures, and that He should have power over the winds and waves had probably never entered their minds. Still, it is obvious, that they turned to their Master in peril, as a child does to its parent, expecting at least to find Him solicitous about them. If our Lord had asked them, as soon as the wind rose, "Shall you, if a storm should come, feel safe because I am with you?" they would have answered, and answered truly, that they would. But their Oriental disposition to panic lay deeper in them than their newly born confidence in their Master, and the sudden emergency brought the depths to the surface. Their trust, we may be sure, advanced after that night both in intensity and breadth.

The miracle in the country of the Gadarenes, into which our Lord went, brings out one point which belongs to my subject[1]. This miracle I

---

[1] In "Trench on the Miracles" this miracle and the question of the demoniacs in the New Testament are thoroughly discussed. I

regard as a practical illustration of the lesson of the parable of the Tares, inasmuch as both one and the other bear on the great puzzle of God's tolerance of evil in the world. While the parable and interpretation are yet fresh in the minds of the Apostles, the case of this Demoniac comes before them. It may have struck them—as it must often have struck ourselves—how often after having learnt something one day we come, unaccountably, on an instance or illustration of it on the next. The circumstance was this, an evil agency was, so to say, taken prisoner by our Lord; should it be deprived of existence, or at any rate of activity at once? Men generally would answer "Yes." They would regard it as something that had escaped God's eye and which God's servants ought to destroy whenever they could. This is not Christ's view. Evil is not regarded by him as an oversight of God. God has allowed it to exist in the world, and so it has probably some function to perform. It is not to be extirpated with ruthless hand. The tares are to grow until the harvest. On the same principle our Lord will not send the Spirit into the pit. He is the Son of Man, and men he has come to deliver; of the man therefore this evil agency must loosen his hold; but, saving this, he may pursue the vocation he was following when Christ crossed the Lake. Our Lord rescues the

purposely confine myself to what bears on the education of the Apostles. See also above Chap. 2, p. 48.

man, because to do good unto men He was sent, but for property he is not concerned. If the Demon must be about some evil, but will be content with turning to the swine, to the swine he is at liberty to go; he is not sent to them, but neither is he interdicted. The plague on men is, as was observed above, turned into a murrain among swine[1]. The destruction of the swine was the act of the Divine government only in the same sense that the losses by the cattle plague are so now. As we go on we read:

"And they began to beseech him to depart from their borders[2]."

It would be hard upon this people to say that they counted the deliverance of their brother a less matter than the loss of their swine; they were terror-stricken at the display of superhuman power, and they wished to be rid of their cause of fear.

In the above verse we find the first instance of indifference or aversion among those to whom our Lord went.

The schooling of the Apostles leads them steadily on; step by step they advance into the rougher ground of actual life, and one such step is noted here.

It was well, as I have said, that a glow of success should at starting rest upon their path,

---

[1] See above, p. 49. [2] Mark v. 17.

but they could never grow into hardy wayfarers if all the ways were smooth and all the weather bright; there were in them many qualities, good and hard, which could only take their proper lustre by rubbing against what was rough. So they were early taught to expect opposition, and they saw in what spirit it was dealt with by our Lord. Men, thinking only of the contest, are apt to lose sight of the matter in debate, and make it a point of honour not to give way. They are often made obstinate by being opposed. Our Lord counts the fact that opposition exists to be material in the case and allows it its weight. Here the people pray Him to go and He goes. He could do them no good by staying against their will. He returns at once to the western side of the Lake, and soon after his arrival we read of the raising of Jairus' daughter. With the miracle itself I have nothing to do; I am concerned with the choosing of Peter, James and John, to witness the miracle[1], but this is an instance of the principle which will form the subject of the next chapter and will there be discussed.

After this, according to my view of the chronology, our Lord paid a second visit to Nazareth accompanied by His disciples. He may have supposed that the news of His doings would have turned His townspeople towards Him; but the old impression is still strong among them. A man

[1] Mark v. 37.

from God, they thought, must come they knew not whence, whereas Jesus and His brothers they had known all their lives; and although it seems that His mother and brethren had gone to live at Capernaum[1], His sisters were still among them in Nazareth. We may gather from these two events that the faith of the disciples had by this time grown strong enough to encounter opposition without harm. A strong conviction is confirmed by attack; it takes up a firm position on its bases of support; while a stripling faith bends and quivers at every gust of disbelief.

It was soon after this rejection at Nazareth, and possibly from the neighbourhood of that place, that our Lord sent forth the Twelve on their mission journey, giving them the very remarkable injunction, which I print below. St Luke tells us of another mission of seventy disciples; how long a time elapsed between the two missions, or whether the Apostles were among the seventy, we do not know; inasmuch as the circumstances of the two journeys, and the directions given are very similar, and the educational purport of the two is alike, I shall print both the narratives here, and consider the two events together. St Mark's account is as follows:

"And he called unto him the twelve, and began to send them forth by two and two; and he gave them

---

[1] Compare Mark iii. 32 and Mark vi. 3.

authority over the unclean spirits; and he charged them that they should take nothing for their journey, save a staff only; no bread, no wallet, no money in their purse; but to go shod with sandals: and, said he, put not on two coats. And he said unto them, Wheresoever ye enter into a house, there abide till ye depart thence. And whatsoever place shall not receive you, and they hear you not, as ye go forth thence, shake off the dust that is under your feet for a testimony unto them. And they went out, and preached that men should repent. And they cast out many devils, and anointed with oil many that were sick, and healed them[1]."

St Luke gives this account of the sending of the seventy.

"Now after these things the Lord appointed seventy others, and sent them two and two before his face into every city and place, whither he himself was about to come. And he said unto them, The harvest is plenteous, but the labourers are few: pray ye therefore the Lord of the harvest, that he send forth labourers into his harvest. Go your ways: behold, I send you forth as lambs in the midst of wolves. Carry no purse, no wallet, no shoes: and salute no man on the way. And into whatsoever house ye shall enter, first say, Peace be to this house. And if a son of peace be there, your peace shall rest upon him: but if not, it shall turn to you again. And in that same house remain, eating and drinking such things as they give: for the labourer is worthy of his hire. Go not from house to house. And into whatsoever city

[1] Mark vi. 7—13.

ye enter, and they receive you, eat such things as are set before you: and heal the sick that are therein, and say unto them, The kingdom of God is come nigh unto you. But into whatsoever city ye shall enter, and they receive you not, go out into the streets thereof and say, Even the dust from your city, that cleaveth to our feet, we do wipe off against you: howbeit know this, that the kingdom of God is come nigh[1]."

In the account of St Matthew we find some small differences. The discourses delivered on the two occasions are perhaps combined[2].

It so rarely happens that practical directions as to conduct or behaviour are given to the Apostles by our Lord, that we may be convinced that there is strong reason for His so doing in this case. A lesson of great moment was to be taught by this mission; much depended on the spirit in which it was carried out. This spirit would be affected by the external circumstances, and these are therefore so ordered as to give the greatest possible impressiveness to the lesson in view.

These missions have another singularity. Our Lord, contrary to His usual practice, explains the part they bore in the education of His followers. In a few words spoken to the Twelve, as He was leaving the chamber on the way to Gethsemane, He throws abundant light on the whole purport of these journeys.

The words are these:

---

[1] Luke x. 1—11. [2] Matth. x. 5—15.

"And he said unto them, When I sent you forth without purse, and wallet, and shoes, lacked ye anything? And they said, Nothing. And he said unto them, But now, he that hath a purse, let him take it, and likewise a wallet: and he that hath none, let him sell his cloke, and buy a sword. For I say unto you, that this which is written must be fulfilled in me, And he was reckoned with transgressors: for that which concerneth me hath fulfilment. And they said, Lord, behold, here are two swords. And he said unto them, It is enough[1]."

From this it is seen that all these provisions and directions had a definite purpose, tending to give certain strong impressions to the Twelve, one of the most important being that the Twelve might trust themselves to Christ's guardianship even when He was not by.

They were sent without purse and scrip and shoes, and they found that those among whom they came would not suffer them to lack anything: all went smoothly as they proceeded with their work in the Lord's name. They were to be kept free from sordid anxieties and harassing bodily wants, in order that their minds might be open to higher lessons; and that they might gain the habit of trusting—not indeed that Christ would send them on every occasion just what they desired—but that He would not suffer them to be tried beyond their strength. Possibly, on that journey all their needs were supplied so easily, that it may hardly have

[1] Luke xxii. 35—38.

struck them as strange that they never had felt the lack of anything they required. They may never have thought that what seemed to come by accident was really the Lord's doing and part of His plan, until He Himself recalled this mission to their minds.

Our Lord goes on to teach them that these journeys of theirs to the cities, compared to the missions awaiting them in the actual life on which they so soon would enter, were only what the mimic fight on a day of review is to the conflict of real war; or what the exercise of a swimmer in a school, within reach of his instructor's help, is to the crossing a river for his life. In the exercise ground one lesson, or one set of motions is taught at a time; but when the faculty acquired is brought into actual practice all a man's capacities and endowments are wanted to work together at once. So, in Christ's schooling also, one thing is taught at a time. Two leading qualities only, viz. trustfulness in Christ's spiritual oversight and a helpful self-reliance, were cultivated and tested by this preparatory mission; but in the actual work itself which awaited the Twelve, every gift of nature or fortune, and every faculty of their being would have to be brought into play and turned to the best account.

They went on their way through the cities without purse or wallet, and they found then that no money or provision was needed; but in the real work awaiting them, in the open world, they must take thought beforehand for all their needs; and those who have worldly means are to use them in God's service just as they must do their talents or their strength. They are to be wise as serpents as well as simple as doves. Prudence and a good judgment are entrusted gifts whose true worth is most apparent when they are turned to the service of God. It is not only piety for which God has a care; He claims for his service all endowments of fortune and body and mind; station and wealth, health and skill of hand, judgment, utterance, and clearness of thought—all these are held on trust for Him. The Apostles had been sent on the mission without any provision, in order that they might learn this one particular lesson— what it was to abandon themselves to the guardianship of Christ. In the real work now lying close before them, He bids them use the same forethought and the same practical good sense in all that relates to God's service as in what relates to their own. They went to the cities without arms, and they were unmolested on their way; but now they are told to provide weapons of self-defence, even though they should sell their garments to buy them. It is not the arms themselves that are the gist of the matter, but they stand for a symbol of that personal courage which would have to play no small part in the work of the Christian Church.

Again these words of our Lord throw a stream of light upon what was His object in the plan He pursued; they shew that the training of the Apostles was carried on continually and systematically from the first, and was among the things always uppermost in His mind. When the Twelve set out on this first mission journey it seemed to them a passing act in the regular course of ministerial duty, but after a year had gone by, it is brought back to their minds by our Lord; and they learn the significance of that which they had almost suffered to pass out of mind. It is cited, not with regard to what it effected directly—not for the good it did to those who were taught—but for the qualities it fostered in the preachers themselves.

That these preachers rendered service to those to whom they were sent there can be no doubt, but the notice of our Lord calls attention, not to this, but to the lesson which the Apostles learned. There are some points in these directions which it is hard to explain if we suppose them given solely with the practical view of furthering the Apostles' work, as Christ's forerunners in making known to the people the advent of the Kingdom of God. We do not, on such an hypothesis, see why they should have gone without food or raiment or have saluted no man on the way; they would have made no fewer converts if they had taken purse and scrip and wished "God speed" to those they met. They might, indeed, have *done* the same good, but they would not have *got* the same good. We shall see presently how these instructions were calculated to make them feel that they were God's servants, dignified by their duty, and withdrawn by their special overmastering vocation from the ordinary intercourse of man with man.

The effects of this journey were twofold. There was an outside good to be done by the workers in the world, and an inside good to be done within themselves. This last was brought about by the mental processes and motions they went through in doing the *outside* good to which only they gave their thoughts at the time. They supposed that they were sent on this mission because their Master wished the Kingdom of God to be preached in the cities, and they regarded the particular injunctions,—if they thought about them at all,—as the set rules of garb and procedure for preachers of the Kingdom. It never occurred to them that by all this they were being made to grow inwardly in the way that Christ desired. They could not be told unto what end they were being educated, for self-consciousness would have spoiled all. They would have got no *inner* good, if they had not believed they were doing *outer* good, and good no doubt they did. Moreover they never thought about themselves at all. Christ's disciples are always led away from doing so. They are, with sedulous care, kept so occupied in body and mind that at last self is lost sight of, and they become absorbed in their love for their Master, and in the glory of feeling that they have a share in His work.

Along with the lesson of confidence in their Master's care, there went another, not less prominently insisted upon, that of the dignity of the work they were being consecrated to do. They were to go in Christ's name, preaching the Kingdom He had declared, and affirming its presence by such Signs as He had Himself shewn. This dignity belonged, not personally to themselves, but to the Lord whom they represented; they felt secure, just as the Ambassador of a power feels Sacrosanct because he represents the Majesty of his State.

They were to be possessed with the sense of the greatness of the charge laid on them, and all their being was to be concentrated in this. Their eyes are never to be off their goal; hence the minute precautions against distraction.

The directions for their equipment will be seen to further the growth of the impressions desired.

They are to go two together; this is a rule always observed. Our Lord sent "messengers before his face[1] into a village of the Samaritans to make ready for him;" it is not said that they were two in number, but as James and John are

[1] Luke ix. 52.

loud in their indignation, it is not improbable that they were the messengers. Two disciples are sent to find the colt before our Lord's entrance to Jerusalem[1], and Peter and John together are sent to make ready the Passover[2]. Afterwards, in all the Apostolic journeys the Church followed the practice. In these mission journeys of the newly chosen Apostles we see how well it suited the objects in view that they should go in pairs. If three or more had gone together the sacred character of their journey might more easily have dropped out of sight. Conversation on indifferent points would have been more likely to arise and dissension might have ensued; two might have differed in opinion and each have tried to gain over the third. They could hardly have remained so absorbed in their purpose, as when they went two together, full of the one matter in their hearts and rarely interchanging a word.

Neither would it have been well for them to go one by one. A man by himself has many dangers. He may grow downcast, and a depressed condition is not favourable to the growth of Faith; or he may harp upon one idea, and having no one with him to criticise it and reduce it to its right proportion, it may overshadow his whole mind and degenerate into a craze. The solitary missionary might find danger also in success. If the cures he

[1] Luke xix. 29. [2] Luke xxii. 8.

wrought excited admiration, he might be inclined to take some of the glory to himself: or he might be tempted to go beyond his commission to preach the Kingdom, and try to establish some notions of his own about Jesus as the Christ. The presence of his colleague would recall him to his true position and remind him that he was not about his own work but his Master's. If one of the pair were inclined to take too much on himself, or to allow the people to exaggerate his own part in the wonder wrought, he would be sure to find a silent monitor in his colleague's eye. When two men go together not only does each represent to the other the purpose with which he is sent, but also each supports the other. When one is inclined to despond the other feels forced to take a hopeful tone and this does good to both.

The Apostles were to salute no man by the way; they were not to join in any trivial wayside talk. This served to impress upon them the solemn nature of their work; all their thoughts were to be centred in that, it was to supply the master purpose of their lives. They had God's work to do and God's message to give, and there should be no room in their hearts for any thing but this. This severed them for the time from the rest of the world. They were to go, side by side, with their staves in their hands, not looking this way or that, but having the fixed gaze and steadfast air of men who are marching determinedly to their goal.

When they come to the city where they will stay they are not to plead for hospitality; they have not come of themselves or for themselves—they are God's messengers; they are to go to the house which they think fittest, and, if denied, they are to shake off the dust from their feet and go elsewhere, and, when admitted, there they are to abide as of right. There is to be no shifting of quarters; disturbance and unsettlement is studiously avoided, as in all other proceedings of our Lord. Many among the householders of a village might strive to have a share in entertaining the prophets of God; and the passing of these from house to house would bring into play little worldly jealousies and call off the attention of the missionary from his single object. Where they are admitted, they are told, "there abide and thence depart."

The Apostles are given minute directions as to outfit and demeanour but very little as to what they were to say. They were not to be mere mouthpieces, they were teachers as well, and were left to teach in their own way. To use responsibility was the highest part of the lesson they had to learn, and if they had been tied down too precisely this responsibility would have been lost. We have no record of their preaching on this journey—they are sent to proclaim one truth and one only "That the Kingdom of God was come.'

This truth they might enforce in any way they chose—they might preach to many or few, in houses or synagogues or on the mountain side—and if any disbelieved that God's Kingdom was come, they were to assure their hearers that it was none the less about them on every side, because they did not choose to believe it was there[1]. On their return, they relate what they had taught[2].

There is another point. They are not directed even to name our Lord; He would not suffer them to proclaim Jesus of Nazareth, for He had not "come in his own name[3]." This law is most steadily observed; the seventy say on their return, that the devils were subject to them through our Lord's name, but though they may have used His name when they wrought cures, they do not seem to have declared that the expected Messiah had come; they kept to what they were told to do. The wonder is that no one on this mission should have announced Jesus as the Messiah: they could not have been warned against doing so, because to warn them specially would have been to suggest the notion of that which was to be avoided. A similar circumstance may have been one cause of the fervent thanks which our Lord renders to His Father on the return of the seventy[4].

How long this journey of the Apostles lasted we do not know; the exigencies of harmonists have

---

[1] Luke x. 9—11. [2] Mark vi. 30.
[3] John v. 43.   [4] Luke x. 21.

THE MISSION TO THE CITIES.

led some of them to reduce it to a day or two, but I should suppose it to have occupied at least a week. Neither do we know in what districts the journeys took place; but that the Twelve started from the neighbourhood of Nazareth in the spring of A.D. 29, and the seventy from the Northern border of Judæa or from Peræa in the following autumn, is a plausible guess. The words, "Go not into the way of the Gentiles," &c. which St Matthew puts at the head of our Lord's directions, I think refer to the mission of the seventy. In Peræa they were close to Gentile countries and Samaria lay in the way to parts of Galilee and Judæa. They are told not to abide in any Samaritan city or set foot at all in a Gentile land; our Lord is first sent to the lost sheep of the house of Israel. All went well on both occasions. On the return of the seventy our Lord saw in this success of His disciples in their ministration, an augury of the establishment of His Church. Men, it was plain, could be trusted for the great work in view; and in this success of the disciples in setting it afoot our Lord seemed to behold the Power of Evil falling from the sky. Our Lord pours out His soul on this occasion in thankfulness to His Father.

"In that same hour he rejoiced in the Holy Spirit, and said, I thank thee, O Father, Lord of heaven and earth, that thou didst hide these things from the wise and understanding, and didst reveal them unto babes: yea,

Father; for so it was well-pleasing in thy sight. All things have been delivered unto me of my Father: and no one knoweth who the Son is, save the Father; and who the Father is, save the Son, and he to whomsoever the Son willeth to reveal him[1]."

This thankfulness of our Lord assures us of one point; these seventy must have been exposed to the possibility of failure. Our Lord's joy is that of one delivered from a great anxiety. This instance bears out the view that our Lord's knowledge of the immediate future was, partly at least, in abeyance during His stay on earth. Indeed, if He had been free from all feeling of uncertainty, His life could not have been truly human. The course of daily events depending on the will of others did not in general lie spread out to His view.

Another illustration of this occurs on the return of the Twelve; our Lord goes to the desert seeking quiet, but in this He is disappointed, for He finds Himself attended by five thousand people.

St Mark tells us

"And the apostles gather themselves together unto Jesus; and they told him all things, whatsoever they had done, and whatsoever they had taught. And he saith unto them, Come ye yourselves apart into a desert place, and rest a while. For there were many coming and going, and they had no leisure so much as to eat. And they went away in the boat to a desert place apart[2]."

This rule of our Lord to give the Apostles rest

---

[1] Luke x. 21, 22. [2] Mark vi. 30—32.

and leisure after a period of mental strain, or when much food for reflection had been taken in, is almost invariable. Our Lord's intention is, in this case, frustrated by the zeal of the multitude, who running together from the villages, go round the head of the Lake and meet Him on the shore near the northern end. St John speaking of this matter says:

"Now the passover, the feast of the Jews, was at hand. Jesus therefore lifting up his eyes, and seeing that a great multitude cometh unto him, saith unto Philip, Whence are we to buy bread, that these may eat[1]?"

We see that St John attributed this great concourse of people to its being the time of the Passover. Now the road from Damascus to Jerusalem went past the north end of the Lake, and it has been supposed that the great caravan of Syrian Jews was passing on its way to the feast, and that to this the "great company" belonged. St Matthew, St Mark and St Luke, however, all imply that the multitude came from the neighbouring cities, and St John says that they "*followed* Him (i.e. from the villages of Gennesaret) because they beheld the Signs;" and St Mark tells us that the people "saw them going and many knew them." The crowd therefore could not have been strangers from Damascus. St John, however, would not have here mentioned the Passover, if

---

[1] John vi. 4, 5.

there had not been some connexion between it and the presence of the crowd. The connexion, I believe to have been this. He means to account for the crowd by saying, "It was feast time, no work was being done, and large bodies of men were therefore at leisure to follow." Some think that the Evangelist may have seen in this miraculous meal a substitute for the Paschal feast, which our Lord and his followers can hardly have kept according to due form.

In this miracle, I am particularly concerned[1]. In speaking of it in an earlier Chapter I observed that our Lord's rule of abstaining from using His miraculous power to provide for the physical wants of His followers or Himself, holds in this case, inasmuch as our Lord's party had enough for themselves; this proceeds on the supposition that the loaves and fishes belonged to the Apostles, although if they had had the money, and bought what would just have sufficed for themselves, the law would have held good.

It may be asked, "Had the Apostles the loaves with them or did they buy them of the lad?"

As a matter of explanation, I think it more consistent with the narrative of the other Evangelists to suppose that the lad mentioned by Andrew[2] was carrying provisions belonging to the party, than that he had brought them for sale and that the disciples bought them.

[1] See p. 22.   [2] John vi. 9.

St Matthew, St Mark and St Luke speak as though the loaves and fishes belonged to the Apostolic company, while St John says "There is *a lad here* who has &c." The supposition that the lad was employed to carry the provisions does not, it is said, agree with the received notions of the poverty of the Apostles. We find, however, that they had the use of various boats, and St Mark speaks of "hired servants" in Zebedee's boat[1]. I suppose that one of these servants, not being wanted while the boat was ashore, was employed to carry the sack of provisions for the party. It supports my view that the two common articles of diet should *both* be brought by the same lad, in just such quantity as to suffice for our Lord's company. The words "How many loaves have ye? Go and see" shew, that our Lord supposed them to have brought a supply[2]; moreover the quantity of provisions was nearly the same and they were of the same kind, as those which the Twelve had with them on the subsequent occasion of the feeding of the four thousand[3]. It is unlike the East, as we now know it, that there should have been no bargaining, and that *one* lad should have seen the opportunity of selling his commodities and followed from one of the villages, and that no other should have done so.

Whether the provisions belonged to the dis-

---

[1] Mark i. 20.   [2] Mark vi. 38.
[3] Mark viii. 5—7.

ciples or were[1] purchased at the time, the wants of our Lord's own party, as I have just said, could have been supplied without miraculous intervention; and the rule, answering to the refusal to turn Stones into Loaves, would hold. These rules, or Laws as I have called them, treated of in Chapter V. are not formally imposed by our Lord on Himself, or alluded to in express terms. They are *uniformities observed* in his conduct, which harmonise with the course taken in the Temptations. We need not suppose that He said to Himself "I will always adhere to this rule or that," but He observed the rule because to follow it best forwarded in each case the end in view. Our Lord's company are never in straits for food, but our Lord once implies that if they had been so His power might always be trusted as a means of supply[2]. He would not have adhered to His practice narrowly, when it would have weakened the lesson of Trust. Philip may have been charged with the care of provisioning the party, just as Judas Iscariot carried the purse; this conjecture would account for our Lord turning to him with the question, "Whence are we to buy bread[3]?"

What our Lord said on this occasion to the multitude we do not know; we are told only that

---

[1] That the disciples habitually carried loaves with them on their journey is clear from Mark viii. 14.

[2] Mark viii. 16, 17.   [3] John vi. 5.

"He began to teach them many things[1]," and in listening they lost all count of time, so that when our Lord had finished, it was too late for them to go and buy bread. After the meal He perceived that they "were about to come and take him by force to make him king[2]." The people must have just heard of the execution of John; they may have been exasperated against Herod and thought they had found in our Lord one who would treat the Romans like Sennacherib's host. We hear of no outbreak of enthusiasm, no clamorous demonstration of fervour; they were perhaps too much possessed by reverential awe for that, at any rate their orderliness is very remarkable.

No malice on the part of the scribes could have been so fatal to what our Lord had in view, as this giving of a political turn to the movement which He was setting afoot. The erroneous impression would spread fast and become ineradicable, so that the work of saving the world might have to be begun over again in another way. He hurried the disciples on board that they might not catch the contagion of this idea.

"And straightway he constrained his disciples to enter into the boat, and to go before him unto the other side to Bethsaida, while he himself sendeth the multitude away. And after he had taken leave of them, he departed into the mountain to pray[3]."

---

[1] Mark vi. 34. [2] John vi. 15.
[3] Mark vi. 45, 46.

Solitary prayer on our Lord's part commonly betokens some important step in his course of proceeding. Here it precedes His leaving Galilee; possibly this political manifestation made it advisable; at any rate, very shortly after this, He goes to the borders of Tyre and Sidon and sees little more of Galilee during his life.

On the passage of the Apostles back to the western shore, occurred the miracle of the Lord walking on the sea.

"And when even was come, the boat was in the midst of the sea, and he alone on the land. And seeing them distressed in rowing, for the wind was contrary unto them, about the fourth watch of the night he cometh unto them, walking on the sea; and he would have passed by them: but they, when they saw him walking on the sea, supposed that it was an apparition, and cried out: for they all saw him, and were troubled. But he straightway spake with them, and saith unto them, Be of good cheer: it is I; be not afraid. And he went up unto them into the boat; and the wind ceased: and they were sore amazed in themselves; for they understood not concerning the loaves, but their heart was hardened[1]."

This miracle is one mainly of instruction, it is a step in that ascending course, whereby the Apostles were led to the conception of the crowning truth that Christ was "ever with them unto the

[1] Mark vi. 47—52.

end of the world." The experience of the journey taught that they "lacked nothing" when on duty for Christ; they were now to obtain assurance that in moments of danger He was at hand to protect. It is worth notice that they were doing their utmost for themselves, "toiling in rowing," when Christ comes to their help. In like manner the miraculous draught of fishes was not given to men who had lightly accepted disappointment, but to those who had toiled all night[1]. I know of no Gospel instance of Divine assistance granted to men sitting with folded hands, and leaving Providence to do all. From this miracle they would learn a truth which was much more fully taught after the Resurrection, viz. that their Master was ever by them, and might assume a body not subject to the forces affecting matter, and become apparent at any time.

These lessons would be graven on the Apostles' memory, and would come upon them from time to time in after life. They would naturally look back to the days when they went forth on their first mission, full of hope and not without exultation; and when they recalled how all had gone well with them, how the devils had been subject to them and how all their needs had been provided for as it were by chance, it would come home to them that matters may be Divinely guided without the finger of God being suffered to

[1] See pp. 199, 200.

appear. Many a time they may have cheered one another saying "Christ provided for us when we went forth with only our staves in our hands. He will not desert us now;" and many a time also in sore days of distress, the Apostles may have reminded one another that they were doing their very utmost—not sitting still and praying for help when the sea ran high—at the time when their Master appeared and said:

"Be of good cheer: it is I; be not afraid[1]."

[1] Mark vi. 50.

CHAPTER X.

TO THOSE WHO HAVE, IS GIVEN.

The Teaching by Parables.

WE have, on our way to this point, while tracing the course of Christ's Schooling of the Apostles every now and then caught sight of the working of the principle, "to whomsoever hath, shall be given."

This apopthegm is recorded to have been three times spoken; first, as has been just mentioned, when our Lord gave to His disciples His reasons for teaching in parables, and again as the moral at the end of the parables of the talents and of the pounds. We draw from it that our Lord was about to exercise selection and deal with different hearers in different ways. Up to this time He had put His lessons into terse sayings, like pearls strung on a string; a hearer could easily carry a single one away, he had only to listen and learn. For a multitude who came and went like the shifting atoms of a cloud, this was the most that could be done. But among those who now listened to the parables at Capernaum were apostles, disciples, and listeners variously disposed, and they received a lesson from which different hearers drew profit in very different degrees.

The time now began to draw in sight when the most momentous duties that ever fell to men, would be laid on the Twelve, and to them our Lord now turned with an interest which daily grew more intent. The Apostles were not mere recipients as the crowd had been. They were not mere passive hearers receiving and storing wise sayings. What they heard was meant to set their minds at work, and the good they got from it depended on themselves.

In the crowd on the Lake shore which stood listening to our Lord as He spoke from the boat, there were characters of all sorts disposed towards Jesus in every variety of way. There were many followers and some foes, while perhaps nearly half were neither the one nor the other, but merely the loiterers who throng every eastern town: these would go where others went, glad of anything which broke the sameness of the day. They had come to listen—after their way of listening, taking no heed how they heard—many a time before, and no good had come of it, though the teaching was so plain that he who ran might read; with all their opportunities they had got nothing, and so from them was taken "what they seemed to have," that is to say, these very opportunities themselves. They now heard only what appeared to be the story of an every-day event, and they wondered what good it could do to them. Thus, this mode of teaching sorted out its auditory by a self-acting mechanism. It threw off the light, while it attracted earnest and enquiring minds who, never doubting of a deep meaning in all our Lord said, asked themselves and one another what this meaning could be.

The aphorism "that to him who had, more was given" was, as applied to material wealth, in some form or other probably familiar to the shrewd men of the time, just as the saying, that "nothing succeeds like success" is among ourselves now. But what was startling was, that this principle should be adopted by Christ and laid down as one of those upon which God's government is carried on. For this inequality in human conditions, and the tendency to rise faster the higher one gets and to sink faster the lower one falls, was a thing that was commonly regarded as a defect in the world's arrangement, due to some inherent perversity in matter or in man.

People's minds, in those days, were possessed by the notion that God must have intended to make things fair and equal for all, but that inequality had slipt into the world in the making, when God's eye was off it for a moment: soon, however, the Messiah would come and set this right among other things. Hence it startled our Lord's hearers to find this defect, as they deemed it, in the order of the world brought forward by Him, and not only not explained away as they would have expected, but set forth as among the Laws according to which the Spiritual Order of the world was carried on. From the prominence given to this statement in the narrative of the three earlier gospels we see what a deep impression it made.

Our Lord applies this aphorism, solely, to the advantages and opportunities which men should have for learning the ways of God. But the analogy between this principle and some observed principles of economic and organic science is very striking and interesting, to say no more; while in education the working of this rule is abundantly obvious in every school. That the world is ordered on a basis not of equality but of inequality, is a patent fact; and lately it has been shewn that it is of inequality that all progress comes. One little superiority, due to what seems an accidental variation, gives an advantage for gaining a greater superiority and so on. Uniformity, indeed, implies stagnation. If all men had just the same powers and minds and characters, would not such a world stagnate from its insupportable dulness and the want of stimulus for the faculties of men? If, at every step, it grew harder to get farther on, then no one could go very far. A bullet fired into a tree, which hardens from the bark to the core, is brought to a standstill very soon. Such a state of things would preclude exalted eminence; mediocrity would reign supreme and the onward march of mankind would be checked.

Our Lord, as a fact, asserts not only that inequalities widen, but also that they are purposely so widened. As the explorer advances, he is brought into more open ground and is better recompensed for his toil. Spiritual progress was to be brought about after the plan upon which all other human progress proceeds. It was to originate in individuals, who should push forward, seize upon posts in the foreground and hold them till the rest came up: it is not the way of Humanity to advance in line along the whole front. All progress comes of individual excellence and the world is so ordered as to favour the growth of one beginning to out-top the rest. It is an aid in this direction, that in education advance becomes commonly easier, and always more pleasurable as we proceed. Education moreover sorts out men. A hundred boys, near of an age, thrown together in a school seem at first nearly on a par; but an aristocracy develops itself wonderfully soon, both in the school and out of doors, and every half year the distinctions between boy and boy grow wider and become more strongly marked. However conscientiously the teachers may distribute their pains, the abler boy gets more attention, because he asks more intelligent questions and, seeing his interest in his work, the teacher's thoughts in spare moments revert to him. The same holds of spiritual life, for when a man attains a sense of communion with God he becomes conscious of an inward joy, which illuminates his life, and this helps him on. Nothing is more striking in the Acts than the "exceeding great joy" which with the Apostles was the habitual state.

A very material point as to the bearing of this principle is brought out in the two parables in which it occurs. What is spoken of as that which a man *hath*, is not what has been given him or what he has inherited, but only what he has acquired for himself. It is not so much the possession of the pounds or the talents which is the ground of reward, as the assiduity, energy and intelligence, by which they have been earned.

I will consider the pair of parables[1] just mentioned, before the discourse in which the saying first occurs, although they stand later in the history, because they shew most clearly what Christ's meaning was. In both parables we remark the following points.

(1) The rewards are proportioned, not to the amount of the original arbitrary gifts, which, I suppose, stand for natural advantages, but to

[1] Matth. xxv. 14—30; Luke xix. 11—27.

what has been obtained by turning these gifts to account.

(2) What the servants are recompensed for is administrative efficiency. This shews that our Lord had in view some active service in God's cause and not internal self-improvement alone.

(3) The rewards are not such that the servants can use them for their own gratification, they are not given money for their own use, but they are promoted to wider governments. He who has made five talents is given the rule of a larger province. And the servants are not so promoted merely for their own sake, the general welfare of the ruler's domain is the paramount object, and in order to promote this those who have proved themselves the ablest are given the amplest charge.

In the parable of the talents, the "man going into a far country" entrusts to his servants sums varying in amount, "to each according to his several abilities." With these they are to carry on business on his behalf during his absence. One of them, he who was of the lowest capacity, received only one talent—with him I am not now concerned; but the rest double the capital which had been put into their hands and all of these, those who have made two talents as well as those who have made five receive the same reward. To each is said "Well done, thou good and faithful servant: thou hast been faithful over a few things, I will set thee over many things: enter thou into the joy of thy Lord." Here the rewards are not in proportion to the original gifts, which were as five and two, but are in proportion to the rate of profit, which was in both cases the same. All have shewn the same diligence and all are recompensed alike.

The same principle appears in the parable of the pounds. The like sum, one pound, is entrusted to each servant; and the difference in the returns, one making ten pounds and the other five, is wholly due to the difference of judgment or diligence in using the money. The reward is exactly proportional to the amount which each servant has earned.

The greater charge is given to him who had made ten pounds—not purely as a *reward*, but because he has shewn himself twice as well adapted to govern the ten cities as the servant who had only made five pounds.

A few words in the parable of the pounds shew how well our Lord knew what the prevalent notion about equality was. The notion I mean that God must have intended men to share all advantages alike. When the pound is taken from him who has left it unused and given to him who has turned his own pound into ten, the bystanders in the parable, who, we may suppose, represent common current opinion, are surprised, not at the pound being taken away, but at its being so bestowed as to augment the inequality. They would have looked to see it go to him who had made five pounds, so as to bring the conditions of the two servants more nearly to a par. They say, "Lord, he hath ten pounds," implying "Why give more to him who has so much already?" Men are jealous of God's prodigality in reward, although such reward may not diminish what they obtain themselves. The master in this parable makes no reply to the bystanders, and our Lord concludes the parable with the moral,

"I say unto you, that unto every one that hath shall be given; but from him that hath not, even that which he hath shall be taken away from him[1]."

The pounds in this parable, be it observed, are not bestowed on the servants as absolute gifts, they represent money held on trust, and this is the case not only with the original pound, but with the profit as well. The Lord (St Luke xix. 23) evidently regards all the produce as his own. The ten pounds have never been given over to the servant who gained them, so as to be absolutely his. Neither is the forfeited pound bestowed on him as a free gift, it is only an addition to the ten pounds of profit, which formed a fresh amount of capital in the hands of the most diligent of the servants to be used in his new employ. All this agrees with the view which I have

[1] Luke xix. 26.

taken, that the question in the parable is not one merely of reward and amercement but of putting the greatest opportunities into the best hands. In like manner our Lord looks to a practical end and adopts practical means. The paramount object that He has in view is the effective carrying forward of God's work; and those who shall prove most efficient are to receive as their reward,—not anything they can sit down to and enjoy,—but a wider sphere of activity, an extended range of opportunities, and of duties answering thereunto.

This remark of the bystanders, so casual in its form and so weighty in its substance, exemplifies our Lord's way of dealing with erroneous ideas. A hint is dropped, attention is called to what many had taken for granted, and there the matter is left. It might be many days before the world would find the seed thus cast upon the waters, but found, some day or other, it would be. When there is question of practical evil our Lord is plain and positive enough. The Pharisees are upbraided sharply, for making the Law of no effect by their traditions, and the Sadducees are told that in denying the resurrection "they do greatly err." But as regards the enigmas of life He only drops hints, which men may take or not.

I now come to the discourse, which I had put aside for a moment that the parables might be discussed.

As soon as our Lord had ended the parable of the Sower

"The disciples came, and said unto him, Why speakest thou unto them in parables[1]?"

Observe the words *unto them.* It is not about themselves that they ask, but the crowd. They were desirous to see our Lord's influence increase, and were perhaps anxious that new proselytes should swell their number, and so they were puzzled at this new form of teaching, which seemed calculated to repel converts. "In order to win men over," they would say to themselves, "it would surely be best to speak in the plainest and most direct way."

The fullest version of the reply is that given by St Mark.

"And he said unto them, Unto you is given the mystery of the kingdom of God: but unto them that are without, all things are done in parables: that seeing they may see, and not perceive; and hearing they may hear, and not understand; lest haply they should turn again, and it should be forgiven them[2]."

This is followed by the interpretation of the parable of the Sower. And then comes a discourse explaining for what purposes the teaching by

---

[1] Matth. xiii. 10.
[2] Mark iv. 11, 12. See also Isaiah vi. 10.

parables was employed, which throws a strong light both on this matter and on education in its highest sense. Here the principle comes to the front, that it is not so much what is done upon the man, or for the man, as what is done by the man himself, that transforms him into a higher creature. "Unto you," says our Lord, turning to the disciples and the Twelve, "is given the mystery of the kingdom of God." The mystery was given not to save their thinking but to set them thinking on a right track. What bore on the practical conduct of life had been preached to all, but the glimpse of the underlying spiritual order was vouchsafed to few : all must learn to tell time from a clock, but all need not know how it works. It is not the application of the parable which is here the difficulty—that is told the hearers at once—but it lies in the original differences between men, how far these come of men's own selves, how far of heredity, and how far men are answerable for their own dispositions; here we come on great difficulties which beset all creeds alike. In the parable of the Tares we are confronted with the origin of moral ill; the Apostles are to *contemplate* these mysteries, and they are given a way of looking at them which will serve for the practical purposes of life, but they are by no means led to believe that they can see to the bottom of them.

The second passage brings out a positive use of parables. They are not primarily meant to hide truth but to show it. The matter is only for a moment put out of sight, in order that men may search after it, prize it when found, and, bringing to it eyes sharpened by keen search, may discern all particulars more truly and well. The sifting of the auditory of which I have spoken above was only a secondary and subordinate use of the parable; its primary one was this; it enshrined an abstract truth in such a portable concrete form that it was made accessible to men; it put it into a shape, familiar to Orientals, a shape to which the Eastern tongue lent itself with ease, and which fitted readily into the minds of men; they could carry the story about with them, and they would in so doing learn its lesson by degrees.

There was also another point; the meaning of these new utterances gave men some pains to find, and when they had found it, they delighted in it as something they had conquered for themselves. Our Lord lets men into this secret of all learning. Did they suffer those words of His which "were Spirit and which were Life" to fecundate their hearts," turning them over in their minds again and again? The words "with what measure ye mete[1]" have no bearing on outward dealings here; what they mean is, "In proportion to the pains and attention which you bestow in searching out all that my words contain, so will the profit be. If you bestow thought freely, and time as well,

[1] Mark iv. 24.

freely will God requite the same—something will you then have, and more shall be given you." To him who had been faithful over a few things a wider range of duties, and that alone, would be given as reward.

I note a connection between the introduction of the new form of teaching and the course of events. When our Lord began to teach in parables "His departure which he was about to accomplish at Jerusalem[1]" was shaping itself more and more definitely in His mind. Time was getting short, and so He now spake for those only who had ears to hear. The nature of this departure was too shocking to Jewish notions and too inexplicable to be declared in plain terms to the mass. We know that even the Twelve were bewildered with the hints that our Lord drops about the end, and we can easily see how ill-suited such declarations would have been for the people at large.

Again, we can understand that as the end in all its awfulness came more and more distinctly into view, our Lord should confine His teaching very much to those to whom was committed the mystery of the Kingdom of God; and, inasmuch as the Twelve differed in spiritual capacity among themselves and higher duties were to be laid on some than on others, within that body a further selection had to be made. Peter and James and John form an inner circle, they are

[1] Luke ix. 31.

chosen as witnesses of the things that were not to be proclaimed until the Son of Man should come[1]. It is worth noting that in St John's Gospel we find no trace of the preeminence of these three; this falls in with the hypothesis of the author being the Apostle John, who carefully avoids mention of himself.

This choosing of the Three Apostles who should be preferred before the rest touches my purpose closely in another way; it was no insignificant part of the Schooling of the Twelve. They would learn from it that Christ gave what charge He would to whom He would; that in God's service it is honour enough to be employed at all; and that no man is to be discouraged because he sees allotted to another what appears to be a higher sphere of work than his own. We all know how heavily jealousy among subordinates who administer affairs clogs the wheels of the state, and it was of the highest importance that this vice should be eradicated, with a view to the practical business of the Church.

So the great lesson taught to the Apostles—and in the end it was taught more completely than ever men were taught it before—was self abnegation. They came at last not to think about themselves at all. This unselfishness is never preached to them, because it cannot be

[1] Three it would seem is the number adopted for *witnesses* just as two is that for missionaries on their way.

taught by preaching. If a man has self-surrender pressed incessantly upon him, this keeps the idea of self ever before his view. Christ does not cry down *self*, but he puts it out of a man's sight by giving him something better to care for, something which shall take full and rightful possession of his soul. The Apostles, without ever having any consciousness of sacrificing self, were brought into a habit of self sacrifice by merging all thoughts for themselves in devotion to a Master and a cause, and in thinking what they could do to serve it themselves.

Have not most of us known cases of men, seemingly immersed in amusements and frivolities, who would gladly have flung these to the winds, if only we could have found them something which would fill their hearts. If such people are selfish, it is not because they really care very much for themselves; but because self seems a little more real and a little more under their own control than anything else. They have found unreality in many things; perhaps when they have attempted to do good they have been thrown back by ridicule or discouragement, and are thereby brought to feel at a loss for an interest in life; and in this case an evil one, who is always by, has seemed to whisper, "Do good to thyself and the world will speak well of thee." If now, at the right moment, you could shew these men a real good, they would be glad enough to throw aside the *self* which they have been only trying to persuade themselves that they cared for, and would seize upon anything which appeared to answer to the secret hope, asleep, but still alive in their hearts.

It is a good test of the nature of the devotion above spoken of to be able to endure the preference of others to ourselves. If the Apostles generally had resented the preeminence of the three, it would have shewn that they had not realised "what spirit they were of." We see from St Luke xxii. 24 that they had not quite overcome all personal feeling, but we hear at this time no word of murmur, though they ventured pretty freely to murmur when they were displeased: from this I gather that, little by little they were losing personal ambition and merging themselves in their Master's cause. Thus this selection of the Three out of the body carried with it a lesson in the postponement of self.

This reserving of special attention for those only who shewed promise is, as I said just now, connected with the appearance on the horizon of the End at Jerusalem. "Times and seasons" the Father "had put in His own power," and it may not have been till a year before the Passion that our Lord had known how short a time was left for Him on earth. Before He had preached unto all alike, now, his time and pains were reserved for the hopeful few. Something of this same reservation of teaching for those likely to profit by it, was seen when the Apostles were sent out two and two. They were only to be a few days away, consequently they were to waste no time over cases that were hopeless; when one city would not receive them they were to go to another.

Resumption of the Narrative.

I left the narrative at the point where the vessel with the Apostles, whom our Lord had joined upon the sea, had just reached the shores of the country of Gennesaret. The multitude sought Him on His arrival bringing their sick to be healed. Our Lord's words addressed to them suit the occasion so exactly, that we may be sure they belong to this place. The discourse[1] is preserved only by St John. It was probably begun upon the shore and was afterwards continued by our Lord in the synagogue.

This discourse is very ably treated by Mr Sanday[2], and the doctrinal matters of which it treats do not fall within my sphere. It is the character of St John's versions of our Lord's discourses that we find it hard to trace in them the progress of thought. One or two points usually form the burden; in this case these points are "I am the bread of life" and "I will raise him up at the last

---

[1] John vi. 25—65.
[2] W. Sanday, "Authorship and Historical character of the Fourth Gospel."

day." This mannerism suits with the supposition that St John's Gospel was written by a very old man; for this recurrence to the dominant topic is a marked peculiarity of the utterances of old age. St John had probably preached on these discourses over and over again, and he set them down in the Gospel in the form in which they were most familiar to him, with, possibly, something of the amplification required to adapt them to homiletic use.

This speech is pitched in so high a spiritual key that it was not all who had ears to hear it: it notably effected the purpose of separating the chaff from the wheat. What the people expected of the Messiah, and what they looked for in the future life may be gathered from the gospels or from Jewish books[1]; our Lord's words gave no promise of His fulfilling these hopes of theirs, and so we read—

"Upon this many of his disciples went back, and walked no more with him[2]."

Another cause of offence arose at this time.

---

[1] Speaking of the beliefs of the Rabbis as to the days of the Messiah, Dr Edersheim, quoting from the Rabbis, says: "In that vast new Jerusalem (not in heaven but in the literal Palestine) the windows and gates were to be of precious stones, the walls of silver, gold, and gems, while all kinds of jewels would be strewed about, of which every Israelite was at liberty to take.......The land would spontaneously produce the best dresses and the finest cakes." "Jesus the Messiah," Book v. p. 438.

[2] John vi. 66.

The Pharisees and certain of the Scribes who had come from Jerusalem had seen that some of his disciples ate their bread with defiled, "that is unwashed hands." These persons had not come from Jerusalem at this time—Passover time—without serious intentions, and these we may be sure were not friendly to our Lord. They fasten on this point of washing before meals, a process not enjoined by Moses but resting on a "tradition of the elders." The stress however laid on it by the Rabbis was excessively great[1], and the provisions with regard to it were so minute and troublesome that only those classes who possessed leisure could possibly observe them. Here we come upon a self-righteous exclusiveness; but what was worse than all was the low idea of God involved in the notion that He gave or withdrew his favour according as men were or were not punctilious about trivial acts.

Our Lord turns the attack against His assailants, "Full well," said He, "do you reject the commandment of God that ye may keep your traditions." He shews how by a Rabbinical fiction they evaded the natural duty of maintaining their parents in their age.

"And he called to him the multitude again, and said unto them, Hear me all of you, and understand: there is nothing from without the man, that going into him can

---

[1] Cf. John iii. 25.

defile him: but the things which proceed out of the man are those that defile the man[1]."

It is to be noted that here our Lord turns *to the multitude*. He calls—not only disciples and not only scribes, but every one—to listen to this vindication of the ways of God. These are our Lord's last words to the people of Capernaum, and the discourse in the synagogue is nearly His last utterance in a place of worship. He would not leave them without a denunciation of that stress upon outward observances, which prevented spiritual religion from growing in their souls. His words are wide, I believe intentionally so, and sweep away those ordinances about meats clean and unclean, which, as sanitary measures, had done good, no doubt, in their time, but which now led one man to think that because he did not eat what another did, he stood religiously on a higher level than his brother. For spiritual religion to become possible, men must be freed from the idea that God's favour depended on what they eat or drank.

This notion however was, by heredity, part and parcel of the mental constitution of every Jew. The disciples regard this statement of our Lord as so bold that it cannot be intended to be taken literally, they call it "the parable." We can understand, they would say, this about eating

[1] Mark vii. 14, 15.

with unclean hands, but the Master's words would go to do away with all distinction of meats, and this surely He cannot intend. No explanation does our Lord give; He restates in the plainest terms what was matter of offence. He expresses wonder that the disciples should be startled at His words—there was that in store which would offend them more—

"Many therefore of his disciples, when they heard *this*, said, This is a hard saying; who can hear it? But Jesus knowing in himself that his disciples murmured at this, said unto them, Doth this cause you to stumble? *What* then if ye should behold the Son of man ascending where he was before? It is the spirit that quickeneth; the flesh profiteth nothing: the words that I have spoken unto you are spirit, and are life[1]."

As far as affection and loyalty went our Lord carried them with Him. But their minds had not kept pace with their hearts, habit was their master still. That many who had counted themselves disciples should have taken offence at this bold assertion, "whatsoever from without goeth into the man it cannot defile him," is easily conceived. It did away with a ready source of self congratulation. If a Jew's conscience pricked him, he turned for comfort to the thought that he had never eaten anything unclean.

So many fell away that our Lord's company

[1] John vi. 60—63.

was reduced to a handful. He had expected, and probably intended, to thin it considerably, but the withdrawals among the disciples appear to have surprised Him, He says to the Apostles, "Will ye also go away?" Puzzled by our Lord's declarations no doubt they were, but of one thing they were sure: having known Christ they could follow no one else but Him. The mountain journey clenched their devotion and their faith.

"And from thence he arose, and went away into the borders of Tyre and Sidon. And he entered into a house, and would have no man know it: and he could not be hid[1]."

Now at last does our Lord find for the Apostles the rest which He had desired to give them before. It is not a missionary journey, He does not preach to the people; and the miracles which He performs are no longer illustrations of God's Kingdom, but works of beneficence wrung from Him by the sight of suffering. The cures are wrought as privately as is possible. The Syro-Phœnician woman obtains what she desires by her exceptional openness to Divine impression: when He entered into a house "and would have no man know it," she sought Him out. The man who was deaf and had an impediment in his speech, is taken "aside from the multitude privately," and our Lord charged the witnesses "that

[1] Mark vii. 24.

they should tell no man[1]." So again with the blind man at Bethsaida (probably Bethsaida Julias at the head of the lake)[2] "He took hold of the blind man by the hand and brought him out of the village," and at the end "He sent him away to his home, saying, Do not even enter into the village[3]."

Our Lord appears to have returned southwards along the valley and down the eastern side of the Lake, where the miracle of the feeding of the four thousand took place.

This country on the east of the Sea of Galilee, contained a mixed population, of which only the smaller part were of Israelite descent. The four thousand had followed day after day seeking cures; but there was no fear of these men trying to make Jesus a King, for there was little nationalist feeling on that side the sea. Our Lord might therefore exert His beneficence without imprudence. It seems strange that the disciples should not have thought of the feeding of the five thousand; but they may have thought that it was out of the question that a miracle should be wrought for people who were mostly heathen; or it may have been one of those not uncommon cases in which a man has seen his mistake and supposes that he can never make it again, and yet when circum-

---

[1] Mark vii. 33—36.
[2] Bethsaida means Fishertown; many places were so named. Dr Edersheim.
[3] Mark viii. 23—26.

stances arise, similar except for some slight variation, he does exactly what he did before.

When the four thousand were sent away, our Lord takes boat and crosses the lake to Magada in "the parts of Dalmanutha." Of this region we know nothing except that it must have been on the western side of the lake. Here our Lord again finds himself among the haunts of men, and, since wherever there was a town population Pharisees were to be found, these "came forth, and began to question with him, seeking of him a Sign from heaven, tempting him[1]."

Perhaps they had heard of the feeding of the four thousand and wanted to put Him to what they considered a conclusive test. "Could He shew a Sign in Heaven?" This iterated cry shewed the poorness of the soil, they had nothing else to utter but a demand for credentials. If our Lord had worked a "Sign in Heaven" they would have examined it to find a flaw, and even if they had been driven to admit that it was valid, no change whatever would have ensued in the men themselves. Chronic evil requires, not a passing shock but a long continued reparative process for its cure. So, here, to those who have not nothing is given, indeed nothing could be given to any purpose, and they soon lose even what they had, viz. our Lord's presence, for He leaves them and goes elsewhere.

On the way across the Lake, while this circum-

[1] Mark viii. 11.

stance is still in His mind, our Lord warns the Apostles against this Pharisaic spirit, the leaven of the Pharisees, which would kill all that is spiritual in religion by reducing every thing to matter of dry proof and dead authority. On the mistake of the disciples, "It is because we have no bread," I have already spoken (p. 7), it is to me a proof of the genuineness of the story. Who would have introduced it, and who has not met scores of people who would have clung to the literal sense of the words just as the Apostles did?

Our Lord and the band of apostles travel along the upper valley of the Jordan to the neighbourhood of Cæsarea Philippi. Most if not all of the outer disciples had by this time fallen away, and the opportunity for giving His higher inmost teaching had come.

Never yet, except to the woman of Samaria, had Our Lord spoken of Himself as the Messiah. The notions of the Jews about the Messiah varied greatly, but the notion of an era of material physical enjoyment was dominant in all, and this had the demoralising effect of leading men to regard sensuous well being as the supreme good. If our Lord had proclaimed Himself the Messiah, crowds would have rallied to his side, hoping to have found one who would give them what they desired. This would have been fatal to all spiritual growth. Our Lord's reticence about the Messiah and also about His own nature, is very significant:

I think it means that truth absolute about heavenly things is not within the reach of man.

What follows, is so important, that it must be given in the words of St Matthew whose narrative is the most full.

"Now when Jesus came into the parts of Cæsarea Philippi, he asked his disciples, saying, Who do men say that the Son of man is? And they said, Some *say* John the Baptist; some, Elijah: and others, Jeremiah, or one of the prophets. He saith unto them, But who say ye that I am? And Simon Peter answered and said, Thou art the Christ, the Son of the living God. And Jesus answered and said unto him, Blessed art thou, Simon Bar-Jonah: for flesh and blood hath not revealed it unto thee, but my Father which is in heaven. And I also say unto thee, that thou art Peter, and upon this rock I will build my church; and the gates of Hades shall not prevail against it. I will give unto thee the keys of the kingdom of heaven: and whatsoever thou shalt bind on earth shall be bound in heaven: and whatsoever thou shalt loose on earth shall be loosed in heaven. Then charged he the disciples that they should tell no man that he was the Christ[1]."

The doctrinal and ecclesiastical bearings of this passage are beyond my scope, they have been fully treated over and over again; but one point belongs to my special province—Peter's knowledge had not come from anything he had been told. Our Lord had not breathed it to him, but it had

---

[1] Matth. xvi. 13—20.

grown up in him as great truths have grown up in prophetic souls by the prompting of God. This is the true inspiration of God; He whispers thoughts into the hearts of men, some nurse them and bring them to maturity, with others they take no hold. Blessed are those with whom they rest. Our Lord had said in the synagogue at Capernaum

"No man can come to me, except the Father which sent me draw him: and I will raise him up in the last day[1]."

Peter had been drawn towards Him in this way.

Another point is to be noted. Henceforth the Apostles had a secret—they were to "tell no man that he was Jesus the Christ."

So long as the belief in our Lord as the Messiah was only a surmise, growing in Peter's mind more and more into positive shape, he was not lifted up by it; but now he had become, as he thought, a species of chief minister, and he looked to the declaration of an earthly kingdom; so that when, immediately after the promise of power, our Lord speaks of sufferings and death, Peter replies, "These things be far from thee." He never doubts but that our Lord would use His powers in self-defence. He looks on His words only as evil boding, and it strikes him that it is

[1] John vi. 44.

impolitic to utter them, because they will confuse and dishearten both the disciples and the Twelve.

This remonstrance of Peter's drew from our Lord the first stern words which an Apostle had received from His lips, and very stern they were.

"But he turned, and said unto Peter, Get thee behind me, Satan: thou art a stumblingblock unto me: for thou mindest not the things of God, but the things of men[1]."

It will help us to understand what moved our Lord so deeply if we go back to the Temptations. St Luke ends his account of the Temptations thus,

"And when the devil had completed every temptation, he departed from him for a season[2]."

The words "for a season" imply that Temptations recurred from time to time, and that our Lord, now and again, heard inward voices harping on the old themes, one of the most persistent being that which said "Employ supernatural might to bring your Kingdom about." Peter now spoke in the same strain. Could it be that even His "own familiar friend" had gone over to the foe.

The following discourse sounds a new note. Now for the first time our Lord speaks of the sufferings that awaited his followers.

"Then said Jesus unto his disciples, If any man

[1] Matth. xvi. 23. [2] Luke iv. 13.

would come after me, let him deny himself, and take up his cross, and follow me. For whosoever would save his life shall lose it: and whosoever shall lose his life for my sake shall find it[1]."

The Apostles understood this probably as applying to the hardships and vicissitudes of the campaign which would result in the restoration of the Kingdom to Israel; for they looked for such a restoration up to the last (see St Luke xxiv. 21). This notion might have been removed no doubt; but what could have been put in its place? the idea of a Kingdom over men's consciences, could not be implanted in men by words or in a short time. It could come about only by long experience in seeing and sharing suffering and toil, and by turning again and again to the abiding recollections of the Cross. Notions mischievously erroneous would have sprouted up in the Apostles' minds from any thing they could have been told in a few words.

One promise however made at this time must have seemed to them to afford just what they wanted.

"And he said unto them, Verily I say unto you, There be some here of them that stand *by*, which shall in no wise taste of death, till they see the kingdom of God come with power[2]."

I understand this verse in a way with which not every body will agree.

---

[1] Matth. xvi. 24. 25. [2] Mark ix. 1.

I take it as referring entirely to the Transfiguration, and I consider that the strong expression "shall in no wise taste of death" means that the witnesses should see what is spoken of during their actual earthly lives. Many might be blessed enough to behold this after death; but what was to distinguish the chosen witnesses from other men was this, that *while in the body* they should see the Kingdom of God come with power. This boon is given, not to those who needed assurance, but to those who possessed it most; it seems given only to those to whom it is superfluous. The Law of the working of Signs (see pp. 142, 143) is rigorously observed. The vision on the Mount of Transfiguration coerced no one into belief.

During those six days we may suppose that the Apostles were busy in their minds, they would wonder who these "some" were to be, and why, supposing that the Kingdom of God came with the kind of power they looked for—a legion of angels for instance—why they should not all see it at once. Of the Transfiguration itself and the lessons it contains, the superseding of the teaching of the Law and the Prophets by the revelation of the incarnate Word, I have spoken fully in Chap. IV. (p. 94). We shall see as we go farther on, that our Lord is careful that there shall be nothing so rigid in His teaching as to prevent its being applicable to all races and conditions of men. It was no longer Moses, and no longer the prophets embodied in the person of Elijah, to whom men were to listen now. Hitherto all had rested on authority —on the letter of written Law. In the place of this were given words which "were Spirit and which were life." Henceforth for their knowledge of God they were to turn to Christ. He manifests God unto the world, both in His own Personality depicted in the Gospels and by Spiritual Communion, whispering unto the end of the world to those who are ready to hear.

One point that was gained by this manifestation may be noted here. Supposing that the foes of Jesus had dispatched Him at the Feast of Tabernacles, still something would have been already accomplished, something secured for the world. There would have been three witnesses—men not given to visions or dreaming—who could declare that a voice from Heaven had sounded in their ears, and that while Moses and Elias were standing by, a voice from Heaven had declared that they were superseded as the Divine teachers of men by Jesus of Nazareth, of whom it declared, "This is my beloved Son, HEAR HIM."

As soon as these words are uttered, all that is wondrous disappears. The Apostles find themselves with their Master on the mountain top, and all is as it was before He had begun to pray. If there had been but one witness he would have found it hard to convince men that he had seen all this with his waking eyes; but there were three

Apostles to say "we were together and awake when we saw it." Is it likely that three men should have fallen asleep together and have waked at the same moment, having all dreamed the same dream?

The supposition, however, of a vision affords a means of escape from accepting the narration. This exemplifies the Law that in every revelation delivered to men not already convinced, room is left for them to disbelieve if they like, because assent to proof which is irrefragable is not moral belief at all. There were people who would have said of this Transfiguration "we would rather believe that you all three slept and dreamed the same dream than that your story is true." And some ground is left for such men to stand upon, though we who believe may think them straitened for room. With the three Apostles themselves, the conviction that their Master was Divine, already formed part of their being, it could hardly be strengthened; acceptance was not forced on them for they already accepted all. What they beheld did not act upon them as additional proof, but as a glimpse of another world, a revelation of new modes of existence—something to give shape to that message of eternal life which is henceforth the ground theme of our Lord's teaching.

It may seem surprising that this revelation of their Master's glory should cause so little disturbance in the Apostles' minds, or in their freedom of intercourse with the Lord. If one whom we ourselves held in honour changed his mortal guise in the way described, not only would the shock upset our judgment but never after could we approach our friend in the old familiar way; he would belong to another order and have his true existence in another plane. We read, it is true, that the Apostles were for a moment "sore afraid," but this was superficial fear due to the spectacle, to impression on the outward sense. St Peter, who is persuaded that they have been removed to a strange and blessed country, quickly regains self-possession. Following his instincts as a worker with his hands, he bethinks himself at once, as was said in Chapter VIII. (p. 248), of what is to be done. When our Lord and the three take their way down the mountain we find again the old confident relation of Master and disciple existing among them, it was so deep-rooted that all were sure that nothing could disturb that. Their Master's spiritual exaltation did not put a gulf between Him and them, because they were so far one with Him that they were in a measure uplifted together; what was His, was also in part their own; whether in earth or heaven, or wherever their Master's Kingdom should be, they felt sure they must be by His side. They could not be estranged from Him by awe of a newly discovered dignity, for they had been sure of His possessing this before, and only wondered that it had not come more patently to light.

Thus the complete love of the three which transfused their being into Christ and rendered the idea of separation inconceivable, made it possible for them to receive that as a blessing which if given to others might have proved a bewilderment. They already possessed something which made them capable of receiving more.

Our Lord makes no comment on the manifestation witnessed by the three beyond charging them "that they should tell no man what things they had seen, till the Son of man were risen from the dead[1]." What they had beheld contained a varied store of lessons, and men in the after times of the world would draw out one or another according to the turn taken by their thoughts. The Apostles, at the moment, only understood a small part of what this revelation conveyed. No exposition given in words could have brought to the comprehension of the three a perception of the whole bearing of what they had seen, but they would live into more of its meaning in time. If our Lord had discoursed on this manifestation, and represented its purport in this view or in that, men might have supposed that He meant His account to be exhaustive, and that the fact contained no lessons beyond those which He Himself set forth. Here we come I think upon a possible reason why our Lord is sparing of exposition regarding the facts of revelation. He could not

[1] Mark ix. 9.

briefly point out *every* truth that a fact embodied, and if in an exposition, which was seemingly full, He should pass any lessons by, these it might be supposed He intended to exclude; in this way His reticence preserves for us the many-sidedness of Divine truth and engages men to ponder on it for themselves.

For the Apostles to have been allowed to spread abroad the story of the solemn scene upon the Mount would have been damaging to the work both for the world and themselves. The old cry might again have been raised to take Jesus and make Him a king; or the people might have been seized with a fever of curiosity, and the scribes would have grown all the more bitter in their hatred from its being leavened with awe. The ill effect on the Apostles of becoming authorised to promulgate such momentous tidings is easy enough to perceive. When people run about to disseminate some scrap of news which they alone possess the result is usually not beneficial either to character or to mind. From this temptation the Apostles were guarded. What they have seen and heard is not matter which they may use to magnify their importance or excite envy—it is a sacred trust. This signal manifestation besides being a light to help to the understanding of what Christ meant by eternal life, was to furnish them with a reserve of certitude. The three might never need to draw on it for themselves, but it would be of no slight avail with Jewish converts to be able to assure them that Christ had visibly appeared in Glory and that God had directed men henceforth to listen, not to the Law or the Prophets, not to Moses or Elijah, but to Him.

It is significant that this is to be kept secret not only until our Lord's death but until His Resurrection. The three were not allowed to use it to comfort and reassure the rest as soon as their Master had suffered on the cross. The nine were to go through this trial unaided, eight stood the test, and held together in Jerusalem. When the Resurrection came, the Apostles "were glad when they saw the Lord," and then in the delight and exultation of that moment the three may have poured forth the secret they had in store.

The Apostles were not surprised at being told that they were to tell no man; they had received the same charge when they had seen Jairus' daughter raised to life; but they were greatly puzzled by the words "till the Son of man were risen from the dead." They believed probably in a Resurrection, but that was to be ages hence, whereas this rising of Christ from the dead must take place in their own lifetime, because after it had happened they were to be free to speak of the Vision on the Mount. They asked each other what this rising could be, and perhaps some fancied that our Lord would permanently assume the glorified existence of which He had given them a glimpse.

Then came the question of Elijah. Our Lord turns the allusion to the prophets towards His coming rejection. Men had ill-treated the prophets; they will set at nought the Son of man too. "Even so shall the Son of man also suffer of them[1]." This news is broken to the disciples gently and little by little, but they never believe that it is literally true. Their cause must, they were sure, succeed in the end, Christ would not have engaged them in failure. What leader ever prophesied his own discomfiture and death? Our Lord first broke this truth to Peter at Cæsaræa Philippi, then to the three, and again, as we shall see presently, to all the Twelve on their way to Capernaum; thus the stream of communication broadens out.

We learn from St Luke[2] that it was not till the next day that our Lord "came down from the hill and much people met him," so that in the night, and in the long day's walk down to the inhabited country, the Apostles had ample time for quietly thinking over all that had taken place. Our Lord is always careful to leave time for one impression to fix itself, before another takes its place.

[1] Matthew xvii. 12.   [2] Luke ix. 37.

CHAPTER XI.

FROM THE MOUNT TO JERUSALEM.

THE spot at which our Lord had left the disciples when He went up to the Mount of the Transfiguration must have been well peopled and provided with synagogues, for our Lord on His return finds a "great multitude about them and scribes questioning with them." The people were greatly amazed either at His sudden appearance or at something uplifted in His air. The Scribes were holding an altercation with the disciples, possibly exulting over the failure of these to cure the child, and our Lord, addressing the Scribes who were, it would seem, the assailing party, asks

"What question ye with them? And one of the multitude answered him, Master, I brought unto thee my son, which hath a dumb spirit; and wheresoever it taketh him, it dasheth him down: and he foameth, and grindeth his teeth, and pineth away: and I spake to thy disciples that they should cast it out; and they were not able. And he answereth them and saith, O faithless generation, how long shall I be with you? how long shall I bear with you? bring him unto me. And they brought him unto him: and when he saw him, straightway the spirit tare him grievously; and he fell on the ground, and wallowed foaming. And he asked his father, How long time is it since this hath come unto him? And he said, From a child. And oft-times it hath cast him both into the fire and into the waters, to destroy him: but if thou canst do anything, have compassion on us, and help us. And Jesus said unto him, If thou canst! All things are possible to him that believeth. Straightway the father of the child cried out, and said, I believe; help thou mine unbelief. And when Jesus saw that a multitude came running together, he rebuked the unclean spirit, saying unto him, Thou dumb and deaf spirit, I command thee, come out of him, and enter no more into him. And having cried out, and torn him much, he came out: and *the child* became as one dead; insomuch that the more part said, He is dead. But Jesus took him by the hand, and raised him up; and he arose. And when he was come into the house, his disciples asked him privately, *saying*, We could not cast it out. And he said unto them, This kind can come out by nothing, save by prayer[1]."

Our Lord's question to the father is just what a physician would ask, "How long is it since this hath come to him[2]?" It may have been that the longer the standing of the complaint the greater would be the effort required for the cure; for

---

[1] Mark ix. 17—29.   [2] See page 95.

that in working these cures some physical strain on the nervous energy was incurred may be inferred from our Lord's feeling that "virtue was gone out of Him," when the woman touched the hem of His garment in the press round the house of Jairus[1].

This force depended on spiritual life, and if this were lowered in the disciples by their Master's absence, or by any little rivalry or thought of personal display in the cure, we can understand that in this difficult case—for our Lord distinctly recognises its exceptional difficulty—they should fail of success. The words "faithless and perverse generation" may apply to all those whom he finds wrangling, more or less the disciples were faithless, and the Scribes perverse. He came from a region of serene peace and heavenly communion, and the contrast of that with what He finds as soon as he comes to the resort of men, draws from Him these stern words. From the disciples' surprise that they could not cast the devil out, it may be inferred that they had succeeded in what they regarded as similar cases before. The narrative proceeds thus

"And they went forth from thence, and passed through Galilee; and he would not that any man should know it[2]."

Our Lord now lays aside for a time His setting forth of God's Kingdom to the people at large, and

---

[1] Mark v. 30. [2] Mark ix. 30.

devotes Himself entirely to preparing the Apostles for what was to come. He now breaks to all the Twelve the news of what His end on earth would be. He speaks in the plainest terms but they do not understand: their own preconception firmly holds its ground. Some perhaps thought that this death spoken of would be like a temporary trance, from which their Master would rise to a life in the body such as He had led before.

Our Lord, we may be sure, did not suppose that they would understand, nor was He careful that they should do so, if He had been He would have asked them questions and commented on their replies. If the whole sad truth had been unfolded, they would have had no heart for daily work; the cloud in the future would have overcast their souls. Thus it is that our Lord does not dwell upon the end. He says nothing of its meaning, He utters no word of doctrine, but He states the facts in the barest form. His intention in doing this is made known to us in words spoken long afterwards:

"But these things have I spoken unto you, that when their hour is come, ye may remember them, how that I told you. And these things I said not unto you from the beginning, because I was with you[1]."

It was not His object that they should know beforehand what was coming, but that when

---

[1] John xvi. 4.

circumstances furnished the key, they should understand that all was taking place in the way He had foreseen: neither should they be made to grieve while the bridegroom was with them.

When the Crucifixion came, it would be some support to the disciples to mark that it was a fulfilment of their Master's words. They would get a larger view of God's plans by marking that what came about was part of a purpose worked steadily out, on lines long before laid down.

Whatever our Lord's words might mean, no doubt about the final restoration of the Kingdom to Israel entered the Apostles' heads. Come what might this was to them a certainty, and the notion of a Kingdom over the hearts and consciences of men, without the sanctions or appurtenances of royal sway, was one which neither they nor any others of those times could conceive; it had to appear, indeed, as a fact, before it could be entertained as an idea.

The Apostles were ready enough to admit that vicissitudes of fortune might befall them and their Master on their way, but that their cause must finally triumph was a conviction which formed part of themselves. They made light of the conflicts and dangers which beset the road, for they saw behind all these an empire settled for evermore and stretching over the world. This material view brought with it at the time the ills that cling to error. It made them think of what they should themselves receive. Their care for self, which had passed almost out of sight while they devotedly followed their Master over the mountains or the Lake, swelled out greatly now. Our Lord, so tolerant of merely speculative error, is made anxious by the symptoms of rivalry displayed. Mistaken opinions, or illusions, due to the traditions in which they had been reared, events already impending would dispel; but self-regard among the founders of the Church would be fatal to the work.

"And they came to Capernaum: and when he was in the house he asked them, What were ye reasoning in the way[1]?"

We get here a glimpse of the Apostolic company taking their road along the path which had been chosen as being unfrequented[2]. We may picture them journeying on, with our Lord a little in front, with them but not quite of them—for always He is essentially alone—close enough to hear a medley of voices and to catch the tones which indicated contest, but not near enough to distinguish words—and after Him the Apostles following in knots of two or three which now and then came together into one group. Our Lord is not quick to interrupt; He is singularly sparing of interposing the Master's hand, He does not

[1] Mark ix. 33. [2] Mark ix. 30.

turn on them and chide. The Apostles would not have grown to what they did if they had been checked at every turn.

The dispute has died away, their journey is over and they are together in the house at Capernaum which they had left some months before, when our Lord asks the question in the text just quoted shewing that He knew their hearts, and they held their peace. Our Lord sat down and called the Twelve; from this they might be sure that He had something of moment to say.

St Mark gives his words thus,

"If any man would be first, he shall be last of all, and minister of all[1]."

This evangelist's way of putting what was said makes it look like a penal provision against seeking the mastery; as if he who was convicted of aiming at the highest place was to be put down to the bottom of the scale. But St Luke's version points to a view more consistent with Our Lord's usual way. He makes our Lord say, "for he that is least among you all, the same is great[2]." Christian greatness is born of willingness to lay the lowliest duties on yourself, and the way to be first is to be ready to remain last.

Our Lord goes to the root of this matter of greatness. He makes them put it to themselves what they meant by being greater one

[1] Mark ix. 35. [2] Luke ix. 48.

than another. He recalls them from what is worldly and ephemeral, from gradations of precedence and authority, to what constitutes the real greatness of a spiritual being, his favour in God's sight.

St Matthew's account of this discourse is the most full, and if we take out of it the denunciations of offence, and suppose them put subsequently as St Mark gives them, it makes it easier to follow the connexion of thought.

"In that hour came the disciples unto Jesus, saying, Who then is greatest in the kingdom of heaven? And he called to him a little child, and set him in the midst of them, and said, Verily I say unto you, Except ye turn, and become as little children, ye shall in no wise enter into the kingdom of heaven. Whosoever therefore shall humble himself as this little child, the same is the greatest in the kingdom of heaven. And whoso shall receive one such little child in my name receiveth me: but whoso shall cause one of these little ones which believe on me to stumble, it is profitable for him that a great millstone should be hanged about his neck, and *that* he should be sunk in the depth of the sea. Woe unto the world because of occasions of stumbling! for it must needs be that the occasions come; but woe to that man through whom the occasion cometh!

* * * * * * * *

See that ye despise not one of these little ones; for I say unto you, that in heaven their angels do always behold the face of my Father which is in heaven[1]."

[1] Matt. xviii. 1—11.

A child does not feel that he is humbling himself by helping even in the lowliest matters in his parents' work; rather is he elated at being found to be of use. The Apostles could take a lesson by children in this particular; and in order to learn this lesson, they could hardly do better than try to win children to them, not counting them lightly because they were children, but feeling a reverence for childhood, because Christ claimed children as His own, and, what was more, declared that in heaven their angels always beheld His Father's face.

This gentleness of our Lord in rebuking, has an effect which gentleness often has, it awakens compunctions in those to whom it is shewn. A child, who by severity is set on its defence or drawn into falsehood, is often melted into full confession by being loved and trusted more than it deserves. While our Lord was speaking of offences, St John had been asking himself whether he had ever put back any who were pressing toward Christ in their own way, whether he had ever chilled a nascent faith; his conscience is not clear and he must come out with what troubles him. They had seen one casting out devils in their Master's name[1] and the evil spirit of exclusiveness

---

[1] This incident shews that the Apostles even while journeying along with our Lord were sometimes out of His sight and acted independently. Perhaps they were in some degree dispersed when they halted for the night. This forbidding cannot have taken place while our Lord was in the Mount because John was there with Him.

had come over them. Their Master they thought was wholly theirs, and no one who did not become altogether one of themselves was to have any part in Him; there is a touch of truth to nature in this which makes us sure that what we read took place. Our Lord's reply is again gentle; to be hard on a fault that was confessed would have dried up that confidence which flowed so freely. They were to take the large view, they are told "He that is not against us is for us." Man is a weak being and where there is good, however partial, there is hope. Spirits, on the contrary, we may suppose are either good or evil and do not change their nature; so when speaking of them, not of mankind, in the reply to the charge that He cast out devils by Beelzebub, we find the opposite statement.

"He that is not with me is against me; and he that gathereth not with me scattereth[1]."

It is commonly supposed that it was at this visit to Capernaum that the half shekel was demanded of Peter, which was provided by the stater found in the fish's mouth; of this miracle I have spoken already, but I may have occasion to recur to it again.

We find in St Matthew's Gospel[2] a lesson delivered at this time by our Lord on the forgiveness of offences. St Peter,—characteristically ready to bring out what is in his heart—is willing to

[1] Matthew xii. 30. [2] xviii. 21, 22.

accept the duty of forgiveness; but he cannot get rid of the notion in which he has been trained, that all conduct must be ordered by definite rule. He would forgive his brother as he was told to do, but he must know how many times he was to do so. He could bring himself to acts of forgiveness, but he did not yet feel that it was more blessed to forgive than to resent. A parable is spoken expressly for him, it is that of the king who made the reckoning with his servants. Later on, when he had himself needed and received forgiveness for denying his Master, a new light in this direction streamed in, no doubt, upon his soul.

This discourse of our Lord precedes His setting out for Jerusalem to the feast of Tabernacles, and may be supposed to contain his parting directions to the body of disciples left behind at Capernaum. Nothing would be so disastrous as the breaking out of rivalry among them; His injunctions therefore, like those which He gave to the Apostles at the last, are to the effect that they should forgive and love one another.

At the end of the 9th Chapter in St Mark, we have a hard passage which has suffered from interpolation[1]; this I believe to have been the close of the lesson given to the Twelve in the house at Capernaum, when our Lord called them round Him and sat down.

---

[1] Compare the Revised Version with that of 1611.

"For every one shall be salted with fire. Salt is good: but if the salt have lost its saltness, wherewith will ye season it? Have salt in yourselves, and be at peace one with another[1]."

When our Lord says "every one shall be salted with fire" I believe that He is thinking of that fire which He had come to send upon the earth; that new sense of communion with God, which Christ awakened in the consciences of men and which has been a mighty transforming agency in the world.

The Apostles who were to be instinct with this Spirit were the salt of the world. This Spirit should be to them what salt is to that which it seasons and preserves; but if the preserving principle, embodied in the Apostles, and which was to emanate from them should itself prove corrupt, then where could help be found? If they, the chosen ones, became selfish, if they wrangled about who should be greatest; then the fire which our Lord had come to send upon earth was clearly not burning in them, and whence could it be kindled afresh. So our Lord parts from the body of disciples, going with a few on His way to the feast, and His last injunction is that they should have salt in themselves and be at peace one with another.

At this point, the end of the ninth chapter, we

[1] Mark ix. 49, 50.

lose the guidance of the Gospel of St Mark. All that the writer gives for the events of half a year, lies in this verse:

"And he arose from thence, and cometh into the borders of Judæa and beyond Jordan: and multitudes come together unto him again; and, as he was wont, he taught them again[1]."

It would seem as if it was the Galilæan ministry that he had set himself to relate, and that when our Lord passed into Judæa and Peræa he—being perhaps no longer a constant eye witness and not willing to speak from hearsay—broke off his tale. The narrative is supplied here by St John (Chap. vii.) and also by St Luke who, in a section of the Gospel which has driven formal Harmonists to despair (Chaps. ix. 50 to xviii. 15), preserves matter of the greatest value belonging apparently to this time.

St Luke speaks of a journey to Jerusalem, and of our Lord's coming to a village of the Samaritans on the way[2]. This journey is identified with that to the feast of Tabernacles (St John vii. 10) which must be the same as that spoken of above by St Mark. It is doubtful whether our Lord saw Capernaum again before His death, but He may have done so just before the final journey to Jerusalem.

A word or two must be said about St John's

[1] Mark x. 1.   [2] Luke ix. 51, 52.

account of the circumstances under which our Lord set out: his account is this.

"Now the feast of the Jews, the feast of tabernacles, was at hand. His brethren therefore said unto him, Depart hence, and go into Judæa, that thy disciples also may behold thy works which thou doest. For no man doeth anything in secret, and himself seeketh to be known openly. If thou doest these things, manifest thyself to the world. For even his brethren did not believe on him. Jesus therefore saith unto them, My time is not yet come; but your time is alway ready. The world cannot hate you; but me it hateth, because I testify of it, that its works are evil. Go ye up unto the feast: I go not up yet unto this feast; because my time is not yet fulfilled. And having said these things unto them, he abode *still* in Galilee. But when his brethren were gone up unto the feast, then went he also up, not publicly, but as it were in secret[1]."

This disbelief was not, in our Lord's brethren, grounded on an opposition of will like that of the scribes. It came from the "slowness of heart" of men who had not imagination for things Divine. What came before their eyes was never doubted by them; they did not explain His miracles away as His enemies did, only they did not see what the possession of this power implied. After the Ascension they are found among the believers[2]. Like the rest of the people at Nazareth they admired "the wisdom given unto this man" and "the

[1] John vii. 2—10.   [2] Acts i. 14, "with his brethren."

mighty works wrought by His hands[1]," but they could not imagine that one who had grown up along with them had a nature of a different order from theirs. Our Lord never upbraids them; they worked their work and He His. They were blameless commonplace men, wondering at their brother's powers and also that, with all His wisdom, He should fail in the practical sense necessary for turning His superiority to account. What was the good of these wonders being wrought if nobody knew of them? That He must aim at notoriety seemed to them too much a matter of course to need saying; and now when the great feast to which all Israel gathered was at hand, it was inexplicable that He should not join the company that travelled from Galilee, and thus enter Jerusalem with a following at his back.

The voice which, at the Temptation, had whispered, "Use your superhuman power to lend material aid to your designs," spoke in His brothers' advice as it had done by Peter. They were not unconcerned for His safety, if they had foreseen danger they would have kept Him away from the Feast (St Mark iii. 21), but they either underrated the hostility of His foes or assumed that He would protect Himself by His superhuman power; for that, possessing miraculous powers as they knew He did, He should hesitate, on an emergency, to exert them in self-defence was to them an idea too

[1] Mark vi. 2.

unreasonable to be entertained. The deep truth unconsciously uttered by His foes, "He saved others, Himself He cannot save," was one which their minds were not constructed to contain. Our Lord foresaw that a public entry into Jerusalem would lead to commotion, and, as afterwards happened, might bring about His death. A man's life, if he have a great matter in hand, is the more precious to him until this be done: so it was with our Lord. Until He had finished what was given Him to accomplish, He took such precautions for personal safety as a prudent man would. To have made light of danger, trusting to baffle it by superhuman means, would have spoiled the lesson and the moral of His life.

When the brethren spoke of His "going up to Jerusalem," they thought of the journey in public as much as of the feast itself. Half Galilee would be upon the road, men would mix and converse freely on the way, and Jesus, they thought, would, by travelling thus, come in contact with a number of zealous men and increase His following largely. But herein lay one of the dangers which made our Lord shun this course. The people, proud of the great prophet from their own district, might have revived the project of making Him a King, and by a turbulent entry to Jerusalem have alarmed the Romans as well as the scribes. Again, the turmoil of this journey would have disturbed those processes of growth in the Apostles' mind over which our Lord held watch; the feast of Tabernacles was, above all, a festival of joyousness, and the journey to it was made an occasion of pleasure and social union. For the Apostles to have joined the crowd would have been unfavourable for the germination of the solemn thoughts of which our Lord had dropped the seed on His way from the Mount to Capernaum. By going up privately in the middle of the Feast these dangers were avoided. There was no public arrival, no welcome. The Romans would know and care nothing about a new preacher who appeared in the Temple, and the priests, in face of the diversity of opinion about Jesus of Nazareth, would hesitate to lay hands upon Him. For the Apostles too, the journey through an unfriendly country would give plenty of occasion for turning over in their minds the strange words they had heard about the sufferings of the Christ, and the injunctions to "have salt in themselves."

What gives this journey its great interest to me, with my particular purpose in view, is the refusal of hospitality to our Lord by the Samaritan villages, and the enquiry of James and John, whether they should not call down fire from heaven; wherein the "Sons of Thunder" justify their name.

"And it came to pass, when the days were well-nigh come that he should be received up, he stedfastly set his face to go to Jerusalem, and sent messengers before his face: and they went, and entered into a village of the

Samaritans, to make ready for him. And they did not receive him, because his face was as though he were going to Jerusalem. And when his disciples James and John saw this, they said, Lord, wilt thou that we bid fire to come down from heaven, and consume them? But he turned, and rebuked them. And they went to another village[1]."

"Some ancient authorities," as we read in the margin of our Revised Version, "add, *and said, Ye know not what manner of spirit ye are of.*"

This is so exactly after our Lord's manner, not only in the quality but in the *quantity* of rebuke, that I have no doubt but that it is a genuine saying of Christ preserved by tradition whether it were originally in St Luke's Gospel or not. It is like our Lord to drop a word indicating error and leave the real correction to grow up in the learner's mind as though it was supplied by himself. He rarely dilates on what is blameworthy and never recurs to a failing that has been noticed at the time.

James and John, we must recollect, had just witnessed the Transfiguration, this helps to explain their mood of mind. They dwelt upon the recollection of this all the more because it was a secret possession of the three. The contrast of their Master's inherent greatness and the humiliation to which He was subjected moved their indignation. The Lord of heaven was refused hospitality by a village in Samaria, and this not

---

[1] Luke ix. 51—56.

out of niggardliness—that would have moved the Apostles less—but from an old animosity about where men should worship. They, no doubt, regarded their "jealousy for the Lord God" as something commendable, and were surprised at our Lord's rebuking them and telling them that they knew not what Spirit they were of. The fact was, that our Lord detected in this fierce proposal a further growth of that tendency to spiritual arrogance which had been indicated by their forbidding the man who followed not with them, and this seems to cause our Lord concern. He treats it as a spiritual affection which it would require care to remove. He does not inveigh against it, but His parables and the drift of His teaching militate against the propensity to exercise "Lordship" over men.

Our Lord subsequently takes occasion to exalt the blessing of forgiveness and to teach that overmuch must not be expected or demanded from men. He gives the parables of the Prodigal Son and of the unjust Steward, of which last I shall speak in the next chapter. Peter saw that when our Lord said, "Blessed are those servants whom the Lord when He cometh shall find watching," He had His eye upon the future rulers of His community.

"And Peter said, Lord, speakest thou this parable unto us, or even unto all? And the Lord said, Who then is the faithful and wise steward, whom his lord shall set over his household, to give them their portion of food in due season? Blessed is that servant, whom his lord when he cometh shall find so doing. Of a truth I say unto you, that he will set him over all that he hath. But if that servant shall say in his heart, My lord delayeth his coming; and shall begin to beat the men-servants and the maidservants, and to eat and drink, and to be drunken; the lord of that servant shall come in a day when he expecteth not, and in an hour when he knoweth not, and shall cut him asunder, and appoint his portion with the unfaithful[1]."

There is a hint of possible priestly oppression in the mention of the ill-treatment of inferiors by those upper servants, who, forgetting that their master might at any moment return, deal with the possessions as their own.

I said a little while ago that in this matter the "Sons of thunder" justified their name. If we had not this passage, critics would wonder how such a surname could have been chosen; St John, it is true, forbade the working of cures by one who "followed not with them," still we regard him as the Apostle of Love, and in the Gospels we hear nothing of St James. This coincidence, though in a small matter, is worth noting. This incident preserved by St Luke shews that there was at the bottom of the natures of these two, loving though they were, a fund of impetuousness and wrath, and that they could break out into a storm of indignation, bearing out the name imposed. It

[1] Luke xii. 41—46.

is worth mentioning that this falls in with what we read in the Acts, viz. that when "Herod the king put forth his hands to afflict certain of the church" the first on whom he seized was "James the brother of John[1];" this shews that James was a vehement, energetic character standing in the front, who to the political authorities was a marked man. For this was a political execution; if the priests had dealt with him for blasphemy he would have been stoned, not "slain with the sword." Our Lord gathered round Him men of very various temperaments; it is not only one type of man, but those of all types, the impetuous as well as the gentle, for whom Christ finds place in the realm of action.

On arriving at Jerusalem, Jesus "went up into the Temple and taught[2]." His discourse is addressed to the crowd; and as many visitors would come from the cities of Asia, the tone of it is necessarily very different from that of His sermons in Galilee. It is even possible, as many of the strangers had lost their Hebrew, that He spoke in Greek[3], this would account for the disuse of parables, a form of speech which went with the Hebrew tongue. During all His stay, in or near Jerusalem, possibly of some weeks' duration, broken by Mission

---

[1] Acts xii. 2. [2] John vii. 14.

[3] That our Lord spoke Greek when required is inferred from His being understood by the Syro-Phœnician woman and by Pilate, who probably knew no Hebrew, see John xviii. 33—38. See also John vii. 35, Revised Version.

journeys, we hear nothing of the disciples; all our Lord's discourses are with "the Jews," and in general with "the Pharisees." (See St John, Chaps. vii. and viii.) The Apostles, or at least some of them, may have been absent on mission duties, for St Luke places the sending out of the seventy near this time.

The question may be asked, where during this time did our Lord reside? During the feast Jerusalem was thronged with strangers, it was a time when all were keeping holiday; every family left their house, and lived in a tent or booth decorated with vine branches and flowers. Jerusalem at any time, was not, as I have said in an earlier chapter[1], favoured by our Lord as a residence for His disciples, and He is not likely to have suffered them to stay there long during the turmoil of the feast. At the beginning of the fragment concerning the woman taken in adultery we find a line which points to Bethany as the place where our Lord sojourned. This document, which I regard as genuinely historical, begins abruptly thus[2]. "And they went every man unto his own house. but Jesus went unto the mount of Olives." It looks as if the writer was speaking of the breaking up of a gathering, towards nightfall. Bethany was just beyond the Mount of Olives, something more than two miles to the east of Jerusalem. It was there, St Luke tells us, that "A certain

---

[1] Page 191.   [2] John vii. 53; viii. 1.

woman, Martha," received our Lord—but, as far as appears, not any disciples—"into her house." This was on some subsequent journey, but our Lord's affection for Lazarus and his sisters may have arisen, or at least have grown up, during the weeks following this feast. Bethany would furnish for such of the Apostles as were with our Lord just the retreat desired.

At this point I shall cease to attempt to follow the order of time. We can indeed trace our Lord's movements in St John's Gospel, and we can find in St Luke's account indications of journeys which may be made fairly well to correspond with these movements, but much uncertainty must attend the assigning of particular events or parables to their proper occasions.

St Luke in this part of his Gospel had lost, it would seem, the guidance of the original memoir which is supposed to have been the basis of the rest, but he was in possession of much valuable matter, a part of which was, very possibly, in the form of detached documents, which he does his best to arrange in order of time. We can understand that parables, such as those of Lazarus and the Prodigal Son, would be copied and circulated and handed from preacher to preacher, as would also incidents of particular interest, or discourses of our Lord. This part of St Luke's Gospel seems drawn from such sources and the connecting matter is sparingly supplied.

Nothing, then, will be gained by endeavouring to keep any longer to chronological order. Henceforth, therefore, I shall treat the points of interest as separate topics and, passing over all that does not immediately bear on the Schooling of the Apostles, I shall take the matters connected with it, about which I have something to say, and discuss them one by one.

NOTE.—The passage from St Luke, xii. 41, &c. (quoted at p. 367), contains the only mention of St Peter in all the Gospel narrative, between the going up to the Feast of Tabernacles (October) and the final journey to Jerusalem (April); although occasions occur in this interval, such as that when Thomas says: "Let us also go, that we may die with him" (St John xi. 16), when we should have expected that Peter would not be silent. In St John's Gospel he is not named between Chaps. i. and xiii. The question arises, was Peter continuously in attendance on his Master during this last winter; or was he, during part of it, learning to feed his Master's sheep by holding together the disciples at Capernaum? If when his Master was in Judæa, he only went backwards and forwards to him, this would account for the omission of the history of this half year in the Gospel of St Mark, for which Peter furnished the materials, and also for the brief mention of the Temptation; for I suppose our Lord to have given the fuller history of this to the disciples, when he was near the banks of the Jordan, after the Feast of the Dedication (St John x. 40). See p. 119. St Peter, who may not have been present, would probably limit his narrative to what he had himself seen, or heard from his Master's lips.

CHAPTER XII.

THE LATER LESSONS.

Different cases receive different treatment.

St Luke ix. 57—62.

"And as they went in the way, a certain man said unto him, I will follow thee whithersoever thou goest. And Jesus said unto him, The foxes have holes, and the birds of the heaven *have* nests; but the Son of man hath not where to lay his head. And he said unto another, Follow me. But he said, Lord, suffer me first to go and bury my father. But he said unto him, Leave the dead to bury their own dead; but go thou and publish abroad the kingdom of God. And another also said, I will follow thee, Lord; but first suffer me to bid farewell to them that are at my house. But Jesus said unto him, No man, having put his hand to the plough, and looking back, is fit for the kingdom of God."

What caught attention and led to the collocation of these two (and in St Luke three) instances was the diversity of our Lord's treatment of cases apparently similar. The disciples saw that our

Lord repelled one who was willing to follow him at once, and imperatively summoned two others who asked for delay. But though they might be puzzled at this inconsistency, they felt sure that there was a purpose and a meaning in it; so they transcribed these contrasting cases side by side, to show that for different conditions of soul Christ had different treatment ready. The second and third[1] of these colloquies probably took place at a different time from the first. They seem to have been held between our Lord and some of the disciples who were summoned to go out on the mission of the seventy, for St Luke inserts this document in his history just before his account of the mission. Thus St Matthew in his narrative puts the passage where the first incident occurs, while St Luke fixes its place by the second and third.

This *individualising* in our Lord's treatment of men struck the disciples as something new; they do not indeed point it out as a novel feature, for they never remark upon our Lord's ways, but the care of the Evangelists in preserving the most striking instances of this diversity of treatment shews that it caught their notice. To our Lord's eye every human being had a moral and spiritual physiognomy of his own. He saw at once, what it was in each man which went to make him

---

[1] The third is preserved only by Luke.

emphatically and distinctly his very self, and He addressed Himself largely to this.

I will now consider the separate instances one by one.

St Matthew, in the passage parallel to part of this[1], tells us that the first speaker was a scribe, and it appears that he was, in some sort, also a disciple of our Lord, for on coming to the next case St Matthew speaks of "*another* of the disciples."

It was, I think, in Galilee, as St Matthew tells us, that this profession of adhesion was made. At the time he speaks of, popular feeling in our Lord's favour was at its greatest height, and it was owing to the thronging of the multitude to the Lake shore near Capernaum that our Lord gave orders to depart unto the other side. The circumstances tally perfectly with the language of the passage, for our Lord was then going into a wild country. But where the passage stands in St Luke, our Lord is travelling "as it were in secret" from a village in Samaria to Jerusalem. In this journey, rapidly made, he would not have been likely to have fallen in with the scribe at all, and, as He did not preach as He went, we cannot account for the emotion which the scribe displays; moreover, it could hardly be said that at Jerusalem, He would not have "where to lay His head."

What most particularizes the scribe is his impulsiveness. We have here another example

[1] Matthew viii. 19.

of that mistrust of emotional fervour which our Lord uniformly shews. The woman who cried "Blessed is the womb that bare thee[1]," the scribe in the case before us, and St Peter, when he said, "I am ready to go with thee both to prison and to death[2]," all are answered by our Lord in the same tone of repression[3].

Sudden transports and ebullitions of feeling like those just named, come mainly of temperament and of passing physical conditions which subjugate the agent, and our Lord does not regard them as betokening a character on which he can depend.

It speaks well for the right feeling of this scribe that he forbears to press his suit. He divined, with the delicacy of a well bred Oriental, that our Lord's reply, though apparently only discouraging him from following for his own sake, shewed that He held it best that he should stay behind. He is satisfied that our Lord's judgment will be right and he yields at once. A man with less perception might have protested against the imputation on his endurance, and have declared that he would go with the Master though he should have to lie on the bare earth.

---

[1] Luke xi. 27.
[2] Luke xxii. 33.
[3] See also Luke xiv. 15. The exclamation, "Blessed is he that shall eat bread in the kingdom of God" is met by the parable of the Great Supper.

That, however genuine his devotion may have been, it was best for the scribe to stay at home is easy to understand; he had been used to an indoors life and under hardships and exposure he would have broken down; besides, while being a burden to the rest, he could, as a jaded man, have gained little in moral or spiritual growth. He was moreover, both as to culture and social caste, of a different type from the rest, and his presence would have made the party less homogeneous. Another important consideration was this; by remaining where he was, he might do that particular kind of good for which he was suited by temper and condition better than by following our Lord. The course which had taken hold of his imagination may not have been that in which he could do the best work. By remaining in Galilee and mixing with other educated men, he, like Joseph of Arimathea and Nicodemus, might help to spread tolerance and leaven the mass.

The two cases which follow, no doubt, puzzled the disciples much. Our Lord had so strenuously enforced a man's duty to his parents, that they would have expected these pleas for delay to be admitted without a word. They are however very positively rejected, and the refusal is put in so impressive a form that I cannot but infer that our Lord intended these colloquies to be recorded.

It has commonly been taken for granted, that the father of the spokesman in the first of these cases was lying dead when our Lord met him and bade him follow; but Eastern usages almost preclude this view, for the Jews buried within twenty-four hours of the death, and for a son to be seen in public while his father was lying dead would to their minds have been highly indecent. Some think that, the father being in extreme age, the son asked to be allowed to stay with him till he died; what seems to me more likely is that the completion of the ten days of strict mourning was regarded as part of the obsequies, and that the word "buried" applies to this. The father might have been laid in the ground, but the ten days not having expired, the funeral solemnities were not considered over.

I think that our Lord meant in this case to leave a lesson, and that the lesson was this. Family ties and duties, blessed though they usually are, must not be turned into idols or suffered to hamper the "clear spirit" in its ascent to God. There is such a thing as the tyranny of family just as there is of social usage or public opinion, and from each and all of these our Lord would set men free. This kind of freedom would cost a struggle as other kinds also would, and owing to divisions caused by change of Faith even parents might be set against children and children against parents —a heavy price indeed, but one that vanishes compared with the opening of eternal life to mankind. Supposing, as I do, that these disciples were summoned by our Lord to go forth with the seventy, I find in this inflexibility which our Lord displays something quite of a piece with the order to "salute no man by the way[1]," and to wipe off the dust from their feet when not received; all this is consistent, when taken together, and viewed as a lesson in the dignity of consecration to God and the imperative character of the charge imposed.

It is important to observe that though these disciples make excuse, and our Lord has usually little tolerance for excuses, yet, instead of being dismissed, these men are despatched to preach the Kingdom of God. This shews that the defect in them was not organic, and that it had not touched the vital centres. Their malady was of a different order from that of the guests invited to the great supper who said, "I pray thee have me excused," for these latter made light of the invitation; while, if my view be correct, these two men were terrified and overawed by being called to duties which their imagination painted as beyond their powers. They were sensitive and distrustful of self, with highly strung nerves, and the suddenness of the call to preach the Kingdom of God took away their breath. They do not refuse, but they beg for delay. If they had obtained such a postponement it would have been all the worse for them, because they would have been working themselves into a fever all the while. They are panic stricken

[1] Luke x. 4—11.

at the idea of going into strange districts proclaiming the Kingdom of God. They were quailing under a nerve-storm and by devising excuses they only gave it greater force; every moment that they lingered increased the hold of the morbid impression: a foreign will must come to their help and take the place of that which was failing. Such a will acts most effectively in the form of an imperative command, calling the patient to immediate positive action. This treatment is followed here. These two men, no doubt, followed as they were bidden. They yielded to authority and herein they found their cure; they, like the rest, set out with only their staves in their hands and came back exulting that the devils were subject to them through the Lord's name. Thus each of the three personages receives the proper specific for his case; Christ divines the treatment that every particular diathesis requires.

But the crowning case of all is yet to come. It belongs to a later time than the above, and is related more at length. It was soon after our Lord had entered on his final public journey to Jerusalem, teaching and discoursing as He went, that a young man, "a certain ruler," in St Luke's words, ran to Him and threw himself at His feet. St Mark's account is the most full of detail.

"And as he was going forth into the way, there ran one to him, and kneeled to him, and asked him, Good Master, what shall I do that I may inherit eternal life?

And Jesus said unto him, Why callest thou me good? none is good save one, *even* God. Thou knowest the commandments, Do not kill, Do not commit adultery, Do not steal, Do not bear false witness, Do not defraud, Honour thy father and mother. And he said unto him, Master, all these things have I observed from my youth. And Jesus looking upon him loved him, and said unto him, One thing thou lackest: go, sell whatsoever thou hast, and give to the poor, and thou shalt have treasure in heaven: and come, follow me. But his countenance fell at the saying, and he went away sorrowful: for he was one that had great possessions[1]."

Behind the young man's question there lay this view. He regarded eternal life as the reward of certain good works and the punctilious observance of what was divinely enjoined. Our Lord on the other hand represents it, not as being granted or withheld according to the record of performances, but rather as coming "of congruity[2]" along with the fitness for it which has been acquired in the whole education of a life. The man's works have no doubt had very much to do with making him what he is, but other influences have acted as well.

Our Lord rejects the appellation "Good Master." In these terms, scholars addressed the Rabbi at whose feet they sat, they accepted his dicta, and gave up all independent judgment of their own.

[1] Mark x. 17—22.
[2] Articles of Religion, XIII.

But our Lord, fostering and, in some sort, respecting the individual principle in each man, would free them from fetters of all kinds, those of the Rabbis among the rest. Here He would say, "Why do you run to a human master"(for as such only could the mass regard our Lord)"to tell you what it is right to do? About this no authority can be absolute but God, and His commandments you know." These commandments the young ruler had kept, indeed it was hardly possible that one in his position could have done otherwise, but an empty place was still left in his soul. Life he felt sure must have a higher meaning and more satisfying occupations than any he had yet found. Surely he thought "The Master cannot mean to put me off with telling me to keep the commandments;" and he was right. He had known of no other guide to virtuous life than rules of conduct, and so he had come asking for a fresh set of such rules; but a new light was breaking on his soul and what he really wanted was for the clouds to be cleared away. This young man had a noble soul and our Lord "looking on him loved him." The scribe, spoken of above, would do best by remaining where he was; but this young man would do best by following. He was worth rescuing from the conventionalities and littlenesses of his every day life and lifting into communion with God. Had he the force to wrench asunder the bonds, slender singly but countless in number, which fastened him down, and to give up, not merely soft living—that he would abandon with joy—but the social consideration and what went with it, personal connections and all, which he would fling away by doing as Christ bade? This was the question.

Our Lord had not told the scribe to sell all he had and give to the poor. He laid no such rule on His disciples, but here it was these possessions and, more than all, the position they conferred that clogged the soul and prevented its rise. The "giving to the poor" is not enjoined merely as benevolence; in that virtue it was not likely that this young man would fail, it is only a means of disposing of the weight that drags him down; the magnitude of the sacrifice required staggered the young ruler and he went sorrowful away; but perhaps there was more hope of him than if, at our Lord's word, he had impulsively surrendered all that he had. He may have been one of those who afterwards sold their land or houses "and brought the prices of the things that were sold and laid them at the Apostles' feet[1]." From this interview our Lord draws the moral, "How hardly shall they that have riches enter into the Kingdom of God;" this is not a denunciation of the rich but rather a commiseration of them, owing to the peculiar and insidious temptations to which they are unceasingly exposed.

The Apostles are "astonished exceedingly[2]"

[1] Acts iv. 35. [2] Mark x. 24.

at our Lord's severity, they had perhaps been pleased at the prospect of the accession to their community of a man who was rich and high in station and well spoken of on all sides. As soon as they had heard him told to give up all and follow, Peter, with a touch of almost infantine nature which stamps the narrative as authentic, looking to his own case says, "Lo we have left all and have followed thee." This was no boast or our Lord would not have answered as he does; it was rather an expression of relief at finding that this special difficulty which beset the young ruler no longer stood in their way. They had been called to leave settled homes and they had done so. Peter, we know, had a wife, and James and John had a father and mother alive. Our Lord seems to give them very positive comfort. Those who had left home or family or lands for His sake and the Gospel's should now, in this time, receive the same a hundred fold[1] as well as life hereafter.

We seem to find here a direct promise of worldly benefit, which would be strangely out of accord with the general tenour of Christ's words; but then comes a clause, preserved only by St Mark, which alters all the meaning. It contains but two words "with persecutions." This appears to unsay all that was said before; for of what good, in the way of enjoyment, are family and possessions "in

[1] Mark x. 30.

the midst of persecution"? Our Lord, to my thinking, in this passage has His eye on a certain time to come; the "brethren and sisters and mothers and children" must mean the great Christian family, and the "lands" are the possessions of that community which, while the Church was confined to Jerusalem, had all things common, "When the multitude of them that believed were of one heart and soul: and not one of them said that aught of the things which he possessed was his own[1]." In the exaltation of spirit in which that community lived, persecution would seem only a superficial ill, without which their happiness would have been too ecstatic for permanent spiritual health. Their condition as we know from the Acts was replete with joy; over and over again we are reminded of the gladness which filled the souls of the early converts. The reward promised, when qualified by this phrase, might rightly be set before the Apostles, for it was no reward at all except to spiritually minded men. These two words, which are omitted by St Luke, enable us to understand —what seems a little strange—why this promise is not accepted with joy and with eager questions as to when this happy time should come; it puzzled the hearers. Any rising exultation is checked by the words, "with persecutions," and the hearers are perhaps set wondering why Christ

---

[1] Acts iv. 32.

often drops difficulties into His speech, just when He seems to be going to reveal what men particularly want to know, and why, when holding out a promise, He should dash the cup from their lips.

Parable of the unjust Steward.

ST LUKE XV., XVI.

More and more, as our Lord's work draws near the close, do we notice that His eye, somewhat diverted from what is passing about Him, is directed to a condition of things foreseen "being yet far off." It is to provide for this that He is ever taking thought and imparting lessons; and if no state of things had come about in which these lessons might find a field of exercise, we should be at a loss to understand what they meant or why they were there. The explanation is found in the early history of the Church of Christ. In the parables and discourses of the later ministry there is one image to which our Lord again and again recurs. It is that of men labouring in a Master's service, and most commonly in that of a Master who is away from home and may at any time come back. It may be that the Master is a great King, in which case the labourers are his ministers, and frequently there is mention made of diversity of office and of some who exercised authority over "men-servants and maid-servants." In these cases we frequently find, either in the parable itself or in the "hard saying" which commonly closes it, an allusion to some special danger attaching to delegated power.

One such moral danger there is besetting those entrusted with any charge, and above all with a spiritual charge, which is very insidious, and more easily corrected by a lesson given in a story than by direct reproof; it is that of the severity and rigour which comes of over-scrupulosity and over-zeal. The trustee of a property will sometimes feel morally or legally bound to exact the very uttermost, and to use a hardness which he would never think of shewing in his own affairs; and by habitually constraining himself to use hardness he may become actually hard of nature himself. When we come to matters spiritual and ecclesiastical all this is true in an intensified degree.

The more exalted the priest's notion of his function and the more genuine his appreciation of the Majesty of God, the more impossible it seems to him to abate one iota of God's claims. Things sacred, he has been taught to think, differ in kind from things secular, and demand rules of management of their own. He holds it unlawful to make composition with offenders against God; he is the appointed upholder of the rights and dignities of the Almighty and he dares not bate a hair. Honestly awe-stricken at the tremendous responsibility, he flies where he can to a written Law, and, pointing to the letter, he takes refuge in the sacerdotal "non possumus" as an answer to every extenuating plea.

I believe that when our Lord delivered the parable of the unjust Steward, He had in view this particular evil which is all the more dangerous because it wears the garb of "jealousy for the Lord God."

If the Apostles, feeling that they formed the personal staff of a King endowed with all power from on high, had *not* been lifted up and shewn some touch of imperious and exclusive spirit, they must indeed have been more or less than men. That symptoms of such a spirit had appeared and caused our Lord concern may be gathered, not only from the positive instances, such as, the forbidding one who followed not with them to cast out devils in the Lord's name; the demand to be allowed to call down fire from heaven; and the rebuking of those who brought to Christ "their babes that He might touch them;" but, even more certainly, from the repeated animadversions, in the later teaching of our Lord, on personal ambition and the over-straining of authority. Moderation, as to what may be expected from human nature, though not enforced by positive injunctions, is commended to us, after our Lord's way, by a gentle influence everywhere present, and by a current in the teaching setting steadily towards the point in view. Our Lord had been speaking to the people in a series of parables—the lost sheep, the lost piece of silver, the Prodigal Son,—all set in one key, all bearing on the "joy in the presence of the angels of God over one sinner that repenteth[1]," and He then turned to the disciples, with, as I believe, the same thought still uppermost in His mind, and urges them as the "pastors and masters" of the future, not, by insisting on the utmost, to make reformation too hard.

The parable of the unjust Steward was addressed, we are told, to the disciples, and as the disciples had no worldly goods at all, it cannot be the main drift of the parable, as has been sometimes maintained, to inculcate Christian prudence in the use of these. I find in this parable a closing comment in a very terse form; this leads me to suspect that the key to the main purport lies therein. The verse is this, "For the sons of this world are for their own generation wiser than the sons of the light[2]." The drift of the parable is, indeed, to teach a kind of prudence, but not one in which *money* is concerned. The administration of property is only the vehicle in which the lesson is conveyed. What I take to be inculcated here is true Christian wisdom as to the exercise of authority—spiritual authority above all. The moral that I discern is this; that the Apostles and their

[1] Luke xv. 10.   [2] Luke xvi. 8.

successors may do more good by shewing a little indulgence—by conceding something to weak human nature, not enforcing Jewish formalities, and not insisting too inflexibly upon every point which they think may touch the honour or the privileges of Christ's Church—than by adhering to the strictest regard for observances, and imposing rules for sanctity of thought and conduct with which only a chosen few would be able to comply. How many have been repelled from religion by the rigour, which Priests or Puritans fancied themselves under compulsion to employ, and how has this fretful anxiety for discipline sometimes soured the natures of those who had it in charge!

I proceed to a short examination of the parable, of which I will quote the whole.

"And he said also unto the disciples, There was a certain rich man, which had a steward; and the same was accused unto him that he was wasting his goods. And he called him, and said unto him, What is this that I hear of thee? render the account of thy stewardship; for thou canst be no longer steward. And the steward said within himself, What shall I do, seeing that my lord taketh away the stewardship from me? I have not strength to dig; to beg I am ashamed. I am resolved what to do, that, when I am put out of the stewardship, they may receive me into their houses. And calling to him each one of his lord's debtors, he said to the first, How much owest thou unto my lord? And he said, A hundred measures of oil. And he said unto him, Take

thy bond, and sit down quickly and write fifty. Then 7
said he to another, And how much owest thou? And he
said, A hundred measures of wheat. He saith unto him,
Take thy bond, and write fourscore. And his lord com- 8
mended the unrighteous steward because he had done
wisely: for the sons of this world are for their own generation wiser than the sons of the light. And I say unto 9
you, Make to yourselves friends by means of the mammon
of unrighteousness; that, when it shall fail, they may
receive you into the eternal tabernacles. He that is 10
faithful in a very little is faithful also in much: and he
that is unrighteous in a very little is unrighteous also in
much. If therefore ye have not been faithful in the 11
unrighteous mammon, who will commit to your trust the
true *riches?* And if ye have not been faithful in that 12
which is another's, who will give you that which is your
own[1]?"

I do not pretend to have made out for every
particular in the story of the parable a spiritual
parallel after my own view, indeed I think that interpreters sometimes look for too complete a correspondence. I can quite understand that a detail
might be introduced which should give life to the
story and so help to fix it in the hearers' minds,
which might have no analogue in the spiritual
interpretation at all. This parable is, as we are told,
addressed neither to the people nor to the scribes,
but to the disciples, and, as it must have been
delivered during our Lord's journeys in the north
of Judæa or its neighbourhood when He was but

[1] Luke xvi. 1—12.

slightly attended, it is probable that when He spoke it few beside the Apostles were by. One peculiarity, which strengthens my impression that it was uttered for the special benefit of the first hearers of it, is, that it turns on a matter which only those who were conversant with the customs of that place and time could fully understand. We know so little of the way in which estates were managed in Palestine, that the relations between the steward and his Lord are imperfectly conceived, and much of the difficulty of this parable arises from this cause: in the other parables the circumstances forming the shell of the story belong to all countries and all times alike. If now, as I have supposed, the primary use of this parable was for those who first listened to it; if it were specially intended to teach the Twelve and their immediate successors not to make too heavy demands on their converts; then it would matter less, if the story should not be so clear for men of later times.

What I regard as the point of the story is this, that it is just as unwise to exact the utmost that is due in moral and spiritual matters—casting off every one who falls short in conduct or differs in religious views—as it would be in worldly business to stand out always for the utmost penny of your rights. The honesty or dishonesty of the steward is not the central point on which the moral turns, it is his tact in remitting part of his claims with a long-sighted view. I do not think that we need now trouble ourselves with the question of who it is that answers to the "rich man which had a steward;" but that he does not represent Providence is clear from the eighth verse, which includes him among the "sons of this world;" for it is his sense in commending the steward which draws forth the moral, "The sons of this world are for their own generation wiser than the sons of the light." This rich man's verdict on his steward's conduct may be taken to represent the view which practically minded men, versed in affairs and regarding matters little on their ethical side, would take of the case in hand; in fact he stands for the public opinion of his class.

Next comes the question, What was the business position of the steward? It agrees best both with the circumstances before us and with such extraneous information as we possess, to suppose that the functionary, called here steward, managed absolutely his master's property, and that he was paid by a poundage on the net receipts, or by some similar method, so that his interest and his master's would, generally speaking, coincide. There is no allegation against him of fraud or corrupt bargaining, and indeed, his being in danger of beggary shews that he is not supposed to have made himself a purse. He is charged with having "wasted the goods," but this may mean in the way of over leniency with creditors or of unproductive outlay, not in that of personal appropriation. He was clearly not treated as though he were liable to criminal prosecution. It is of course meant to represent him as a *bad steward*, and the word here construed *unjust* sometimes means little more than *bad*, as will be seen from Archbishop Trench's note, in the sense of being ineffective and unsatisfactory to his employers.

Dr Edersheim observes as follows[1]:

"It must be borne in mind that he is still steward, and as such has full power of disposing of his master's affairs. When, therefore, he sends for one after another of his master's debtors, and tells each to alter the sum in the bond, he does not suggest to them forgery or fraud, but, in remitting part of the debt, whether it had been incurred as rent in kind or as the price of produce purchased, he acts, although unrighteously, yet strictly within his rights." His master praised his astuteness, he had kept within the law and so long as this was done the current code of morality was satisfied. It is a point to be noted that no bargain is made with the debtors, he trusts to their gratitude to receive him into their houses.

A lesson prominent in the parable and which is brought out in the application is, that as he had made friends by his leniency in administering the substance of the master so they, Christian pastors and masters, should make to themselves friends out

[1] "Life and times of Jesus the Messiah," p. 267.

of something which is called the "mammon of unrighteousness" (about which we shall presently enquire). These friends would, out of gratitude, receive them into "the eternal tabernacles." For these friends are to be in Heaven themselves, and they must have got there—if we are to keep to the story—not only through their pastor's teaching and ministrations, but they must have partly owed their salvation to the loving and merciful treatment they had met with. An offender may be sometimes won over and completely changed for the better by feeling that he has been treated more kindly and leniently than he deserves. The parable implies that these might not have reached heaven if their guides had been more hard with them, if they had exacted every religious duty, and had been severe upon every failing. These men having reached the eternal tabernacles welcomed into them those who by lessening their burdens had been the means of their getting there themselves.

We now come to the hard question, What is meant by the words "the mammon of unrighteousness" or "unrighteous mammon"—which are identical? I think they must mean the temporal authority in regulating things outward which the earliest rulers of the Church necessarily possessed. The word translated "unrighteous" does not here imply inherent badness, but that the seeming wealth has only a value according to worldly judgment and worldly measure, without intrinsic worth in itself. This may corrupt its possessor as much as worldly riches. I give, in a note, Archbishop Trench's discussion of the Greek word[1]. Riches, *as riches*, are never called unrighteous by our Lord. I do not think, however, that wealth in its common sense can be intended by the word "mammon" here, for of "silver and gold" the Apostles would have none. But though the Apostles had not money, yet they had advantages for the use of which they must answer; they had, in authority and position, what answered to wealth; they could regulate the lives of the converts; they could lay hands on those chosen for the Ministry; they could enforce or remit certain of the Laws of Moses. This power dealt with things outward,— contributions, observances, rules of discipline and the like,—and so, if, as the authorities quoted seem to shew, the word here translated *unrighteous* may mean false, in the sense of unreal, as paste to diamond, then this possession of theirs which gave room for the exercise of clemency—this apparel of dignity—might be so termed in contrast with

---

[1] "The use of ἄδικος for 'false' runs through the whole Septuagint. Thus, Deut. xix. 16, μάρτυς ἄδικος, a false witness; and ver. 18, ἐμαρτύρησεν ἄδικα, he hath witnessed falsely. See Prov. vi. 19; xii. 17; Jer. v. 31, 'The prophets prophesy falsely' (ἄδικα), and many more examples might be adduced. So here the '*unrighteous*' mammon is the false mammon, that which will betray the reliance which is placed on it (1 Tim. vi. 17). Thus ἰατροὶ ἄδικοι (Job xiii. 4), 'physicians of no value.'" Trench, "On the Parables," The unjust Steward.

inward spiritual riches, which form part of the condition of the individual man.

Of such real wealth we presently hear. Soon after this "the Apostles said unto our Lord, Increase our faith[1]," but this faith is not to be given from without; it cannot be transferred into them as though it could be poured from one receptacle into another. They are to fit themselves for it and grow into it in the exercise of their work; when attained it would move mountains, it would be a wealth that no man could take from them, something inalienably bound up in their existence, comprising the blessing of feeling God present in their souls. Here indeed is a treasure compared to which not only silver and gold, but power and authority and the right of ordering of matters in the churches, would seem trifling and unreal like glass beside the gem.

Again what is the "little" and the "much" of verse 10? According to my view the "little" answers to the externals of religious management, and the "much" to the spiritual verity which passes from soul to soul: those who are unfaithful in matters of administration which are comparatively little, will find that this spreading laxity will overgrow their whole nature and that they will soon become unfaithful in that which is great[2].

---

[1] Luke xvii. 5.

[2] It is clear that "unrighteous," in verse 10 means "superficial" and "unreal," because it is contrasted with "true." The opposite of ἄδικος is here ἀληθινός.

If God's servants had not been faithful in administering their rule, if they had not in God's affairs used good sense and judgment, such as men employ in their own business, if they had not controlled their tempers, disregarded their personal interest and suppressed that temptation to lord it over others which goes with new-born power;— if they had not, that is, been faithful in the use of that wealth which is by comparison unreal, then, not being faithful in the discharge of this delegated trust, "that which is another's," who would give them that "clear-eyed Faith," that sense that God was abiding in their hearts, which would be essentially their very "own."

Thus we reach what I take to be the close of the parable; for the verse about serving two masters, which occurs also in the Sermon on the Mount, does not, I think, belong to this parable, but has only been *attracted*, so to say, into its place by the occurrence in both passages of the rare word "mammon," which induced St Luke to put the two together.

I need hardly say, how far from positive I must be about the interpretation of a parable which has caused such an infinitude of comment.

Our Lord refusing to judge.

If we regard the Gospels in the light of memoirs of our Lord's actual life upon earth, it may seem strange that so few occasions are noticed in which we are shewn our Lord dealing with the business of ordinary life. Whenever we do find Him forced to take part in any secular proceeding, He is uniformly careful to avoid such decisive action as would establish an authoritative precedent in regard to things which might be left to men to manage. Some people are now disappointed at His not having furnished a wholly new and perfect scheme of human society. So far is He from doing this, that He will not even put patches upon that which He found existing. God had supplied men with faculties to frame social institutions for themselves, and these faculties Christ would leave free to work. If He had interposed to set the world right by absolute power, it might have been asked, Why this had not been done before? and, Whether it was owing to accident that the world had been let to go wrong?

Living among the people as our Lord did, He must commonly have conformed to Jewish usages. He could hardly have performed any act without coming into contact with their ways. If the particulars of every little occurrence in His private life had been set down, perhaps we might have realised, what we now hardly perceive, that in the Gospel we are reading of Jewish life in Galilee two thousand years ago. This absence of what is called "local colour" is partly due to the omission of small particulars. An outline can be more general and more universal than a picture of minute elaboration; and the portraiture of our Lord would have lost much of its singular character of belonging to every age as its own, if the draughtsman's attention had been distracted from what was characteristic, in order to present every detail with equal care.

Now arises the question, How far did our Lord Himself determine which among His doings and sayings should be recorded and which not? If He had Himself left a record, every word would have been regarded as inspired, and the Christian church would have been ruled, not by an indwelling Spirit, but by a book written once for all. It could not have been ruled by both,—for men cannot walk after the letter and after Faith at the same time—and that wooden fixity which characterised Rabbinical Judaism, would have affected Christianity as well. It pleased God that it should be left to men to tell the tale, and so other men may venture to use their judgment about it. But as Christ passed on His course, He must Himself have felt that this or that incident or discourse ought to be handed down. How could He effect this without miracle of any kind? It seems to me that He may have selected, as it were, matters for preservation thus. When He desired an incident to be known, "Wheresoever the Gospel shall be preached throughout the whole world[1]," He em-

[1] Mark xiv. 9.

phasizes it, by some action or declaration, as above, viz. by letting drop some vivid expression which takes hold of the minds of men. Thus the story of the denials of Peter is rendered indelible by the words, "before the cock crow twice." The hard saying or striking expression, sometimes because it touched the quick of men's understandings, and sometimes because it puzzled them to make it out, was thought of again and again, and remained by them as part of themselves. The incident which called the saying forth, or the colloquy in which it occurred would have to be recorded to explain the saying itself: a mass of the matrix would go along with the precious metal embedded in it. What it was not thought needful to preserve, was not enriched with these pregnant sayings and has not survived.

Hence I believe that the withdrawal from us of those "many other things that Jesus did" was not without design. The consequences of this may be of service to us in many ways, but the only one of which I shall speak is this. If every detail of our Lord's acts had been set down, many more of those matters of daily life, on which judgment is now left open, would have been determined for us by the recorded example of our Lord. Many Christians would have felt bound to act as Christ had done, even in those concerns of ordinary life which might well be left to the individual; and many inexorable necessities—many rigid lines for which there was no occasion—would have traversed the field of Christian action.

That our Lord should have thus placed a limit on the particulars that should be recorded about Him falls in with the views taken in this book, viz. that He was anxious to preserve individual freedom of action, and that He looked forward with a general prescience to the course of events.

It is my opinion that our Lord foresaw, that, in time to come, men of different races and under different conditions would desire to fashion their lives after His, and that therefore He purposely freed the account of Himself that should come into their hands from all that was immaterial, and particularly from all that was exclusively Jewish in its garb; but whether this were so or not, the fact remains that no particular national institutions or social usages are consecrated by our Lord's words or practice. Supposing that our Lord knew that posterity would regard His example as a sacred rule, and that He wished men not to be hampered in this way, but to retain free play of thought and will, it is hard to devise for Him a course more expedient for the end in view than that which he actually took.

Several instances occur in the Gospels, of appeal being made to our Lord about vexed matters belonging to the life of that time. Such appeals He always meets much in the same way. He puts the matter aside, either by positively refusing

THE LATER LESSONS.   403

to judge or by giving the question an unexpected turn.

The cases to which I shall refer are, (1) the disputed inheritance, (2) the woman taken in adultery, (3) the paying of the didrachma, (4) the judgment on the tribute to Cæsar.

1.   It seems to have been during the ministry in some city, either in Judæa or Peræa, when the people were pressing on one another to get near our Lord, that one of the multitude said to Him, "Master bid my brother divide the inheritance with me[1]."

This man was influenced by some notion that he had been wronged, a notion which was very likely born of cupidity. This greed he carried always about him, it was uppermost in his mind, and when he found the crowd listening to the Preacher of righteousness, he thought that he might turn the influence of this Preacher to account for his own ends. If, by an *ex parte* statement he could get Christ's judgment on his side, possibly his brother would do His bidding. The Jewish Law of inheritance was plain and courts of Law were accessible, but perhaps his claim had been disallowed; at any rate he thought it a cheaper plan to get the great Preacher to interfere.

Our Lord repudiates in strong terms the notion that He is a "judge or a divider," Judges and dividers through many ages had been provided for

[1] Luke xii. 14.

regular duty in a regular way; but Christ's coming was an act standing by itself in the History of the race. It had nothing to do with the internal concerns of this people or of that. Its influence was worldwide. He was to kindle the new fire, to set alight the spiritual passion in mankind. He notes how, in the man who appeals to Him, every affection had been absorbed and killed by his covetousness. He turns to the multitude and inveighs against this insidious vice, and delivers to them the parable[1] of the rich man who would pull down his barns and build greater. There is no hidden meaning lying behind this parable as there is in those in which He set the Kingdom forth, it is only an instructive story for the hearers to carry away. Then, turning to the disciples, He puts the matter in a higher light. His moral is ever this, that to improve a man's well being, whether of a material or a social kind, you must begin by making the man himself as good as you can. Such material well being as is needed for society will follow on the moral and spiritual improvement of individual men. "Seek ye *first*," says He, "the Kingdom of God and His righteousness, *and all these things shall be added unto you*[2].

Let us suppose for a moment that our Lord had listened to this man and reviewed his case and left a judgment. What would have been the result? We should have had an isolated

[1] Luke xii. 16—20.   [2] Luke xii. 36. Matt. vi. 25.

case of the Law of inheritance, on which an irreversible decision had been pronounced. Every code framed for Christian lands would have had to accept and embody this. Endless comments on this particular case would have been written, endless guesses at the circumstances of it would have been made, and every one who contested a distribution would have endeavoured to shew that this decision covered his claims. Moreover, whenever the Christian missionary came to a new country, instead of holding a purely spiritual position he would have brought with him a new law of inheritance as part of the new religion, and people could not have accepted his teaching without changing usages to which they clung.

(2) Next comes the case of the woman taken in adultery (see p. 370). In the criminal jurisdiction of Moses the leading thought was to "put away evil;" but men had grown less cruel, and pity for the offender and hope of his reformation were coming into play. If the Lord had given judgment either in one way or the other we should have been landed in endless perplexity. The difficult questions of the distinction between a sin and a crime, and whether it is advisable for a state to enforce morality, would have been complicated by a Divine decision in a case of which the relation would not, unless the account were fuller than the Gospel notices usually are, contain all the particulars that are material.

The two cases that remain refer to polity rather than to law.

(3) The "didrachma" were levied apparently as a tax for the Temple service, enforced by custom, if not by positive law. Those who collected it ask Peter if our Lord does not pay this annual sum, and Peter at once declares that He does. But our Lord will not leave the matter so. The money shall be paid, because to refuse the payment would waken ill feeling and give an impression altogether false; but our Lord will not sanction such a payment with His authority, without protest and explanation. It might have been made the ground of supporting many kinds of religious impost if He had. He puts the question in such a light that His practice can never be quoted in support of any such demand.

(4) Those who came asking whether it was lawful to pay tribute to Cæsar, like those who brought the woman taken in adultery, had a hostile intent. They asked with a view only to entangle, not with a desire to learn. Our Lord always baffles those who address Him in this spirit. In dealing with the question of the tribute, He avoids each horn of the dilemma and teaches a grand lesson to the people who heard. For they were to render to God "the things that were God's," that is to say, not a man's money, but the whole man himself, for he is made in God's image and carries the likeness of it in his personality, just as the

coin carries on its face the name and the impress of Cæsar. Thus, in these words, the whole man is claimed as God's own by Christ.

If our Lord had either enforced or forbidden these two payments, His authority, appealed to on this side or that, would have further embittered questions which are bitter enough of themselves. Men have often pored over Scripture to extract an authority for what they wanted to do, and the case of the tribute money, notwithstanding our Lord's answer, has been pressed into the service of the upholders of imperial power.

Dr Bryce speaking of the Mediæval Empire says :—

"From the New Testament the authority and eternity of Rome herself was established. Every passage was seized on where submission to the powers that be is enjoined, every instance cited where obedience had actually been rendered to imperial officials, a special emphasis being laid on the sanction which Christ Himself had given to Roman dominion by pacifying the world through Augustus, by being born at the time of the taxing, by paying tribute to Cæsar, by saying to Pilate, 'Thou couldest have no power at all against Me except it were given thee from above.'"

In finishing this notice I must remark that there is one social institution about which our Lord does not shun to speak; this is marriage. He upholds the sanctity and inviolability of the marriage tie more stringently than did the Jewish Law. The scribe who came "making trial" of our Lord is confounded—not by being put off without an answer—as usually happens in these cases, but by the singular positiveness of the reply.

"And I say unto you, Whosoever shall put away his wife, except for fornication, and shall marry another, committeth adultery: and he that marrieth her when she is put away committeth adultery[1]."

This exception is not inconsistent with the principles governing our Lord's acts. Christ's teaching was meant for all mankind, and Christianity would have been less adapted for universal use if it had been bound up with particular institutions. But marriage is not a particular institution, it is declared to be as universal as the human race; it goes down deeper than all divisions, it belongs to the stock below the point where the branches sprout. Thus Christ's recognition of the sanctity of marriage does not hamper human legislation, or prevent the growth of Humanity in any manner consistent with its health.

Close by the side of this matter lies another on which I must only say a word. It is one of the Gesta Christi that He has put woman into her right place. Slowly and quietly has this come about, as a growth from seed turned up in the soil, and not a construction upreared by men,— as indeed, with the changes that are wrought by

[1] Matthew xix. 9.

Christ is mostly the way. He says not a word about the social condition of women or their position in the eye of the Law; He puts forward no grievances, He asserts no claim. To have done either one or the other in His day would have been to bring about a violent upheaval, which would have destroyed all chance of the germination of the seed. Nowhere do men cling to old usages with more tenacity than in the matter of relations between sex and sex. These variations of usage may rest upon solid grounds, and it would have stood in the way of the adaptability of what He left to the needs of all races and all times, if by one rigid ordinance He had enforced uniformity, even in the justest way. But though our Lord says little about the right place of women yet He treats them as though that proper place were already theirs; for parts are given them in His great world-drama consistent with those they take in the common life of family and home[1].

One word that our Lord drops has too important a bearing on this point to be passed by. Frequently as our Lord alludes to eternal life, it is rarely that anything as to the modes of this

[1] On the conversation of our Lord at Sychar with the woman of Samaria, Dr Edersheim says: "That Jesus should converse with a woman was so contrary to all Jewish notions of a Rabbi that they wondered." The disciples "marvelled that he was speaking with a woman," John iv. 27; and in a note Dr Edersheim has: "Readers know how thoroughly opposed to Jewish notions was any needless converse with a woman."

life can be gathered from His speech, but in the one passage in which He does touch on this directly, He implies that distinction of sex ceases with the life upon earth.

"But they that are accounted worthy to attain to that world, and the resurrection from the dead, neither marry, nor are given in marriage: for neither can they die any more: for they are equal unto the angels; and are sons of God, being sons of the resurrection[1]."

There is to be no marrying or giving in marriage in the Kingdom of God. All will there be as the angels of heaven. There can be no such thing as a male or female soul. Some may be educated for eternal life in the frame of man and others in that of woman, but when out of the body all distinction comes to an end, and both one and the other, if deemed worthy of the resurrection to life, assume the nature of angels of God. When this comes home to a people and they see that the distinction of male and female is one of a day, while the angelic existence, in which no distinction shall remain, is an everlasting one, then whatever remains that seems degrading in the condition of woman will be in the way to disappear.

I will end this by stating the truth which I have had it in view to bring out.

Supposing that Christ, lest He should hamper

[1] Luke xx. 35, 36.

free human growth, was unwilling to tie down posterity to particular rules touching the affairs of life, and that He also foresaw that in time men would take His behaviour as a model for their own; then the course He actually took, in refusing to sanction by His example this or that course of proceeding in matters coming within man's cognizance, was admirably suited to His end, and met perfectly the circumstances of the case.

Our Lord's action prospective.

But if our Lord's behaviour in secular matters is often hard to explain, unless we suppose Him to have had a glimpse of what has actually come to pass, much more is this the case in what concerns the building of His Church. We know from His own words that He saw His end to be near at hand. We know how He loved the Apostles and we know how His heart was set on His great work; so that it is inexplicable that He should have left the Apostles without directions for their personal conduct, and as to the practical shape they were to give to the work in view. All is explained, if they were merely being exposed to a few hours of trial, and if our Lord meant to commission them with definite duties and give the necessary directions, when He rose again. Apart from any miraculous foreknowledge, our Lord could foresee that His end was near, and that persecution awaited those who for more than two years had formed the chief visible interest of His life. Would He have left them at Jerusalem perfectly at a loss, would He have left them in the position of a boat's crew in the open sea, whose captain has died without giving them their course? If He had not felt certain of being soon again by their side, then indeed we should, with the author of "Ecce Homo," have felt constrained to confess "that there was no historical character whose motives, objects and feelings remained so incomprehensible to us."

After the Resurrection, the forms needful for a religious community are delivered to the Apostles. They are given a rite, marking admission to the body, and sacramental words serving as a symbol and the nucleus of a creed. They are to go and baptize all nations in the name of the Father and of the Son and of the Holy Ghost. Moreover they are told what they are, for the moment, to do. They are to remain at Jerusalem, till they be endowed with power from on high. Christ opens to them the Scriptures and possibly left some instruction as to the earliest form of His Church which, agreeably to His unfailing method, He does not communicate to aftertimes. He will not stereotype the outward garb which he would have adapt itself to the changing wants of men.

Christ's intimations of the future wear the appearance of being given, less to communicate fore-knowledge than that when the event came to pass the hearers might feel that Christ had "told them before[1]:" if He had thought good He would have made the lessons plainer. It may have helped to sustain the Apostles during the terrible hours when their Master lay in the grave, to turn to these words of forecast and from them to gather that all was being carried forward towards a purpose preordained of God. It is true that our Lord had told the Apostles again and again what the end was to be, but they could not believe that He would permit His enemies to prevail, and our Lord hardly seems to expect that they would take His words as literal truth. If, during the last days, they had really believed that He was about to perish on the cross, they would have been paralysed with anguish and dismay, and the last lessons would have fallen on the ears of men who were prostrated and stunned.

That our Lord's action was suited to what did actually happen, and not to what was likely to happen after the judgment of men, appears also in another way.

The Apostles, both in themselves and in virtue of their training, were exactly adapted to the part which came into their hands, but they were by no means of the sort which the leader either of a

[1] Matth. xxiv. 25.

political or a religious movement would have picked out to carry it forward when He should die. They were not men to fascinate crowds and lead them whither they would, they were not men to discover that aspect of a dogma which should commend itself to the understandings of their hearers. They had no skill in policy, no experience in government or in organising bodies of men; their strength lay not in their talent but their truth. If they had possessed brilliant capacity, and all or any of the qualities named above, the danger of disunion or of there being as many different followings as there were Apostles (see 1 Cor. i. 12) would have been thereby increased. We read in History or Philosophy of great men who have left empires or systems for their chosen successors to maintain. Did such successors keep free from dissension and disruption in the way that those did whom Jesus chose and trained? Did any such body answer its purpose as the Apostles did?

The training of the Apostles fitted them admirably, as has been said above, for witnesses who should carry credit with the world; it brought them, by the road of personal devotion to a visible Master, unto Faith in an unseen God; it endowed them with wonderful endurance, it taught them the patience whereby they might "win their souls[1];" it educated their intuitions to discern

---

[1] Luke xxi. 19.

THE LATER LESSONS. 415

God's ways and recognise God's whisper in the voice which spake at their hearts. But they were destitute of eloquence and of many of the gifts with which the founder of a sect would have been careful to see that those were furnished who were to take His place; and this omission only becomes intelligible when we find that the deficiencies are supplied by Christ's presence with them, and by the Spirit from on high.

What was most important of all was, that no act or word of Christ's should seem to shut out from their share in Him any section of mankind. Agreeably with this, He never proclaims Himself the Jewish Messiah. No Greek or Roman would have listened for a moment to one who declared Himself the especial prophet of the Jews. Though of the "house and family of David[1]," He will accept no advantage on this score. He repudiates for the Redeemer of the world the title of "Son of David[2]," which from its nature was based on legitimacy and must rest on the veracity of genealogical rolls. The Apostles were to divine the nature of His Personality by long and close intercourse[3] with Him, more than by canvassing claims or interpreting texts. When His disciples ask to be taught to pray, "as John also taught his disciples[4]," He gives them a prayer very unlike what John

---

[1] Luke ii. 4.
[2] Matth. xxii. 42, 43.   Mark xii. 35—37.   Luke xx. 41.
[3] See John xiv. 9.   [4] Luke xi. 1.

would have given, for it contains not a word of that petition for blessing upon Israel, which, in any prayer that an Israelite offered, contained, to his mind, the gist of the whole. This prayer too was offered, not to the "Lord God of Israel" or the "God of their Fathers,"—as Jewish prayers[1] were; there was not a word in it, echoing their boast that God was peculiarly their own—but every human being is emboldened by it to turn to God as his Father in Heaven. In all this, however, our Lord never loosens the bonds of Israelite life. He proceeds always in a positive and not a negative way; without removing the Kingdom of Israel from view, He lets it dissolve, as it were, into the Kingdom of God.

There is another point brought out in this later ministry; Christ does not look forward to ultimate visible success in the way of making converts. No hope is held out of the whole world being eventually won over to allegiance—of a spiritual conquest, any more than of a material one— "Howbeit," says He—and who would have said this but Christ?—"when the Son of man cometh shall he find Faith upon the earth?" No other than Christ ever dared to tell his followers, not only that their Master would be put to death, and they themselves ill used, but also that it was very doubtful whether their cause, as far as visible appearances went, would finally prevail.

With Christ indeed as with God, there is no

---

[1] See Edersheim. vol. I. p. 110.

speaking of such a thing as either failure or success at all; He moves steadily onward toward the development of the Design of the World. But this men do not easily perceive; adversaries of the Faith are apt to say "If this religion were of God, the world would have been compelled to accept it." But of what good could such acceptance have been? Christianity is not a project of God, which it gratifies Him for men to be made to fall in with. Christ views His word as a winnowing fan sorting out those who are God's, that they may be brought to that knowledge of Him in which eternal life resides. At some epochs of the world's history, the yield will be rich and at others poor; and although Christ may come at a moment when the wheat is almost lost in the abundance of the chaff; nevertheless the grain of earlier harvests will have been sifted out and garnered in heaven, and Christ's work will have accomplished its end. But besides sifting out those who could be educated to eternal life, it is by Christ's words and work that the world has been preserved such that Holiness can grow in it; without this it might have perished of evil. Wickedness might have so got the Mastery that the world could not have served its purpose as an exercise ground for man's capacity for reaching the knowledge of God.

The whole scheme of Christ's action is made complete by the promise, "I am with you always until the end of the world." Not only is it in virtue of this truth that the Church is a living organism, and not merely a body dispensing doctrines or following directions which have been received once for all, but I also see the fulfilment of this promise in the alacrity and vigour which characterised the Apostles' work. They must have felt that they were something more than a society of men held together by love for a lost Leader; and I cannot explain how the eleven held together, and subordinated every personal care to their Master's glory;—I cannot account for this personal transformation of them, *everyone*,—except by supposing them animated by the feeling that Christ was among them still.

It is far more in harmony with our Lord's ways for Him to put the Apostles, by His spiritual monitions, into the way of organising their Society for themselves, than that He should peremptorily lay down a formal plan to which they must adhere. What Christ left undone, was what it would be good for man to endeavour to do for himself: but if Christ had not been by to whisper, men might never have set themselves to the work at all. The energy and persistent determination of the Apostles could hardly have been maintained without a sense of Christ's abiding presence; and that they had eye and ear open for discerning this I count to have come, partly of God's free gift, partly of their ingrained nature, but in far greater degree to have been the outcome of the gentle and almost imperceptible Schooling of Christ.

Christ washing the Apostles' feet.

ST JOHN XIII. 1—14.

"Now before the feast of the passover, Jesus knowing that his hour was come that he should depart out of this world unto the Father, having loved his own which were in the world, he loved them unto the end. And during supper, the devil having already put into the heart of Judas Iscariot, Simon's *son*, to betray him, *Jesus*, knowing that the Father had given all things into his hands, and that he came forth from God, and goeth unto God, riseth from supper, and layeth aside his garments; and he took a towel, and girded himself. Then he poureth water into the bason, and began to wash the disciples' feet, and to wipe them with the towel wherewith he was girded. So he cometh to Simon Peter. He saith unto him, Lord, dost thou wash my feet? Jesus answered and said unto him, What I do thou knowest not now; but thou shalt understand hereafter. Peter saith unto him, Thou shalt never wash my feet. Jesus answered him, If I wash thee not, thou hast no part with me. Simon Peter saith unto him, Lord, not my feet only, but also my hands and my head. Jesus saith to him, He that is bathed needeth not save to wash his feet, but is clean every whit: and ye are clean, but not all. For he knew him that should betray him; therefore said he, Ye are not all clean.

So when he had washed their feet, and taken his garments, and sat down again, he said unto them, Know ye what I have done to you? Ye call me, Master, and, Lord: and ye say well; for so I am. If I then, the Lord and the Master, have washed your feet, ye also ought to wash one another's feet[1]."

More than once I have characterised certain of "the things which Jesus did[2]" as "acted parables." The cursing of the fig-tree, which is the type of the class, shews what is meant by the term. The washing of the Apostles' feet is another of these parables of action. These acted parables are usually furnished by incidents lying a little out of the main drift of the action; as though Christ, struck by some plant or berry in which virtue lay, should have stepped to the way-side to gather it and preserve it for use.

The drift of the practical lesson of which we read above, I take to be this. There are men, right in heart towards God, who are beset with infirmities which lead them astray. The more alive their conscience is, the more they are distressed by their lapses into ill. This distress may grow morbid, and lead to ruin and despair. Christ in this symbolic action, anticipatory of His Supreme Work, brings healing for such men's woes. He does not merely remit the penalty of sin, He actually "puts the sin away[3]." He is like a physician who can assure the patient that the

[1] John xiii. 1–14. [2] John xxi. 25. [3] 2 Sam. xii. 13.

canker he thought was malignant is only skin-deep, and can be removed at once. The parable speaks of a man who is "bathed," and whose body is therefore clean, but who by travelling along the dusty road has got his feet sullied on the way; he has only to wash them, to become "clean every whit." So a man, righteous and godfearing at bottom, may be taken off his guard and carried away by the stream, or he may contract moral and spiritual ill from a physical irritation akin to bodily ailment; these are the evils contracted on "life's common way." These kinds of spiritual ill answer to the dust on the feet, they can be wiped off; they have not seriously damaged the soul.

This was a cheering lesson, and it was made to bear on the duty of mutual restoration. They were to wash one another's feet. It is not the way of the world to do this. If, in a body aiming at holiness of life, one of the society should go wrong, it might seem the readiest way of upholding the society's good name to thrust out the offending member at once; but Christians are not to deal with one another thus. It is just when a man goes wrong that he most wants his brethren's support. Who else is there to stand by him? So if a disciple does amiss, the rest are told to wash his feet as Christ had washed theirs—not making out that he was clean—fully allowing that he was sullied, but telling him that the soil would wash off; telling him that they had not given him up as being bad to the core, and that they were sure that his Father in Heaven had not cast him off. So doing they might lift him back into self-respect.

It is in St John's Gospel only that this account is found, and it is not hard to understand why the writers of the earlier narratives should have passed it by. They looked for historical matter that was linked on with what came before and after, or else, they took for their material pregnant sayings along with the events out of which they sprang. They may have omitted this incident, because of this washing nothing seemed to come. They did not perceive how significant our Lord's remark on it was. The writers were just coming to the account of the Lord's Supper, their minds were taken up with that, and they went straight forward to this crowning act. They probably saw in our Lord's words nothing more than an injunction to lay upon themselves the lowliest duties in serving each other. But the words, "What I do thou knowest not now, but thou shalt understand hereafter" rested in St John's ear. They implied that behind this washing of the Apostles' feet there lay something more than appeared. What could this be? He turned the matter over and over again in his mind, and a sparkle of the truth was, perhaps, struck out which served to make him careful to set the matter down precisely as it took place, for men to look into when they should have a better light.

Without entering into the controverted question as to whether the Last Supper was the Passover or not[1], I adopt Dr Edersheim's view that the contention for precedence arose as they were taking places at the table. St Luke tells us, "there arose a contention among them which of them is accounted to be greatest[2]." St John omits the account of the contention and St Luke that of the feetwashing, but the two fit together admirably well. Our Lord, by this action of His, gently gives the Apostles the lesson which they had shewn themselves to need. The scene evidently rises before the writer as he takes up his pen, and every movement of our Lord is followed and set down, from His quitting His seat to His wiping the Apostles' feet with the towel which He had wrapped round His waist.

The narrative goes on, "So he cometh to Simon Peter." Peter's individuality is strong and marked in its character. Not only is he demonstrative but he is quick to receive impressions and new emotion soon displaces the old. His Master's

[1] Dr Edersheim, who takes the view that this is the Paschal meal, says that it was usual for the head of the company to wash the hands of the guests. The washing of the feet would therefore only be an extension of a common practice and would excite no great attention. "Life and Times of Jesus the Messiah," vol. II. pp. 495—498.

[2] Luke xxii. 24, 30.

dignity was dear to him, and when he thought this infringed, every other sentiment was lost in his indignation. He says, "Thou shalt never wash my feet." But as soon as he is told that unless his Master wash him, "he has no part with Him," he is transported to the opposite extreme, and begs our Lord to wash—not his feet only—but his hands and head as well.

Throughout the Gospel history we discern our Lord's care to keep men in a fit condition to serve God by active work. All that would impair their efficiency is to be shunned. Now, to repine and brood over some past error cuts the sinews of action; from this the Apostles therefore are always diverted, and they are to be watchful to prevent others from sinking into dejection and folding their hands in despair. A man who is hopeless has no heart for work, but when he is so far encouraged as to be able to exert himself his despondency soon disappears. Thus, by their washing one another's feet, the efficiency of their Society in all ways would be notably increased.

The Apostles seem to have rightly learned the lesson which Christ here inculcates. St Mark had turned back in his first mission journey, but he is afterwards spoken of with affection and found of great service; and St Paul's words, with which I shall close this notice, are quite in the spirit of this acted parable.

"Brethren, even if a man be overtaken in any trespass, ye which are spiritual, restore such a one in a spirit of meekness; looking to thyself, lest thou also be tempted. Bear ye one another's burdens, and so fulfil the law of Christ[1]."

Use of Signs in the later Ministry.

Ever since the time when after the feeding of the five thousand, the people wanted to take Him and make Him a King, our Lord has been chary of working Signs and Wonders; and such as are wrought are no longer used for demonstration; Signs are now hardly if at all employed to attract attention and waken interest. They had already done in this way all the good they were likely to effect, and if they had been employed longer, some of those bye-effects, which potent agencies are almost sure to produce along with that which is intended, might have come into operation with injurious results.

Between the journey to the feast of Tabernacles and the week of the Passion, three only of the leading miracles are recorded; they are the giving of sight to one born blind in Jerusalem, the raising of Lazarus, and the opening of the eyes of the blind near Jericho. This last, of which I shall first speak, occurred on that final journey of our Lord to Jeru-

[1] Galatians vi. 1, 2.

salem during which He seems to have resumed for a moment His earliest function, that of witness of the Kingdom of God to the people at large. We seem to see, once again, the same Jesus who lived at Capernaum and taught the people by the Lake side.

Whether our Lord, on His way to this last Passover, set out Himself from Galilee or joined on the road the great company travelling from the north is left uncertain, but we find our Lord among a throng of visitants to the feast, who are proud of having the Great Prophet of Nazareth among them; and men come to Him—some with real troubles of soul like the young ruler—and others, like the Pharisees, either curious to obtain His decision on some vexed question, or maliciously setting Him in a dilemna between the contravention of Moses' Law, and the retaining of a burden which men were loth to bear. One small event, preserved to us in the account of this journey, gives us the clearest glimpse of our Lord's air and general demeanour that we ever obtain. There was, about Him, that indefinable something which wins children's confidence at sight. The little ones, who swarmed in the hamlets of the Jordan valley, were drawn to Him by something in His look, and—after long gazing out of their dark eastern eyes, in childhood's own intent way—they made out that they would be safe with Him, and stole to His side.

The miracle of healing, worked on the way, that of the cure of the blind men in Jericho, is nearly after the old sort. As Jesus nears the end, He reverts to the ways with which His revelation began. Our Lord was touched no doubt by the affliction of these men and their urgent cry, and this was a miracle of beneficence, but He takes no pains now to withdraw the act from public view, He does not call them "aside from the multitude[1]," and heal them in private as He had done on His way back from the coasts of Tyre and Sidon some months before. This miracle stirred the hearts of many beholders, and this emotion of theirs may have played no small part in the great drama to which this journey was the prelude; for the company that came with our Lord from Galilee formed the staple of that great concourse which shouted

"Blessed *is* the kingdom that cometh, *the kingdom* of our father David : Hosanna in the highest[2],"

and this shout of the people not only roused in the priests that terror which "sits hard by hate," but gave them the very thing they wanted—grounds for calling upon Pilate to prove himself Cæsar's friend.

It is not likely that any of our Lord's doings were without an ordered purpose, and that this cessa-

---

[1] Mark vii. 33. See p. 333.
[2] Mark xi. 10.

tion of Signs certainly was not so, is apparent from our Lord's words spoken probably soon after the performance of the first of those miracles mentioned above. The words are these.

"And when the multitudes were gathering together unto him, he began to say, This generation is an evil generation: it seeketh after a sign; and there shall no sign be given to it but the sign of Jonah[1]."

On this text as given by St Matthew I have already commented; it is only the coincidence of the time when it was spoken with the gradual withdrawal of visible Signs that I have to notice now. Our Lord looks to sowing the germs of spiritual Faith. This would not grow up either from the curiosity of those who sought for Signs, or the stupefaction of those who gazed in wonderment. Henceforth it is "the word of eternal life" which lays hold of men. The questions asked in the deepest earnest turn now upon this[2]. The revelation of it did not come by express statements or descriptions, but rather it grew up in men through their consorting with Christ. They could not believe that He would perish, and He told them that because He lived they should live also[3]. Christ, speaking just before the end, rests His expectation of bringing about the knowledge of God, not on His works but on His Personality. His reply to the words "Shew us the Father," is

[1] Luke xi. 29. See p. 104. [2] Luke xiii. 23; xviii. 19.
[3] John xiv. 19.

not, Have I not done mighty works before your eyes? but, "Have I been so long time with you and dost thou not know me, Philip?"

I now pass to the raising of Lazarus. It is not within my scope to discuss the nature of the miracle, I have to do with it only in its relation to that Law of the working of Signs, which is suggested in the Temptation of the Pinnacle of the Temple. No Sign is given to men whose belief is in the formative stage, in order to force it on; but to those whose belief is already assured a conclusive miracle may be shown, because it does not now constrain judgment but only confirms it. If the miracle had been at once published wherever the gospel was preached, and if it had been supported by testimony which no one could dispute, this would have been an exception to the rule so often marked in our Lord's conduct. This miracle is in its nature appalling and conclusive, and it could not be attributed to Beelzebub; but a loop-hole in point of evidence is left for those indisposed to believe, for it rests on the unsupported testimony of St John. The raising of Lazarus was not, we may conclude, recorded in the Apostolic memoir which some suppose to have been the basis of the Synoptic Gospels. I have said in the last chapter that I think it possible that the entire body of Apostles were not continuously about the person of our Lord during the six months between the Feast of Tabernacles and the last journey. When Thomas said, speaking of the proposed visit to Jerusalem at the time of Lazarus' death, "Let us also go that we may die with Him[1]," I can hardly suppose that Peter can have been by and have held his peace. Supposing then that the writers of this memoir, among whom Peter must have held a foremost place, confined themselves as much as possible to what they knew from *personal knowledge*, they would have abstained from introducing a matter so wondrous as that of the raising of Lazarus, which they had not witnessed themselves. In whatever way this silence is to be explained, the silence itself accords with the above-noted Law.

Passing on to the events of the Passion week, we may be struck by the absence of all public and notable Signs at a time when, if ever, they seemed of vital importance for the cause. A signal miracle wrought before the crowd in the Temple would have rallied the people to the side of our Lord in such numbers and with such vehement support, that none of His foes would have dared to lift a hand. For even if the priesthood should have persisted in persuading themselves that our Lord's power did not come from God, yet, they would not have dared to move, if the popular feeling had been strong, lest they should provoke a riot and the Roman authorities should intervene.

But the people were themselves disappointed

[1] John xi. 16, see p. 372.

by our Lord's working no Sign or Wonder, during these last days of teaching in the Temple. Some looked for the restoration of Israel, and were impatient at the continued delay, while the lower part of the populace had set their hearts on seeing a prodigy, and none came. It may be true that, among the crowd who had shouted "Hosanna," the lead had been taken by the caravan of pilgrims from Galilee, but still, at the time of the triumphal entry, the feeling of the people of Jerusalem went the same way; this had cooled down to indifference when our Lord left the Temple for the last time; and disappointment had turned into contemptuous chagrin when our Lord, after yielding passively to the Temple guard, stood before Pilate apparently as powerless as they would have been themselves.

To Christians of to-day it seems of the essence of Christ's sacrifice that He should have submitted of His own free will to indignity and torment, when, by raising a finger or uttering a word, He might have shivered the power both of the priesthood and of Rome. His behaviour in this point is therefore exactly what we expect. But this truth, inconceivable for the people, had hardly dawned as yet on the Apostles' minds. The multitude would be told and would, in general, believe that the miracles of Jesus, which all had heard of and some had seen, must have been unreal or the work of Beelzebub; while those who had leaned towards

Him would conclude that, if He had ever been endowed with Divine power, it had left Him now, or He would certainly have used it for defence.

But the Apostles were not left without fresh assurance, given to them alone. Although of Signs, notable and public, during this period there were none, still two Signs of a special character there were, which exactly met the requirements of the case; they created no stir, they were not observed by the people, but they served to keep alive in the Apostles' hearts the certainty that God was with their Master still. One was the withering of the fig-tree, the other the foretelling that Peter would deny his Lord; of the first of these miracles I have spoken fully before[1].

This latter miracle is connected with our Lord's strange faculty of seeing what was passing in men's hearts, and of tracing what the outcome of it would be. When men felt that Christ knew their hearts, they were getting near the idea of His spiritual presence with them; so that all this leads up to the crowning point of Christ's education, the rendering the Apostles sensitive to every breath of the Spirit, capable, amid a din of inward voices calling them diverse ways, of discerning with sure ear the tones of God.

This miracle and this event contain a lesson on forgiven error, intended for all time. Here, as before observed, we have an instance of Christ's way of

---
[1] pp. 95, 96, 97.

ensuring that what He desired to preserve should be handed down. This event is stamped with life-like particulars which ensure its currency and its becoming familiar in the mouths of men.

The words "the cock shall not crow twice" give to the incident a reality which vitalises the story and preserves it for ever. Contrast the tale such as we have it, with what it would have been if our Lord had only said, "You will deny me before I die."

As to the miracle itself a few words must be said. It brings out the identity of the idiosyncrasy of St Peter, who is given up to the impulse of the moment.

The Peter who denied and then wept bitterly, is the same man, psychologically, as he who begged his Master to call him to come upon the sea, and whose faith failed. This liability to panic clung to him; years after, we find him at Antioch going along with Paul in freeing the converts from Jewish obligations; but, as soon as "certain came from James[1]," he was alarmed at his temerity and separated himself, "fearing them that were of the circumcision." (See also pp. 423, 424.) Neither by our Lord or any of the brethren is this failing of Peter's ever touched upon again.

This is exactly a case of what was noted at page 421. Christ washes from off Peter's feet the soil contracted on the way, and he becomes clean

[1] Galatians ii. 11—14.

every whit. The evil was only skin deep and had not tainted the blood. For this denial was, I am sure, not due to any base fear. Peter had drawn and struck for his Master, and was naturally bewildered at finding that his Master would neither suffer His disciples to fight nor call the legions of angels to His help. In their utter confusion of mind the Apostles fled, but Peter and John followed a little way off. This they would not have done if they had been in actual terror of being punished themselves. But there was no real ground for any such fear; no attempt is made to apprehend any follower of our Lord. To have tried to do so would have increased that danger of riot, which the rulers shunned. What Peter *did* fear was forcible separation from Christ. He was afraid that, if proved to be a follower of Jesus, he would be turned out of the judgment hall of Caiaphas. He would have said or done almost anything to avoid that. It was, as we have seen, part of his nature to be mastered by the feeling that was uppermost. He clung to his Master's side with the instinctive fidelity of a Highland henchman to his chief. Thrice he might have gone away, but this he will on no account do. After being noticed he on each occasion moves away and returns, only shifting his position; he goes into the vestibule, and finally tries to mix with the crowd round the fire; whence, out of the half-darkness which saved him from recognition, he could still see his Master.

But "his speech bewrayeth" him; he is noticed again as he had been before, and for the third time he denies. Whereupon the cock crows, and turning towards the arcade at the end of the court where the trial was going on, he meets our Lord's eyes fixed upon him. Then, for the first time, it strikes him that he has done wrong. It never occurred to Peter that in saying "I know not the man," he was being disloyal to the Master he loved. He wanted to keep sight of his Master, and did not feel bound to speak the truth to a foe. No words are needed to shew him his fault. One look of our Lord settles the matter; it awakens the higher sense of truth, which had gone to sleep when the old instinct of the Oriental peasant, the habit of confronting authority with a flat denial, became dominant in Peter's breast. When the company of Apostles was scattered on their Master's apprehension, the strength they had drawn from association with Jesus vanished at once; and then Peter dropped from the moral level of a disciple of Christ into the Galilean fisherman he had been before. He had been used to regard officials of Herod, or any ruling power, as his natural enemies, to whom he was not bound to speak the truth, and to this, his old self, he came back now.

But though Peter's heart may have acquitted him of cowardly forsaking his Master,—though he knew that he would, if need were, have gone with him to prison and to death,—yet he felt that this denial was, in words—though only in words—a falling away from perfect loyalty; it made clear to him, as it may have been meant to do, the weakness of his character in the way of yielding to impulse, and awakened floods of self reproach. He went out and wept bitterly; but no trace appears afterwards of a loss of self respect, or of his feeling it possible that he could be in disgrace with his Master; in fact his part in his Master becomes all the greater, owing to his having needed that He should wash his feet.

These two miracles of instruction then, the prediction of Peter's denials and the withering of the fig tree, were an assurance to the disciples that our Lord still retained His superhuman power, and that whether He should drink of the cup or put it away, up to the last, rested entirely with Him. These powers of His could not be displayed to the people without hindrance to the accomplishment of that Baptism with which He "had to be baptised;" even the working of miracles of healing might so have moved the crowd that they would have risen in His defence[1]. The Apostles, however, were to be rendered sure that these powers remained what they had ever been and that they were, for them, in operation still; so that they might never doubt but that, amid all the apparent defeat, it was with the voluntary sufferer on the Cross that the real Victory—the moral Victory lay.

[1] See Preface.

CHAPTER XIII.

THE LESSONS OF THE RESURRECTION.

WHEN contemplating the Passion and the Resurrection of Christ, we have little attention to spare for the subordinate personages in the scene. The effects of these manifestations, in working changes in the hearts and minds of the witnesses, are put out of sight by the brilliancy and intrinsic grandeur of the manifestations themselves, and by the momentous character of their direct consequences, universally affecting mankind. But the transformation in temper, in views, and in habits of mind which converted the Apostles of the Gospels into the Apostles of the Acts—a transformation to me otherwise inexplicable—was consummated and clenched by the hours of hard trial and bitter anguish of that Sabbath day, when there was nothing to be done but to mourn and to wonder; as well as by the burst of gladness when the Risen Lord appeared to the eleven. Throughout all the Post-Resurrection interval, during which the Apostles felt that He was close by and might at any time appear—indeed that any stranger accosting them might turn out to be He—the changes which had been wrought were taking lasting hold.

The data for the history of that Passover season of A.D. 30 must have been furnished by the Apostles, yet we find in it scarcely any mention of themselves; all personal thought was driven from their minds; the narrators, like ourselves, had eyes for the Saviour alone.

From the hour of cockcrow on the Thursday night to the time when it "began to dawn toward the first day of the week" all that we hear of the Apostles, and that comes out incidentally, is that John stood at the foot of the Cross. There is not a word to explain their flight at Gethsemane, they do not tell us, that they stood in the crowd or followed to Golgotha; neither have we, what for my purpose would be invaluable, any word of how they passed that Sabbath day of enforced inaction, which—in accordance with our Lord's way of letting intervals of quiet alternate with times of stress and strain—followed on the violent perturbation and intense dismay of the Crucifixion.

The Apostles could not be perfected for the part that awaited them, unless they encountered some great desolation of soul. Acute suffering, which searches the innermost nature, works after the law which has become so trite to my readers, it gives to those who have. There are some who under its pangs learn that they possess a kind of strength of which they did not know, and find that when some, seemingly more robust, break down in trouble, resource and tenacity are still left in them. This kind of strength the Apostles possessed; they stood the test of being apparently forsaken and were the better for it. Each individual after the trial felt surer that he could rely on himself than he had been before, and each then knew for certain that he could rely on the rest.

They might, as soon as the Sabbath was over, have taken their northward journey, going every man to his own; and, as they did not feel safe where they were—for they had to close their doors for fear of the Jews—and must have been grievously bewildered, this is what some out of the eleven at any rate might have been expected to do. It is the steadfastness of *the whole number* that is so surprising.

The trial to which the Apostles were subjected, during those six and thirty hours, was excessively severe. They were left as sheep without a shepherd, with no rallying point, no organised rule; and not only were they in the deepest anguish, owing to their personal affection for their Master, but the lodestar of their lives, the hope of the Restoration of the Kingdom to Israel, seemed suddenly and totally withdrawn.

The Jewish notion of a Messiah, who would

inaugurate a golden age of national glory and material enjoyment, was so engrained in the Israelite nature that only facts could drive it out. Our Lord never argues against it; if He beheld, in the course of coming events, a fact approaching, which would do more to dispel error than all the arguments in the world, this would explain His silence on these points. The awakening would not be without dangers. It is a perilous moment for a man, when the one dream, the one exalted hope, that has lifted him above selfish considerations is rudely dispelled; and God, whom he had thought to serve, seems to disregard him altogether.

Then self and the world say, "We told you so; now give yourself to us? Our votaries will be found to have taken the right road after all." Of all the temptations that assailed the Apostles this was perhaps the direst; but their loyalty to their Master, born of nearly two years' daily fellowship, held fast. Even if He *were* gone they could be true to His memory still, and that was something left.

One lesson, which the Apostles could hardly help learning, would arise, in this way, out of the discomfiture of their hopes. They might ask themselves, on what this confident expectation of theirs, of a Messianic kingdom, rested by way of grounds. They would have to own that Christ had never spoken of it, but, indeed, had often given hints of what had really come to pass—hints which they had always quickly brushed aside. They had believed in this material Kingdom because everybody around them had done so. They had not formed any notion about it of their own selves; no movement of their own minds had gone towards forming the belief. They had imbibed it and that was all. Hence finding themselves deceived by trusting to a popular belief, there may have arisen in them a healthy mistrust of positiveness about the ways of God. Again, their disappointment might put them in a better direction for finding their way. "Some hope," they might say, "assuredly Christ did hold out to us," and the search after this hope might lead them to recollect that latterly they had heard little from Him of the Kingdom, and much of the future Life; He had told them that because He lived they should live also; and the conception of a Kingdom, not of this world, might arise in their minds, and take the place of that of the expected Supremacy of Israel, which was dissolving out of sight.

Another effect of their affliction was that it drew them closer together. When a family, is orphaned by a heavy blow, what they first feel may be helplessness, but soon follows the feeling that they must cling together and be true to one another, and each in his degree supply the help that is lost. Soon the elder brothers, if there is good in them, learn what duty is, and this new responsibility draws capacity out. Now the

Apostles stood in the position of elder brethren to all the family of Christ's disciples.

It is a striking feature of the change worked in the Apostles, that, after the Resurrection, all thoughts of self disappeared. The Apostles, as the History shews us, had been originally no less prone to wrangle as to "which should be greatest" than the average of men. We find in the Gospel the self-regard that we might naturally expect: sometimes it is of a healthy sort, as when Peter says, "We have left all and followed thee;" and sometimes it is unhealthy, like that soreness on points of precedence, which we mark even just before the Last Supper; but in the Acts we find among the Apostles no trace of self-regard at all. The history in our hands will account for this change satisfactorily enough; for these men were called to a Work, so transcending all human interests, so absolute, that. it would leave no room for any personal thought in their souls. They were to be fellow-workers with the living God. What could be the worth of the difference between this office or dignity in God's service and that, compared with being counted worthy to take a conscious part in God's service at all? Some powerful impression must have been employed to bring about such a moral change as this; and what could better account for such an impression, than to have witnessed Christ upon the Cross? How could they, the servants, cavil about social consideration or dignity, when their

Master had spurned all dignity and cast away all that common men hold dear, and that too, when by speaking a word, all that earth could bestow might have been His. Lastly, the sense that Christ was present with them and knew their hearts, was made so real and effectual by the Post-Resurrection intercourse, that it afterwards dominated their lives. This feeling would still the disposition to rivalry, if any such lingered in their hearts; for, being convinced that their Master knew what went on in them, they would know that He grieved over anything that was wrong, as He had done when He was by their side; and they would shrink from causing Him pain.

The story of the Apostles is unique in History in another way. No one of them endeavoured to draw a following about himself, or to claim succession to the Master's place. Little differences of view and little disagreements as to the course to be followed now and then there were; if, indeed, our records did not speak of such we should suspect that something was kept back. We have cases enough of causes passed on to a company of successors from the dying leaders' hands, but in no instance, that I recollect, have these successors remained united as the Apostles did (p. 414). Monarchs have sometimes left empires in trust to their generals, whose quarrels have finally torn them to bits. Philosophers have left their systems or their discoveries to their favourite pupils, who, taking hold of them by different ends, have set up new philosophies of their own. Kingly dynasties and political parties have bequeathed causes claiming to be sanctioned by Divine right, or to embody immutable principles, and the inheritors have so fallen out over points of policy, that the broad principle, broken up into branching channels, has lost its momentum and disappeared in the sands.

I pass on to the lessons which our History of the Resurrection conveys. The different narratives relate our Lord's appearances, with differing circumstances of persons and place. Herein I find that loophole for disbelief which may be discovered in every miraculous manifestation of our Lord. If the fact of our Lord's Resurrection had been so attested that no sane person could doubt of the fact; if He had appeared in public, and appalled Pilate on his judgment seat or Herod on his throne, then—strange as it may appear—by the very fact of the historical certainty being thus established, the moral significance of the Resurrection would be impaired, for the acceptance of it would be independent of that which I have so often said is essential to religious belief, the concurrence of the free human will.

Although, as to the occasions and circumstances of the appearances, we find in the different accounts rather more than their customary diversity; yet in the *nature* of the appearances the agreement is so singular, and the conception

THE LESSONS OF THE RESURRECTION. 445

involved is so unexampled, that it is impossible for different writers to have lighted at the same time on the idea, and I can find no explanation for the phenomena, except by supposing that the picture was taken from life. The appearances themselves, as we should expect from their nature, leave on the mental retina an impression indelible and distinct; but the traditions about *when* and *how* they occurred, undergo variation as they pass from mouth to mouth.

The character of our Lord's appearances, in all the Gospels, is alike. Most commonly He is not recognised at first, and does not appear in His own form, when other than disciples are by; only to those, who had already mastered the words of eternal life, was it given to see Him Risen from the dead. He comes men know not how, when they are sitting with fastened doors He appears in the midst; He goes they know not where, and the disciples who beforetime were so full of curiosity, do not venture to ask whither He goes or where He abides. But, what bears most of all on my subject, is the mode in which our Lord assuages that dread of a disembodied spirit, which would have paralysed the Apostles' minds. This terror, reasonable or not, certainly existed, and Christ always deals with the fact He finds.

There were lessons still to be taught and for the right learning of them it was needful that the old confidence between Master and learners should still subsist. Could the disciples have listened to the Lord, as their old Master, receiving his direction to go back to Jerusalem and tarry there till they were "endued with power;"—could they have rested gladly on the assurance that He would appear and help them in any need that came, if they had regarded Him as a spectre belonging to another world?

In order to calm their instinctive terror of a spirit, and be again in some degree what He had been on the Lake shore of Galilee, it was necessary for our Lord to assure the Apostles that He had a body even as they. The deep doctrinal significance of this lies beyond the limited purpose of my book, but the point which is within my range—the effect on the Apostles themselves of the conviction of our Lord's existence in the body—is important and full of instruction. It was essential that confidence should be restored, and the course actually adopted did restore it in a wonderful way. Men thought that a spirit might be seen and heard but only a body could be *felt*. Our Lord therefore at once appeals to touch—He eats and drinks before them. He tells them that He has flesh and bones. He suffers them to "handle Him and see." To this corporal presence as a crowning fact St John recurs, saying "That which we beheld and our hands handled[1];" and St Peter says

"Him God raised up the third day, and gave him to be made manifest, not to all the people, but unto witnesses that were chosen before of God, *even* to us, who did eat and drink with him after he rose from the dead[1]."

Our Lord would not Himself establish a visible Church. I have amply set out, p. 236, the difficulties that would have ensued if He had so done; but it was essential that the Apostles should receive some indication—though only so much as was essential to the lines upon which they were to build; and this being a matter of human cognisance was to be given by Christ in His human guise. A phantom, or a voice from Heaven, would have seemed an agency of a different order from the intervention of the Son of Man.

Here I will stop for a moment, to consider these narratives of the Resurrection under a purely literary point of view. These accounts present us with the same general aspect of the risen Lord, and they remain true to the primary conception in unnoticeable points of detail such as no one would have introduced out of purposed imitation. Inasmuch as we cannot suppose that the same wondrous creation of fancy presented itself to different writers at the same time, we are driven to suppose, either that the accounts relate actual facts, as Christians generally believe; or else that they were imagined by one person who disseminated the story. But who this writer can have been

[1] Acts x. 40, 41.

is not only a mystery but a mystery embodying almost a miracle, for here we have a genius compared with whom—in point of dealing naturally with the supernatural—Shakespeare is thrown into the shade; and further this genius, we must suppose, never invented or wrote anything else in that particular line in which he so wondrously surpassed the rest of mankind. The Orientals delighted in tales. Did they suffer the greatest imaginative genius of the world to live and die unknown?

There was nothing in Literature to furnish a hint for the portraiture of the risen Lord; the idea of the Resurrection body must have been due to one man's imagination and have been presented with extraordinary literary skill at a time when imaginative narration was wholly unknown. The writers of the age in which the Gospels appeared could set down events and record colloquies, and depict living personalities with truth and force; but they were no more capable of conceiving a character, of making him act, and putting into his mouth words which should seem to be his own; or of imagining a new supernatural phenomenon, and keeping their account always true to itself; than they were of conceiving the vibrations of an elastic medium. That this phenomenon also, exactly met the requirements of a most singular condition of things adds greatly to the wonder, but in another way.

If the Christian records had been thrown aside and forgotten, while the world, passing on its way reached a mental culture such as we now possess and then, in some exploration, the Gospels had been brought to light: would they not have been regarded by the critics of that day as wholly anomalous, and as refusing to fit in with any theory of the growth and progress of the literary faculty in mankind? The surprise caused by the discovery would have been like that of excavators at Mycenae, if they had found a watch in the treasury of Agamemnon. This aspect of the matter belongs to the realm of critical literature rather than to mine, and I only note it for a hint. The literary aspect of the History of the Resurrection has yet to be written; it would be curious to see it treated from the point of view of one, who, shut out from a knowledge of the religious history of mankind, lighted on it as a mere literary treasure.

There is one point on which I cannot forbear to touch. Our Lord never mentions His persecutors, He never touches on the past. The apparition of a legend usually either reveals a burning secret, or embodies resentment for the past; frequently it personifies hatred or foretells destruction, and its fateful whispers make the blood of enemies run cold. But in all the utterances of the Risen Lord not a word is said of the coming destruction of Jerusalem, not a syllable is breathed of the treason of Judas, or of the persistent malice of the scribes. There is an ineffable grandeur—so unconscious that we may fail to mark it—in the utter oblivion that is passed on the foes who had beset the path of the Son of Man. He no more resents the ills that men had wrought Him on His way through life, than the traveller, who has reached his home, resents the insect plague of the desert or the tempests he has met with at sea. The past is lost to sight, and our Lord displays but one thought and one interest, and that is for the disciples and their work. He has now done with the rest of the world and He belongs wholly to them. He is lifted above all human contention into that serene atmosphere, which we feel ourselves to be breathing, when, reading the story, we seem to find ourselves in the presence of the Risen Lord.

I will now quote St Paul's account of the chief occasions when our Lord appeared; but I can only discuss one or two points of the History.

"And that he appeared to Cephas; then to the twelve; then he appeared to above five hundred brethren at once, of whom the greater part remain until now, but some are fallen asleep; then he appeared to James; then to all the apostles; and last of all, as unto one born out of due time, he appeared to me also[1]."

I take the view, that within a few days of the

[1] 1 Cor. xv. 5, 6, 7, 8.

Resurrection, the Apostles, by our Lord's command, returned to Galilee. If the Resurrection had been immediately followed by a time of agitation—one of persecution for instance—so that the Apostles could not have let their minds dwell on what had happened, the lessons of that period would have been soon effaced; but our Lord, as we have seen, is ever careful to provide seasonable opportunity for reflection, and it was not likely that He would suffer it to be wanting now.

The Apostles in Galilee, engaging again in their old callings, would have leisure to review, not only the last few days, but the whole of the two eventful years since they had been called from their work to follow Christ. It was probably here in Galilee that the Apostles received a command to return to Jerusalem; for we cannot account for the presence there of all the eleven, at the time of the Ascension, together with the mother and brethren of our Lord, except by special direction of our Lord. They would not, without some injunction, have remained at Jerusalem after the Resurrection[1], neither would they have gone up thither for Pentecost, having been so lately at the Passover. Whether the appearance to the "five hundred brethren at once[2]" be, as I think it was, identical with that on the mountain in Galilee recorded in St Matthew's Gospel, c. xxviii., v. 16, is a matter of discussion.

[1] See Chronol. Append., May A.D. 30.   [2] 1 Cor. xv. 6.

But where else, except in Galilee could five hundred disciples have been got together? It could not have been at Jerusalem, at the Ascension, because the brethren there only numbered one hundred and twenty souls[1]. St Matthew, it is true, only speaks of the eleven disciples as going "into Galilee unto the mountain," but others must have been present because we are told that "some doubted," and the eleven would not have doubted. This admission shews that when the writer drew up his account, he felt no eagerness to strengthen the evidence for the Resurrection; and that He had no fear of its being disbelieved by those for whom he wrote. The eagerness that St Matthew does shew is to find instances of the fulfilment of Scripture, not to support his statements of fact. It seems to me likely, that, in Galilee, among His earliest followers, our Lord should have appeared more publicly than He did elsewhere; here only could He find a *body* of believers who should serve as witnesses, and, inasmuch as among these five hundred, there must have been men in different states of belief, it falls in with our Lord's way, so often noted, that He should appear in a form, not indisputably recognisable at once and by all, but with His aspect so changed, by some glorification perhaps, that those who were half-hearted in their belief might remain in doubt or disbelief if they chose; while the faithful and

[1] Acts i. 15.

THE LESSONS OF THE RESURRECTION. 453

loving would be in no uncertainty about their Master's lineaments and voice.

The appearance "to James" which is related by St Paul alone, is important, and calls for special notice.

There are three persons called "James" in the sacred books, and there may be a question which of these it is of whom St Paul speaks. I am of opinion that it is James the brother of our Lord. The Corinthians, to whom St Paul is writing, would hardly know of any other; he was the head of the church at Jerusalem and when Paul speaks of "James" simply, as in Galatians ii. 9, 12, he means always the brother of the Lord. "James, the son of Zebedee," Acts xii. 2, is designated "the brother of John" for distinction's sake, and of James the son of Alphaeus we never hear. Every disciple however in the Church at Corinth had heard of James, the "pillar" of the Church at Jerusalem[1].

Nothing is heard of our Lord's brethren during the week of the Passion; possibly, they were not in Jerusalem, but, from the Acts, as has been just said, we find that they were present there at the time of the Ascension.

"These all with one accord continued steadfastly in

[1] I would point out that in the passage from 1 Cor. xv. quoted p. 450, we have "then to the *Twelve*," and later, "then to *all the Apostles*." May not St Paul have meant the latter term to be a wider one than the former, and, possibly, to include James?

prayer, with the women, and Mary the mother of Jesus, and with his brethren." Acts i. 14.

This adhesion of the brethren falls in with the supposition that our Lord appeared to His brother James after the Resurrection in Galilee. It was natural that James and the younger brethren should have found difficulty in comprehending that their elder brother, who had played among them as a child was of a nature essentially different from their own; and that this exceptional hindrance to belief should be counterpoised by an exceptional, but not absolutely decisive, revelation is what we might expect. It is not inconsistent with our Lord's treatment of doubt; for the difficulty arose out of circumstances and not from adverse will. Of James, our Lord may have felt sure; and Joses and Jude and Simon[1], no one of whom could have been much over thirty years of age, while one or two of them must have been quite young men, may have been brought to full discipleship by what they heard from James.

From what St Paul says, "Am I not an Apostle? Have I not seen Jesus our Lord[2]?" it seems likely that to have beheld the Risen Lord was held to be a condition of the status of an Apostle. St Paul must have meant " seen the *Risen* Jesus," for to have cast eyes on the bodily presence of Jesus, as He journeyed and taught, would have been a distinction shared with thousands.

[1] Mark vi. 3. [2] 1 Cor. ix. 1.

Without some recognition of James by our Lord, such as is related by St Paul, it is hard to account for his being placed at the head of the Church. We hear of no election or form of appointment, but we find him in this position about ten years after this time. It would have been at variance with our Lord's repeated injunctions to the Apostles not to seek authority one over the other, if the primacy had been made a matter of contest[1].

Organisation and graduation of authority grew up in the Church, not after any plan settled and declared, but as the need of it arose. It agreed in this respect with the history of those human institutions that have proved the most enduring. In this, as in all matters, our Lord, wherever it was possible, left His followers free; not but what, when these same followers turned to their Master and prayed for guidance, as in the election of Matthias, they found in their hearts an answer positive and plain.

St Peter, in the earliest days of the Church, stands forth as the foremost personage; but this influence rests on personal qualities and not on any formal appointment. He, as I have said (pp. 248, 344), was the man of action, the person who in every juncture addressed himself at once to the question,

[1] "Clement of Alexandria says that Peter, James and John after our Lord's ascension were not ambitious of dignity, honoured though they had been by the preference of their Master, but chose James the Just as Bishop of Jerusalem." Dr Salmon, "Introduction to the New Testament," p. 565.

"What is to be done?" It was Peter, who took immediate steps to fill up the vacancy which the apostacy of Judas had left. He was the speaker on the day of Pentecost, and he it was who in the case of Ananias sternly repressed falsehood unto God. But the impetuosity of Peter, and his disposition to give himself up completely to the impression of the moment, though it served well to carry forward a great movement at its outset, may have made him ill adapted for the ruler of an infant Church, in which discordant elements had to be welded into one; while the well-poised judgment of James the Just[1] and his practical sense fitted him particularly for this kind of rule. That this admirable selection, this putting of each in his right place, should have come about without dispute; and that those who had "borne the burden and heat of the day" should have admitted to equality—or something more—in outward dignity, one who was "of the eleventh hour," bears out what I have said of the phenomenal subordination of self displayed by the Apostles. It shews that outward dignity and authority—that which I have taken to be the "false mammon" of the parable —was as nothing in their eyes compared to the true riches, the priceless feeling that their work great or small, as men might count it, was all done for God and all accepted by God.

[1] "This James whom the ancients...surnamed the Just." Eusebius, *Eccl. Hist.* 6, ii. c. 1.

The Ascension.

What was said of the Resurrection we may say of the Ascension too. The changes it brought about in the position and characters of those few "men of Galilee" who stood "gazing up into heaven," seem small matters compared with the immensity of its import for the Human Race. But, that our Lord did not leave out of sight the effect on the Apostles of the change in their condition which His departure would cause, is clear from words spoken to the Twelve, which are preserved to us by St John, and on which there is something to say.

"Nevertheless I tell you the truth; It is expedient for you that I go away: for if I go not away, the Comforter will not come unto you; but if I go, I will send him unto you[1]."

This saying the Apostles may have found hard to comprehend; for it must have seemed to them impossible that it could ever be for their good for their Master to leave them; and, why the Comforter should not come, while they all continued together, would by no means be clear to their minds. Neither here nor elsewhere does our Lord explain to the Apostles either the reason of His regimen or the way in which it was to work. He

[1] John xvi. 7, 8.

tells them simply the fact, without a word as to *how* or *why*. He never leads them to examine into the *modus operandi* of His treatment, He would have awakened—what He carefully avoids—self-consciousness, if He had so done. That they could not learn, at the same time, from Him in the body and also from the Comforter in their own souls, arose, not from any "determinate counsel of God," but because the mind cannot perform two operations at once. It rested on the positive psychological fact that we cannot walk by Sight and by Faith at the same time; that we cannot turn one ear to an earthly monitor, and keep the other open to the whispers of a spiritual guide. The posture of our minds when we are hanging on the lips of a living Master, is different from that in which we set ourselves to listen for the Comforting Voice from within. The Apostles would not have learned to hearken to the promptings of the Spirit so long as they could turn to Christ by their side; and it was therefore "expedient for them" that Christ should go away. They would not otherwise have reached full communion with the Spirit on high.

Instances in the Acts shew us in what way the Spirit acted in the hearts of believers. Sometimes, when human judgment and inclination seemed to agree, an unaccountable inward reluctance to follow their dictates was nevertheless felt—a repugnance, not resting on a new argument, but simply saying

"No." When men experienced such feelings, some might overbear them by will; but Paul and Silas recognised in them the voice of the Spirit. For we hear that they "went through the region of Phrygia and Galatia, having been forbidden of the Holy Ghost to speak the word in Asia; and when they were come over against Mysia, they assayed to go into Bithynia; and the Spirit of Jesus suffered them not[1]."

Again Christ's Church was to be everlasting and universal, and this it could only become by changing outward and visible for inward spiritual rule. So long as the Lord was in bodily presence among them, the disciples naturally looked only to Him. Where He was, there and there only to their minds was His Kingdom and His Church. For His sway to become universal it was essential that He should go away, for it is only Spiritual influence that can be everywhere at once. The fire had to be set alight at a particular spot and at a particular time, but it was then to be left to spread over the earth and to go on burning seemingly all of itself.

All through the Gospel we mark how men cling to the Letter, and how Christ, with tender hand extricates the Spirit from it and tells His hearers, that it is this which gives the Letter its worth. A law such as that of Moses has its place

[1] Acts xvi. 6—8.

in the Schooling of a race at a certain epoch of national life; but a code or a creed that cannot be expanded must at last be outgrown. If however a Divine and living Spirit be enshrined in a Church, it may direct its development, and transform the outward tenement as inward need requires.

Christ came to set men spiritually free; but, strange to say, men are slow to take this freedom up. Among some African races, a man set free from a master at once goes and sells himself to another, he cannot be troubled with managing for himself. This is like the way in which men liberated from one absolute and infallible authority have so often handed themselves over to another. They must have something or somebody to take their beliefs and consciences in charge. Fancying that they are to be saved by holding proper opinions—for by belief they often mean no more than taking up and maintaining opinion—they come, asking, "What are we to believe?" just as the Scribe asked, "What am I to do?" Christ's answer to him practically was, that he possessed already grounds enough to frame for himself a rule of conduct such as he required. Might He not answer the others nearly in the same strain?

Belief, in Christ's sense of the word, is not the acceptance of a theory, it is something that will actuate the man's whole being, and which requires the concurrence of an emancipated will. Now this emancipation brings with it a responsibility—a call to mental effort—which a large proportion of mankind steadfastly abhor.

Thus the Israelitish party in St Paul's time and after, hugged the chains of the Jewish Law; then, after turbulent ages of fierce doctrinal dissension, when combative spirits found in polemics the strife which their temperaments required, the Churches of Greece and of Rome took charge of the consciences of men. A revolt at length took place against the external authority of the Church, but there was no more religious freedom under the new regimes than under the old. Confessions of Faith came into vogue, and men tried to tie down after ages to the ways in which the controversialists of the sixteenth century had, with much giving and taking, agreed to regard the insoluble problems of existence. The Bible was now often held up, not to reveal God's will and ways, but to yield texts for weapons in disputes. Christ's care to guard against a bondage unto written matter is apparent in the whole form of His teaching; and especially in His leaving no writings of His own, and no directly accredited record of His life; but the craving of men after an unerring touchstone of truth has wrapped them again in bonds like those from which Christ would have set them free; and the Canonical books have been invested with a character of literal inspiration, not unlike what would have attached to writings of our Lord Himself.

The verses of John, Chap. xvi. 9, 10 which

follow that of which I have been speaking, while leading us to the profoundest Theology, bear on the change from a visible teacher to a spiritual one, and so far they come within my scope. I have only to do with them so far as they illustrate this change. The reason given for the intervention of the Spirit is, that Christ, in the body, will no longer bring home to the world the sense of sin and of righteousness and of judgement.

"And he, when he is come, will convict the world in respect of sin, and of righteousness, and of judgement: of sin, because they believe not on me; of righteousness, because I go to the Father, and ye behold me no more; of judgement, because the prince of this world has been judged." John xvi. 8—11.

I should place the emphasis on the pronouns— He and I. The Spirit is to take the place of the departed Lord. So long as Christ was in the world He Himself brought home to the men who believed on Him the sense of sin; He presented the ideal of righteousness, and He enforced the conviction that moral evil brought doom and destruction upon men. Henceforth the witness to all this would no longer be Christ in the body, whose contact with the world was necessarily limited to one point, but the Holy Spirit, which could speak to the hearts of all mankind at once. It would lead me too far from my province if I enlarged on the topic of *Judgment*; and I turn to another matter.

It may be asked, Why did this Post-Resurrection state last as long as it did and not longer? God's *reasons* we leave aside, but this we can say, Christ never hurries forward processes in the Apostles' mind, and these processes, in this case, needed all the time allowed; also, since a state of watchfulness involves a nerve-strain, it agrees with Christ's carefulness for the body that this condition should not last too long. The *durations* of the different stages of our Lord's teaching—that while He was in the flesh, and that while He wore the body of the Resurrection—seem to me just as wisely ordered for the end in view, as are the other circumstances of the case.

Christ's way of teaching is the very opposite of that which would make the learner a mere reflection of his Master. In the Mission to the cities and in the ministrations of their every-day life, Christ had left the Apostles to act very much for themselves, He had kept their self-helpfulness alive in various ways; we find them bold to question, and not slow to murmur, and both questions and murmurs are readily tolerated by our Lord. But, even with all these precautions, if they had remained too long in attendance on Him, we can imagine that they would have got confirmed in the habit of looking constantly to their Master and of, at once, carrying to Him every difficulty without considering it themselves, and they would thus have lost capacity both to think and to act. They might also have fallen into habits of mind which, serviceable so long as they were subordinates, would stand in their way when they had to take the lead. They might have become faithful to execute, but helpless to plan. When subordinates, or young people, are too long deprived of opportunity for judging and acting for themselves, their minds are apt to become passive and purely receptive; they become slow to start a notion or suggest an expedient; ideas of theirs, they fancy, are not wanted, and so they soon cease to have ideas at all.

Our Lord guarded against this by restricting the period of the Apostles' pupilage. As soon as the ground plan of their characters was marked out, He left them to rear the superstructure for themselves. He was so tender in preserving every line of individuality that He would not shackle freedom of growth in His disciples, even by prolonging His own companionship and instruction beyond the proper time.

But, if the period of our Lord's stay on earth in the body, served its educational purpose all the better from being no longer than it was; so did that also of the forty days after the Resurrection (supposing that we accept the traditional chronology) for the opposite reason, from its being extended so long. Four days would have served as well as forty for the manifestation of the Risen Lord, for the conclusive witness to His Divine nature, and for ratifying the hope of immortality in the bosoms

THE LESSONS OF THE RESURRECTION.

of mankind; within this time He could have given His final charge to the infant Church, and have set it on its way. A higher work however remained which could not be perfected all at once. The Apostles were now to receive the crowning lesson of the course. They were about to pass out of the training ground into the real arena of danger and of toil. They were to be gradually fitted to exercise authority, and to feel trust in the presence with them of a Spiritual Guide.

It took time for their faculties to grow into shape and adapt themselves to the change. Christ always brings His scholars on by gradual progress; He moulds them as nature moulds organic forms; there are with Him no sharp or sudden turns, no jerks in the movements, but all proceeds along one even curve. If the forty days of this transitional condition had not intervened, but the Apostles had been suddenly transformed from disciples into the rulers of a community; if, more than this, they had found themselves all at once exalted into the accredited ministers of the Almighty in the most express and patent of His dispensations, what human beings could have stood the strain? Gradually, during those forty days, they got used to possessing authority. It was not formally conferred; but the other disciples took it for granted that they were to look to them for direction or advice. In this season also, the Apostles acquired a habit of watchfulness over themselves, knowing that Christ was looking into their hearts, and might at any moment appear by their side.

The framing of a society in which Christ's word should be the outer Law and Christ's spiritual presence be the sustaining life, was to be the work of men, because it was to be adapted to human needs. It does not derogate from man's free agency, that he should own and follow the promptings of God, for to do this is part of his proper nature; these promptings are not an alien influence, but belong to his own self as he was intended to be.

With the descent of the Holy Spirit at the end of the forty days, the outward visible training of the Apostles, which it has been my business to trace, was brought to an end; and the guidance of God's Spirit, working in men to will and to do of His good pleasure, came in its place[1].

The fire which Christ had come into man's world to kindle, was now alight, and the special need for Christ's presence on earth did not longer exist. What was it, we may ask, that He left behind? The chief visible outcome of His work was the little band of Apostles; but the mightiest of His influences were imponderable and unseen. Our Lord's sojourn on earth had changed the world in which He had dwelt, so that all subsequent History reads differently from that which goes before. By what means was this change wrought? Christ left no new code of regulations for men to live by. He

---
[1] Philippians ii. 13.

THE LESSONS OF THE RESURRECTION. 467

introduced no changes into Human Society or into any of the forms of Government which He found upon earth. If men might not be left to frame such things for themselves, what had freedom and faculties been given to them for? What Christ did leave, was infinitely more than a reorganisation of Society or a scheme for the reformation of men. On that day of Pentecost a new faculty—that of communing with God's Spirit—came to the birth. And a new force—that of living religion—sprang into existence as a fresh agent in the affairs of the world—a force which Emperors and sacerdotal castes and schools of philosophers had soon to reckon with.

This fire has now and then burned low, but at such times some "circumstance" has often come about, which, answering to some expression of our Lord—perhaps one which seemed till then obscure—has opened out a vista in the minds of men. People say, "Now we see what that hard saying meant," or "Christ must have had this in view when He spoke." Or else—what has sometimes happened—an idea has sprung up in men's hearts, seemingly everywhere at once, and Christ's words have caught a fuller meaning, read by the light of this.

So far we have traced the steps by which the Apostles were taught Faith in the unseen. First by confidence in a Master at their side, next by the assurance that, though unseen, He was close by, and could, if needed, appear and help as of old; and now, lastly, when seeing Him no more, there comes in their hearts an assurance that He is with them to the end of the world.

When I say that the Apostles were *taught* Faith, I use the word *taught* in a different sense from that which it has when applied to the subjects of knowledge. I mean that through wise moral treatment, a quality existing only as a rudiment was so developed as to fit the disciples for communion with God; and not only did they in this sense learn Faith, but—what also need learning, more than we suppose—Love and Hope as well.

I spoke casually just now of the joy which, as appears by the Book of Acts, illumined the Apostles' lives. This came greatly of Love; not merely from the affection of the brethren for each other, but from a general Lovingness, a capacity for Love, which, on coming into action, made them look differently on all they saw. This, like their Faith, had grown up from their being in their Master's company. They felt how He loved them; and if ever one among them was disposed to think lightly or unkindly of a brother disciple, he might recollect how dear that brother—faults and all—was to Christ; and then he could hardly help feeling that if his Master bore with him he might do so too. They marked also Christ's beneficence, His eagerness to render kindness, His readiness to use His wondrous power for the good of those who had no claim upon Him, His gentleness in rebuke, His never recurring to a bygone fault. And this sense of being beloved, this living in an atmosphere of affection, generated in them the capacity for Loving, just as the Home Love that is round a child, not only awakens in it affection to those who shew affection towards it, but teaches it what Love is; and engenders in it a great outcome of Lovingness which it strews broadcast, and bestows, not on persons only, but on animals, and even on inanimate things.

We have had sight of the Apostles at a time when this Love was only half fledged among them, and did not understand itself. It was yet in this state in St Peter when he asked: How often he must forgive the brother who sinned against him[1]. Love with him was then only unfolding in his mind, it was still a thing of bounds and measures; later on he learnt—and his Master's sacrifice crowned the lesson—that it is in essence infinite. By the time when the Apostles had to stand alone and labour for their charge, they had learnt what Love was. From that came the unity and harmony of which I have spoken above. A common interest or even common devotion to a cause would not have gone deep enough down to have quenched all rivalries. Even if paramount interests had put

[1] Matth. xviii. 21.

self out of sight for a while, it would still have been there, ready to reappear when opportunity came. Impatience would have come out now and then. It is Love only which brings others as close to a man as his own self. This lesson of Love was perfected, for the Apostles, by their witnessing Christ's death upon the cross—a death not for friends, not for those under His protection, but for men "while they were yet sinners[1]." They saw, too, that when He rose from the dead in absolute might Divine, He breathed not a word shewing that He remembered His wrongs, but quietly put the past away. All this filled the Apostles' hearts with Lovingness; they could not have gone on with their work, with so little return to shew, unless they had loved the brethren and the converts. The joy which we note in the Apostles, resting like a halo upon them, comes of their feeling sure that God loves them, and of their loving all God's creatures in return. It was this Love that fascinated their hearers; when the words of Paul, notwithstanding that his speech—so they said—was contemptible, went to the hearts of Greeks and Barbarians, as we know they did, what he touched them by was this magic of Love.

A word about the nature of that Hope which nestled in the Apostles' hearts must end my book. If their Master doubted, whether, when He should come at the last, "He should find Faith upon the

[1] Romans v. 8.

THE LESSONS OF THE RESURRECTION. 471

earth;" what, it may be asked, could this Hope of the Apostles have been? Now, that these words of Christ were not spoken in despondency is clear enough for many reasons, but this one reason, that they caused no despondency to the hearers would, to my mind, be sufficient of itself.

What this saying tells us is, that we are not to look for Christ's Kingdom in the shape of a perfected community existing at the last upon the earth. Science and observation seem to point in the same way. Men are never so selfish and so regardless of others as when they are pushing for place in a crowd. Now this globe can only yield food for a time, it must be exhausted of its stores, and even, it would seem, of its reproductive powers, at last; and a half-regenerated humanity would be apt to degenerate back again when they were struggling for standing room and for bread.

To take another point; though science has not settled the future of this planet of ours, yet opinion leans greatly towards our system's having an end. But, if we accept Christ's teaching, Man need not come to an end together with the fabric of the world. The earth is only the spot upon which he is reared and put to proof. Those who come out of the trial we believe to be removed, perhaps after an interval, to another kind of life elsewhere; so that, though this outer fabric of the world may perish, Man, we may believe, will survive, not in a material but in "a spiritual body[1]" whose nature of course we cannot know. Thus the Human episode in the great Epic of Existence, may, as far as life upon this planet goes, come to an end, but the Humanity for which the Christian labours and for which Christ died, will exist for ever; for the Spirits of just men made perfect will have been garnered from age to age into abodes prepared for them from the first. And though Christ, in His wisdom, be sparing of utterances about that which is winnowed away, yet there are not wanting analogies justifying hope.

The education of human souls to fitness for everlasting spiritual life, is of all God's purposes the one which we can most continuously discern. No reign of peace and bliss upon this earth could be of indefinite continuance; a perfected Humanity could only endure for a time. Consequently, if we limit our Love to a Humanity visibly existing on the earth, we give up our hearts to something which must necessarily come to an end: if we make a Deity of this we shall serve but a temporary God. But—although the earth should be calcined to powder, or fly off into regions of space where the temperature is fatal to life—still that Humanity which has the Son of Man for its central and presiding figure may abide with Him for ever, in some of the many mansions of His Father's House.

[1] 1 Cor. xv. 44.

CHRONOLOGICAL APPENDIX.

It will be of service to readers to have a summary of the actions and movements of our Lord, in the order in which they are treated of in the Text. Few of the dates can be fixed with any certitude and it remains a matter of opinion in what order many of the events occurred. The only dates which can be historically determined are those of the death of Herod, and of the beginning (A.D. 25) and end (A.D. 36) of the Governorship of Pilate; with these latter I am not now concerned. When St Luke names the fifteenth year of Tiberius (A.D. 28, A.U.C. 781 beginning on August 19), it is not quite certain whether he means to fix the time when John began to preach, or when Jesus was baptised, or when John was cast into prison. The grounds for fixing the dates of our Lord's birth, His appearance in public, and the duration of His Ministry are given in Tischendorf's "Synopsis Evangelica." I assume, as sufficiently admitted for my working hypothesis, (1) that our Lord was born early in the year B.C. 4, A.U.C. 750, in which, shortly before the passover, as we learn from Josephus, Herod the Great died; and also (2) that the Baptism of our Lord took place in the very beginning of A.D. 28.

I propose to exhibit the order of events, taken month by month, as I suppose them to have occurred. In the greater number of cases I am supported by the authority of Dr Edersheim in his work on the "Life and Times of Jesus the Messiah," and also frequently by Bishop Ellicott, from the Notes to whose Historical Lectures on the Life of our Lord, delivered 1860, I have obtained much help in forming this Appendix.

A.D. 28. *January*. A.U.C. 781.

I place the Baptism of our Lord near the close of the month. This was immediately followed by His withdrawal into the wilderness.

A.D. 28. *February*.

The whole of this month I suppose to have been passed by our Lord in the wilderness.

A.D. 28. *March*.

About the 10th or 12th of March our Lord appears "in Bethany (or Bethabarah) beyond Jordan where John was baptizing." John i. 28.

On the next day, John, Simon and Andrew come to our Lord, and on that which follows our Lord "findeth Philip," and "Philip findeth Nathanael." John i. 43, 45.

Indications in the Gospels of the season of the year in which the events happened are so rare that we catch even at slight matters—one such occurs here—Nathanael is seen "sitting under the fig tree," John i. 48; and as he would hardly have done so if the tree had been bare, it is probable that at this time the fig tree was already in leaf. It might have been so by March 10th; for the climate of the Jordan valley, in the deep cleft of the limestone rocks, far beneath the level of the Mediterranean and three thousand feet lower than the hills of Judæa, was almost tropical; and fig trees, which on the high ground about Jerusalem were not in leaf till April, would be at least a month earlier at this "Peræan Bethany," as the place is called by Bishop Ellicott.

I suppose our Lord to have left "the place where John was baptizing" not later than March 10th and to have been present at the marriage at Cana on or near the 14th. The Passover in this year fell on the 30th of March, and, assuming that our Lord reached Jerusalem on the 28th March, a fortnight has to be accounted for. I have explained, p. 165, what I suppose to have happened in the meanwhile, viz. that our Lord returned with His family to Nazareth, which was 4 miles from Cana, and that, owing to the displeasure shewn by the inhabitants, either at His pretensions or at His having performed His first miracle at another place, He and His mother, His brethren and His disciples removed to Capernaum —"there they abode not many days," John ii. 12. Our Lord then went to Jerusalem, and His family, though not mentioned, may have gone there also. Whether they ever settled again at Nazareth is uncertain. They were at Capernaum in March, A.D. 29, Mark iii. 21, 32. Observe that the sisters of our Lord are not named: they remained at Nazareth, where they were probably married. We read, "Are not His sisters here with us?" (implying that the brothers were not so), Mark vi. 3.

A.D. 28. *April.*

Our Lord during this month was with His disciples at Jerusalem; the events are related in St John, Chap. ii. 13 to Chap. iii. 21.

A.D. 28. *May.*

Henceforth the Chronology depends greatly on the time at which we suppose our Lord's journey through Samaria to have taken place. I place it in May A.D. 28, but many authorities put it in the December of that year. We read,

"After these things came Jesus and his disciples into the land of Judæa; and there he tarried with them, and baptized. And John also was baptizing in Ænon near to Salim, because there was much water there: and they came, and were baptized."—John iii. 22, 23.

This choice of Ænon on account of there being "much water there" points to water having already become somewhat scarce elsewhere. There are in the North-eastern part of Judæa only a few springs which never fail. These are much valued, and one such spring at least was found at Ænon; its site is doubtful (see Bishop Westcott, "St John's Gospel"). If, as some have supposed, it was late in the Autumn when our Lord made this journey, water would be abundant enough in many places, as the streams become full in November. I speak of this because it bears out my view that our Lord's journey through Samaria took place in the May and not in the December of A.D. 28.

In the latter half of the former month, I suppose that our Lord left Judæa and passed, with only a few disciples, through Samaria into Galilee (see pp. 171, 174, 176, 179).

The verse—

"Say not ye, There are yet four months, and *then* cometh the harvest? behold, I say unto you, Lift up your eyes, and look on the fields, that they are white already unto harvest," John iv. 35,

is important in determining the dates.

Some regard the above saying as having been spoken soon after seed time; and think that the first sentence refers to the state of the corn at that moment, when it would have been just coming up, it being then four months from harvest: this would agree with the view that the journey was taken at the end of December[1], and that the "whiteness to harvest" referred metaphorically to the harvest of conversions the Apostles were to reap. Others, among whom is Dr Edersheim, regard the country as being *at the time of speaking* white (that is *bright*) with harvest, and consider the words to have been spoken in May and to bear a literal sense. This latter view seems to me to agree best with the incidents of the journey, many of which—our Lord's weariness, His resting at the fountain[2] and His asking for

[1] The harvest in Palestine ripens at different times in different localities; but as a general rule the barley-harvest may be considered as taking place from the middle to the close of April, and the wheat-harvest about a fortnight later; see Robinson, *Palestine*, Vol. I. p. 431 (ed. 2), and compare Stanley, *Palestine*, p. 240, note (ed. 2). Note taken from Bishop Ellicott's Historical Lectures on the "Life of our Lord," page 106.

[2] John iv. 6. The marginal rendering of the Revised Version is "Jesus...sat *as he was* by the well." The words in italics answer to "thus," οὕτως. This means that He did not call for His cloke and wrap it round Him, as in winter He would have done. This is clearly eye-witness narration.

drink—wear, to my mind, an aspect of summer; moreover, the words "Say ye not" apply better to a maxim of husbandry lying in the minds of the people, than to such an indisputable fact as the time of year when they were spoken. It would have seemed more natural to say "Are we not four months now from harvest?" It was a fact which was in every husbandman's mouth, that the interval between seed time (December), and barley harvest (April) was four months, and our Lord's meaning is, "The husbandman has to wait four months for his harvest, you begin at once to reap; law-givers and prophets and agencies unseen have sown for you."

A.D. 28. *June.*

Our Lord arrives at Cana in Galilee. A "certain nobleman" comes to Him from Capernaum; our Lord heals his son, John iv. 46. The words "whatsoever we have heard done at Capernaum," Luke iv. 23, refer I think to this, if so, they help to fix the date of the Preaching at Nazareth related in St Luke's Gospel, chap. iv. 16—30. For additional reasons for placing the Sermon in the synagogue at Nazareth at this time instead of after John's imprisonment, see above, pp. 164, 165, 179, and also Dr Edersheim, "Life and Times of Jesus," vol. I. p. 430.

It should be noted that we hear nothing of our Lord's mother and brethren. If they had been in Nazareth, they would probably have interposed as they subsequently did at Capernaum where we find them living, Mark iii. 31.

The few disciples who came with our Lord through

Samaria probably went to their homes when He reached Galilee, for St John does not speak of them afterwards.

This account of the Preaching at Nazareth is peculiar to St Luke, I conceive it to have come into his hands as an isolated piece of information, which he fits into the history to the best of his judgment. The events at Capernaum, which in the Gospel of St Luke (iv. 31—44) are related immediately after this sermon, took place after our Lord had come preaching the Kingdom (see Mark i. 21—39). In the Sermon at Nazareth there is no mention of the "Kingdom of God," nor do the disciples seem to have been in attendance. This favours the view that the public Ministry in Galilee had not yet begun.

A.D. 28. *July, August.*

I believe our Lord to have spent this summer preaching in the synagogues, not only of Galilee but also of Judæa. With regard to the verse (Luke iv. 44), "and he was preaching in the synagogues of Galilee," we have in the margin of the Revised Version "very many ancient authorities read *Judæa*." We can understand Judæa being altered into Galilee, to suit the mention of Capernaum, but it is not easy to comprehend a change from Galilee into Judæa (see also Acts x. 37). It agrees with my view of our Lord's course that He should at this time have been exploring the tempers of the people both in Judæa and in Galilee; and I believe the summer of A.D. 28 to have been passed in this work. The Lord may have gone about unattended or nearly so, He had as yet bidden no one to follow except Philip (John i. 43). The 15th year of Tiberius began in this

August, but possibly St Luke might speak of the whole year, from Jan. 1st, by this name.

A.D. 28. *September.*

The feast of John v. which, both by Bishop Westcott and Dr Edersheim, is spoken of as "the unknown feast," I believe to have taken place in this month. I am inclined to identify it with the feast of Tabernacles, see p. 181. It was, as I think, in this month that John was imprisoned by Herod Antipas, who may have feared that the great influence of the prophet would be especially dangerous when the country would be thronged with visitors to the great feast. The Feast of Tabernacles in A.U.C. 781 began on Sept. 18, and lasted till Sept. 29. Josephus, "Antiquities of the Jews," Bk. xviii. Chap. v, Whiston's translation, gives the following account: "Now, when [many] others came in crowds about him, for they were greatly moved [or pleased] by hearing his words, Herod, who feared lest the great influence John had over the people might put it into his power and inclination to raise rebellion (for they seemed to do any thing he should advise), thought it best, by putting him to death, to prevent any mischief he might cause, and not bring himself into difficulties, by sparing a man who might make him repent of it when it should be too late. Accordingly he was sent a prisoner, out of Herod's suspicious temper, to Macherus, the castle I before mentioned, and was there put to death." The Gospel account is not at variance with this, for if John denounced Herod's intentions with regard to Herodias as a violation of Law, this would

CHRONOLOGICAL APPENDIX. 481

be likely to increase the disaffection of the people. When the news reaches our Lord (probably in Judæa) He goes at once into Galilee (Matth. iv. 12, 13; Mark i. 14; Acts x. 37) and His public preaching of the Kingdom of God begins.

A.D. 28. *October, November, December.*

Early in October our Lord comes to the sea of Galilee and calls Simon and Andrew and James and John. Matth. iv. 18; Mark i. 16—19; Luke v. 4.

Following this, comes His residence at Capernaum, and the events of Mark i. 14—45, and Mark ii.

A.D. 29. *January, February.* A.U.C. 782.

The events of Mark iii. may be placed here.

The call of the Twelve (Mark iii. 13, 14; Luke vi. 13) probably took place early in February. Neither St Matthew nor St John gives an express account of the calling, but both refer to it, "And he called unto him his twelve disciples," Matt. x. 1; and, "Jesus said therefore unto the Twelve," John vi. 67. I suppose it to have been near the end of the month when the two disciples sent by John the Baptist came to Christ. Matth. xi. 2; Luke vii. 18.

A.D. 29. *March.*

In this month I should place the following events in the order given below:

(1) The teaching by parables. Matth. xiii. 3; Mark iv. 1; Luke viii. 4.

(2) The visit to the country of the Gerasenes (or Gadarenes). Matth. viii. 28; Mark v. 1; Luke viii. 26.

CHRONOLOGICAL APPENDIX.

(3) The raising of Jairus' daughter, Matth. ix. 18; Mark v. 21—41; Luke viii. 41.

(4) The second visit to Nazareth. "And he went out from thence; and he cometh into his own country; and his disciples follow him;" Mark vi. 1, also Matth. xiii. 54. This mention of "disciples" is one of many circumstances which distinguish this visit to Nazareth from that of Luke iv. 15.

(5) The sending out of the twelve two by two. Matth. x. 1; Mark vi. 7; Luke ix. 1.

(6) Execution of John the Baptist. Tischendorf is inclined to think that Herod was celebrating not his birthday but his accession, which took place on the death of Herod the Great about ten days before the Passover, which in A.U.C. 750 fell on April 2. This conjecture is doubtful. Matth. xiv. 2; Mark vi. 21; Luke iii. 19.

A.D. 29. *April.*

The order of events in this month I take to have been, approximately, as follows:

(1) Herod's misgiving that John had risen from the dead. Matth. xiv. 2; Mark vi. 16.

(2) Our Lord, on the return of the twelve, crosses the lake. Matth. xiv. 13; Mark vi. 32; Luke ix. 10.

(3) The Passover was now at hand, John vi. 4. Feeding of the five thousand, Matth. xiv. 15; Mark vi. 35; Luke ix. 12; John vi. 5. The walking on the sea, Matth. xiv. 25; Mark vi. 48; John vi. 19.

The day of the passover A.D. 29 was the 18th of April. What is mentioned by St Mark, viz. that the multitude sat down on "the green grass," agrees with this indication of the season. It was only during a short time in spring, and then only in a few places, that green grass was found in Palestine. This impressed itself on the narrator, and is an indication of eye-witness work; it is what critics call "autoptic." There is no mention of green grass in the feeding of the 4000 which was in the late summer. This miracle was followed by the return to Capernaum (Discourse on the bread of life, John, chap. vi.) and the controversy with the Pharisees on traditions, Matth. xv. 1, 20; Mark vii. 1—23.

A.D. 29.   *May, June, July, August.*

(1) Journey to the borders of Tyre and Sidon, Matth. xv. 21; Mark vii. 24.

(2) Return from thence.

"And again he went out from the borders of Tyre, and came through Sidon unto the sea of Galilee and through the midst of the borders of Decapolis" (on the east of the sea of Galilee), Matth. xv. 29; Mark vii. 31.

(3) There the feeding of the four thousand takes place (see under April). Matth. xv. 32; Mark viii. 1.

(4) Our Lord crosses the lake "into the borders of Magadan," Matth. xv. 39; or "into the parts of Dalmanutha," Mark viii. 10, this was on the western coast. He then proceeds to the north of the lake; there He heals the blind man at Bethsaida Julias.

(5) "And Jesus went forth, and his disciples into the villages of Cæsarea Philippi," Mark xiii. 33. Con-

fession of Peter, Matth. xvi. 13; Mark viii. 29; Luke ix. 20.

(6) The Transfiguration; Matth. xvii. 1; Mark ix. 2; Luke ix. 28.

(7) Return of our Lord with Peter, James and John from the Mount, to the place where He had left the disciples. Mark ix. 9.

A.D. 29. *September.*

"They went forth from thence and passed through Galilee; and he would not that any man should know it," Mark ix. 30, "and they came to Capernaum," Mark ix. 33.

The miracle of the stater in the fish's mouth (Matth. xvii. 24) is usually placed at this point of the narrative. We have no other account than that given in St Matthew's Gospel, where it seems to be related as happening at this time. But the evidence as to chronology is not conclusive. This stater or half-shekel was the payment for the Temple service, and we know that this was levied in March. That the demand should be made in September is explained by saying that our Lord's absence since April might have prevented the collection of the tax. It is however possible that this event may have taken place in March, A.D. 30, see below.

Our Lord, leaving Capernaum, made the journey through Samaria to Jerusalem, John vii. 3, Luke ix. 51, 56, arriving there about the 18th of September, which in this year was the middle of the Feast of Tabernacles. The sending out of the Seventy took place soon afterwards, Luke x. 1.

A.D. 29. *October.*

Our Lord takes up His residence in Judæa, possibly at Bethany, see p. 370. Incident of woman taken in adultery, John viii. 1. Our Lord in the house of Martha, Luke x. 38—40.

November.

Our Lord probably passed this month in Judæa. Many of the events of Luke, chapters xi., xii., xiii. may have occurred at this time, but we must not conclude for certain from St Luke's account that the events of these chapters all fell together in one short period. Some of them are related by St Matthew in a different connexion; it seems impossible to place them in order.

A.D. 29. *December.*

The Feast of dedication (encaenia), John x. 22, fell in this year on the 20th of December, and lasted eight days. At the end of our Lord's discourse at this feast, St John says "They sought again to take him: and he went forth out of their hand. And he went away again beyond Jordan into the place where John was at first baptizing, and there he abode." John x. 39, 40.

A.D. 30. *January.* A.U.C. 783.

Our Lord may have remained at the place just mentioned, "the Peræan Bethany" (see A.D. 28, March), during this month, having probably only a few followers with Him.

"And many came unto him; and they said, John

indeed did no sign: but all things whatsoever John spake of this man were true." John x. 41.

The people contrast Him with John. This agrees with what is said of the place, viz. that John had baptized there; the people recollected him. The teaching of our Lord in Peræa, of which we have an account only in Luke, chaps. xv., xvi., was probably given about this time.

A.D. 30. *February.*

Early in this month our Lord leaves Peræa, where He had been travelling about, being warned by the Pharisees—

"And he went on his way through cities and villages, teaching, and journeying on unto Jerusalem." Luke xiii. 22.

"In that very hour there came certain Pharisees, saying to him, Get thee out, and go hence: for Herod would fain kill thee." St Luke xiii. 31.

A.D. 30. *March.*

While on this progress the news of the sickness of Lazarus reaches our Lord. He seems then to have been little more than a day's journey from Jerusalem, but outside the limits of Judæa:

"The sisters therefore sent unto him, saying, Lord, behold, he whom thou lovest is sick. But when Jesus heard it, he said, This sickness is not unto death, but for the glory of God, that the Son of God may be glorified thereby[1]." John xi. 3, 4.

[1] This *glorifying* consisted not in its gaining Him glory in the common sense but in its being an event leading Him to the Cross, to the fullest abandonment to His Father's will. This is the true glory. Compare John xii. 28, xxi. 19.

"When therefore he heard that he was sick, he abode at that time two days in the place where he was. Then after this he saith to the disciples, Let us go into Judæa again." John xi. 6, 7.

After the raising of Lazarus, the chief priests and Pharisees "from that day forth took counsel that they might put him (Jesus) to death: Jesus therefore walked no more openly among the Jews, but departed thence into the country near to the wilderness, into a city called Ephraim; and there he tarried with the disciples." John xi. 53, 54.

From Ephraim, the position of which is uncertain, (Dr Edersheim, as I understand him, thinks it may have been near the north end of the sea of Galilee, in Decapolis,) our Lord passes through "the midst of Samaria and Galilee"—St Luke xvii. 11.

This would seem, from the order in which the places are named, to refer to the journey on the way north to Ephraim, but no certain conclusion can be drawn. Towards the end of the month, our Lord joins the company of people on their way from Galilee to Jerusalem, passing by Jericho. The incidents of the journey and the important discourses on the way are related in Mark, chap. x., and in the parallel passages of Matthew and Luke.

The question arises, Where did our Lord join this company? I incline to think that after a short stay at Capernaum, He went with the Galilean company up to the Passover. During the stay at Ephraim, the disciples would have had leisure to turn over in their minds what they had seen and heard; especially the raising of Lazarus, and the words to Martha on eternal life, the plainest our Lord ever spoke; John xi. 25. It is our Lord's way, as I have often pointed out, to leave intervals for reflection. On the way south (supposing that Ephraim was to the north), with His small company of disciples, He may have made a short stop at Capernaum, where, according to my view (see p. 372), St Peter may have partly resided since the feast of Tabernacles, joining from time to time the disciples in attendance on our Lord. Jesus would, on this supposition, be in St Peter's house in the month of March when the officers, in due course, called for the Temple contribution, and in this way we avoid the hypothesis of a payment overdue (see under Sept. A.D. 29). It may be noted that the officers make no question about *Peter's* paying the half-shekel; he was a regular resident and their claim was undoubted, but our Lord had been long absent and was only passing through the place, so that in His case the payment was less obligatory. This is one view of the matter, but I am inclined to think from the form of the collector's question, "Your Master, does not He pay?" (Matth. xvii. 24) that they half expected an objection on higher grounds. The internal evidence, that is to say the tone of doctrine, which appears in the words, "Then are the children free," favours the adopting the later period, inasmuch as it reminds us of the later discourses in chaps. xv., xvi., xvii. of John.

A.D. 30. *April.*

Our Lord may have made His entry into Jerusalem on Sunday, April 2. He returned that night to Bethany after looking "round about upon all things." Mark xi. 11.

Monday, April 3. Cursing of fig tree on the way to Jerusalem (see March, A.D. 28), Matth. xxi. 19; Mark xi. 13. Cleansing of Temple, Matth. xxi. 12; Mark xi. 15; Luke xix. 45. Return to Bethany, Mark xi. 19. Either on this day or the next, the Greeks seek Jesus, John xii. 20.

Tuesday, April 4. Tree is found withered. Parables delivered in Temple. Controversies with Pharisees, Herodians and Sadducees. Our Lord takes leave of the Temple; Mark xi. 20 and chaps. xii., xiii. and parallel passages in Matthew and Luke.

Wednesday, April 5. Treason of Judas.

Thursday, April 6. Last Supper. Our Lord's apprehension.

Friday, April 7. The Crucifixion.

Sunday, April 9. The Resurrection.

I should place the journey of the Apostles to Galilee in the subsequent week. This change would do the Apostles good in many ways. It would relieve the strain on their minds, and was medicine for the shock they had received. For our Lord's care for the physical and mental health of His followers, see text, p. 302, on the words, "Come ye yourselves apart into a desert place and rest a while."

During this stay in Galilee, there took place the appearance of our Lord on the mountain, which I take to be that named, 1 Cor. xv. 6 (see text, last chapter), and at this time I also place the important interview of our Lord with James, our Lord's brother, 1 Cor. xv. 17, and probably with the rest of His brethren, see below.

A.D. 30. *May.*

The appearance at the sea of Tiberias (but see Mr Sanday on the "Authorship of the Fourth Gospel,' chap. XVII.) may have taken place in this month, as also the return of the Apostles from Galilee to Jerusalem with the women and Mary the Mother of Jesus, and the brethren of our Lord. The latter, possibly, had not been in Jerusalem at the Crucifixion, but had at last learned, perhaps through James, the fulness of their brother's greatness. The Apostles as well as the relations of our Lord must have been enjoined to return to Jerusalem, or they would not without exception have gone thither. The Feast of Pentecost was not a sufficiently imperative call to account for their presence. This injunction must have been given in Galilee. If we had only St Luke's account, we should suppose that the Apostles never left Jerusalem; but this would in itself be unlikely and is contradicted by the other Evangelists. The day given for the Ascension by Wieseler, "Chronologie des Apostolischen Zeitalters," 1848, is May 18.

The Ascension was followed by the choice of Matthias.

The day of Pentecost, as fixed by Wieseler, was May 27, A.D. 30.

INDEX OF TEXTS.

GENESIS.	PAGE
iii. 18, 19	44
xxviii. 12	161

DEUTERONOMY.	
xviii. 15	94
xix. 16	396
18	396

II SAMUEL.	
xii. 13	420

JOB.	
xiii. 4	396

PSALMS.	
cxix. 162	232

PROVERBS.	
vi. 19	396
xii. 17	396

ISAIAH.	
vi. 10	321
xi. 1	160

JEREMIAH.	PAGE
vi. 31	396

S. MATTHEW.	
iii. 5	189
iv. 1	117
1—11	114
20	186
vi. 25	404
vii. 17	259
viii. 19	375
ix. 14—17	220
36—38	234
x. 2—6	162
5—15	290
xi. 2—6	262
12	232
21	106
xii. 28	83
30	358
46	180
xiii. 10	321
xiv. 17	22
23	229
xvi. 13—20	327

S. MATTHEW.	PAGE
xvi. 22	126
23	329
24, 25	340
xvii. 12	348
25	133
xviii. 1—11	356
21	469
21, 22	358
xix. 6	408
xxii. 42, 43	415
xxiv. 24	75
25	413
xxv. 14—30	316
xxviii. 16	451
19	250
xxviii. 20	69

S. MARK.	
i. 12, 13	114
14	188
14, 15	83, 195
16—20	195
20	305
22	202

INDEX OF TEXTS.

S. MARK.	PAGE
ii. 16—22	220
iii. 5	19
6, 7	233
13, 14	239
14, 15	229
17—19	161
20, 21	261
26	126
32	288
iv. 11	30
11, 12	321
24	323
35	283
35—40	274
37—40	283
v. 1	48
17	286
19	84
30	351
37	287
vi. 1—6	180
2	362
3	288, 454
7—13	289
30—32	302
30	300
34	307
38	305
39, 40	278
45, 46	307
47—52	308
50	310
vii. 14, 15	331
24	333
33	427
33—35	91

S. MARK.	PAGE
vii. 33—36	334
viii. 5—7	305
11	335
14	306
16, 17	306
23—25	90
23—26	334
ix. 1	340
2—8	94
7	94
9	345
17—29	350
30	351, 354
31	227
33	354
35	355
40—50	360
x. 1	227, 361
17—22	381
24	383
30	384
xi. 10	427
12—14	96
20—22	96
xii. 35—37	415
xiii. 22	75
xiv. 9	400
50	240
xv. 31	139
xvi. 20	84

S. LUKE.	PAGE
ii. 4	415
35	52, 161
iv. 1—13	115
13	339

S. LUKE.	PAGE
iv. 14, 15	179
v. 4	200
8	202
17	218
33	155
vi. 12	239
17—19	253
20	253
22, 23	254
23	79
24—26	255
27	257
39, 40	257
43	259
vii. 18—23	266
20	107
21—23	108
23	264
29, 30	265
35	264
viii. 1—3	276
3	166
26	48
ix. 27	93
31	324
37	348
51, 52	279
51—56	366
52	296
48	355
55	138
x. 1—11	290
4—11	379
9—11	300
11	68, 83
13	106

INDEX OF TEXTS.

S. LUKE.	
	PAGE
x. 18	126
21	300
21, 22	178, 302
22	73
xi. 1	155, 221, 415
20	83
27	376
29	428
xii. 14	403
16—20	404
36	404
41	372
41—46	368
49, 50	150
xiii. 23	428
xiv. 15	376
xv. 10	178, 389
xvi. 1—12	391
8	389
30	144
31	63
xvii. 5	397
xviii. 8	27
19	428
xix. 11—27	316
26	319
29	297
xx. 35	68
35, 36	410
41	415
xxi. 19	414
xxii. 8	297
24—30	423
28	178
33	376
35—38	291

S. LUKE.	
	PAGE
xxiv. 36	240
48	241

S. JOHN.	
i. 32, 33	109
43	156, 182
45	156
46	156
48, 49	160
51	161
ii. 11	152, 163
12	152, 164, 180
16	167
17	152
23	153, 167
24	176, 246
24, 25	167
iii. 2	148
22	153
22, 23	170
25	155, 330
26	170
iv. 1, 2	171
2	153
27	409
31	175
35—38	177
43—45	164
45	179
47	105
48	76, 104
v. 1	179, 181
15—18	182
17	183
26	89
35	189

S. JOHN.	
	PAGE
v. 43	184, 300
vi. 4, 5	303
5	306
8	157
9	304
15	23, 307
25—65	328
44	338
60—63	332
66	168, 329
vii. 2	181
2—10	363
14	369
35	369
53	370
viii. 1	370
ix. 1—3	46
x. 16	269
40	119, 372
xi. 16	245, 372, 430
48	183
xii. 20—22	158
xiii. 1—14	420
xiv. 4—11	101
6	73
9	159, 415
11	102
19	428
xv. 15	176
23, 24	106
27	241
xvi. 4	352
7, 8	457
8—11	462
12	69
xvii. 3	68

S. John.

	PAGE
xvii. 6	68
xxi. 2	156
25	420

Acts.

i. 8	216, 241
14	362, 453
15	452
22	241
ii. 32	241
41	199
iii. 15	241
iv. 32	385
35	383
x. 40, 41	143, 447
34, 35	95
41	241
xii.	139
2	369, 453
xiii. 31	241

Acts.

	PAGE
xvi. 6—8	459
xviii. 21	100

Romans.

v. 8	470

1 Corinthians.

i. 12	174
14—15	155
ix. 1	454
xiv. 24	71
xv. 5—8	450
6	451
44	471

Galatians.

i. 13	97
ii. 9—12	453
11—14	433
iv. 6	68, 72
vi. 1, 2	425

Philippians.

	PAGE
ii. 13	466

1 Timothy.

vi. 17	396

2 Timothy.

iv. 2	173
13	119

Hebrews.

xi. 1	273

James.

i. 20	245

1 Peter.

ii. 23	167

1 John.

i. 1	446

GENERAL INDEX.

Address to newly chosen Apostles, 253—261
Advent of our Lord into Galilee, 188, 189
Andrew, 157
Animosity of people of Nazareth, when first shewn, 165
Apologue, 125, 126
Apostles (The), named in pairs by Matthew, reason suggested, 162; must have been directed to return to Jerusalem for the Ascension, 194, 451; not fit men to promulgate Theological doctrines, 230; general characteristics of the, 247; not men whom the Founder of a policy would have chosen, 249; the chosen three, 325, 327; the crowning lesson of, 465; steps by which they learnt Faith in an unseen presence, 467; taught Love, 468; taught Hope, 470
Ascension, 457; expedient that Christ should go away, 457; Holy Spirit swaying human action, 459

Astonishment produced by our Lord's teaching, 202
Authority manifested by Christ, 167, 203—206

Baptist (The) and his disciples, 153—155; competition with, shunned by our Lord, 173
Baptist's (The) messengers, their arrival, 262; their question and their answer, 268
Bartholomew, 159, see Nathanael
Bethany in Peræa (Bethabara), 119, 161, 168, 189 note
Bethany in Judæa, when did our Lord first resort thither? 370
Bethsaida Julias, 334
Brethren of our Lord, 362, 453

Christ leaves disciples independent, 5; with them after the Resurrection, 9, 274; influence of His Personality, 16, 17; did He from the first see all that lay before Him? 140; explores the tempers of different classes of men, 148; His return from the wilderness, 151; calls to him certain disciples, 151; at Cana and Capernaum, 152; leaves time for impressions to fix themselves, 185; arrives at the Lake of Galilee and calls the brethren, 195—198; His way of proceeding positive, 208; enjoins no system of religious observance, 222; why did He not found a church Himself? 236; lays stress on what men are, as well as on what they do, 259; ceases to have a stationary abode, 270; educational effects of the change of place, 275—279; journey to borders of Tyre and Sidon, 333; at Cæsarea Philippi, 336—338 (see Transfiguration); returns to Capernaum after the Transfiguration, 354; sets out for the feast of Tabernacles, 359—362; refusing to judge, 399; upholds sanctity of marriage, 409; disclaims for the Messiah the title of Son of David, 415; does not look to visibly converting the world, 416; the washing the disciples' feet, an acted parable, 419; always endeavours to set men free, 460; calls the conscience into play, 467; His Kingdom not upon earth, 471

Christian revelation centred in a Fact, 230

Demoniac in country of Gadarenes, 285

Didrachma, paying of, 406

Disciples not in attendance at first visit to Nazareth, 180; doubtful if present at feast, John v., 181; early Judæan, 188

Dives and Lazarus, parable of, 62

Ecce Homo, quoted, p. 412.

Edersheim, Dr, life and times of Jesus the Messiah, quoted, 139, 140, 329, 334, 394; on our Lord's conversing with the woman at Sychar, 409

Eloquence, its small part in the Divine economy, 250

Erskine of Linlathen, quotation, 40

Evil, existence of, 29; functions of, in the world, 43—51

Family, description of a, restrained from knowing evil, 30—36

Feast of the Jews, John v. 1, 181

Five (The) first called, John, Andrew, Peter, Philip, Nathanael, 156

Form of Christ's Teaching, 209

Free Will, 29; implies liberty to go wrong, 41

Galilæans receive our Lord, 179

Galilee, why suited for cradle of movement, 169

Gospel of St John, surely written by a disciple, 151, 157

GENERAL INDEX. 497

Gospels, advantages of narrative form, 13, 461

Herodians, 233

Inheritance, The disputed, 403

James, our Lord's brother, 452—454
James and John, the sons of thunder, 365, 368
Jerusalem, not a favourable spot for the schooling of the apostles, 190; not desirable that the Christian community should originate there, 192
Judas Iscariot, 246

Laws of our Lord's conduct—sense in which term is used, 2, 18—20, 306
Lazarus, raising of, 429
Levi (see also Matthew), 214
Levitical Law, 207

Mammon of unrighteousness, 395—397
Matthew, 214—216; his call a proof that Christ was no respecter of persons, 217
Messiah, what the people expected him to be, 329
Milton, 'Paradise Regained,' 124
Miracle of feeding of the 5000, 304; of Christ walking on sea, 308; of feeding of the 4000, 305
Miracles, standing, not to be expected, 65; use of, 75; Laws of, 112; as works of beneficence, 333
Miraculous draught of fishes, 198, 202
Mission (The) to the cities, 8, 288; referred to by our Lord, 291—293; effects of these mission journeys, 295; directions given, 295—300
Mission of Seventy, 289, 301—302
Moses, 207

Nathanael, 159, 161
Natural Selection, 26, 314
Nazareth, preaching in synagogues at, 79; second visit of Christ to, 287
Negative characteristics of Christ's teaching, 10
Nicodemus, 148, 169, 172

Parables, 312; that of the talents, 317; that of the pounds, 318; intended not to hide truth but to show it, 323; of the unjust steward, 388 and preface
Passover, 2nd, at time of feeding of the 5000, 303; see Teaching
Peter, with our Lord at the Passover, A.D. 28, probably returned to Galilee, 166; how far in attendance before call, 166; his giving himself up on a sudden, to one impression, 244; was he in constant attendance during the winter, A.D. 29, 30? 372 note; his practical character, 248, 455; denials of, 433

Pharisees, their hostility and that of the Sadducees contrasted, 218
Philip, 158, 306
Preparatio Evangelica, 153—194
Preparation, noted in our Lord's ways, 80, 94
Prospective action of our Lord, 411

Receiving a hundred fold "with persecutions," 381
Resurrection, grandeur in the conception of the Risen Christ, 450; appearance of Christ to 500 brethren at once, 451; appearance to James, 453; literary aspect of the history of, 449; duration of post Resurrection period, 464
Revelation, 52—73; "should be written in the skies," this demand considered, 59
Ruler, the young, 381

Sabbath, its value, 219; our Lord's practice in relation to, 220
Samaria, 1st journey through, 175
Sanday, Mr, authorship and historical character of the fourth Gospel, references, 105, 328
Satan, 120, 125
Seed thoughts, 212; see Sermon on the Mount
Sermon on the Mount, not a Code of Laws, 210, 211; contains *seed thoughts*, 212
Sex ceases with life upon earth, 410

Signs and Wonders: their laws, 21; distinguished, 75; functions of, to attract hearers, 77; for selection, 79; for preparation, 80; for setting forth the kingdom, 82; for general teaching, 84; they shew that God does not respect persons, 87; they do not wholly supersede the processes of nature, 88, 89; practical lessons furnished by them to disciples, 91; Laws of, recapitulated, 112
Signs, sparingly displayed after the Feast of Tabernacles, 425; absence of public and notable signs during the Passion week, 430
Silas, 139
Simon the Zealot, 245
Spiritual order, how far analogous to natural selection, 314, 315
Storm on sea of Galilee, 283
Successors inheriting a cause, 414, 443
Suffer me first to bury my father, 377
Synoptists, term explained, 157 note

Tabernacles, Feast of, 181
Teaching in parables, 12, 280—282, 321
Teaching of Christ, its form, 209; that for the multitudes and that for the disciples, 225
Temptation, to turn stones into loaves, 127—135; on the Mount,

134—139; on the pinnacle of Temple, 139—141

Temptations in the wilderness, form of the narrative, 113—117; where communicated to disciples, 119; whether literal history, 119

Transfiguration, 93, 341—348

Trench, Archbishop, on demoniacs, 284; on the miracles, 396

Tribute to Cæsar, 406

Twelve, the, their call, 239; their fitness for the work which fell to them, 239; their character as witnesses, 241—243

Universality of Christ's Kingdom, 10, 415

Wisdom justified of all her children, 264—269

Withering of fig-tree, 95, 432

Witnessing to Christ the first function of the Apostles, 216, 241

Woman taken in adultery, 405

BY THE SAME AUTHOR.

A SERVICE OF ANGELS. Crown 8vo., 3s. 6d.

"Originality of treatment and freshness of style make Mr Latham's *Service of Angels* a delightful book."—*Church Quarterly Review.*

"Whether its tendency be orthodox or not, his book is certainly a curious and attractive contribution to the study of the question of angel ministry, which has a peculiar charm of its own."—*Scotsman.*

THE RISEN MASTER. A Sequel to PASTOR PASTORUM. Crown 8vo., 6s.

"Mr Latham's theory, which we find so convincing, about the discovery of the grave clothes, is admirably illustrated by a drawing which shows the tomb as he conceives it. We call this the groundwork of the book, but those who know the author's previous work will understand that such a theory subserves a higher end than the gratification of curiosity as to facts...... We could find many things in the book to criticize, but these very things suggest devout thought—not flippant doubt. It has faults, but no book could do more to stimulate and corroborate faith. Our advice is to buy it and read it, to keep it and read it again."—*Church Times.*

"Mr Latham has unquestionably rendered a real service to all thoughtful students of the Gospel records. Those whose vocation is teaching will perhaps find less to help them in this volume than in *Pastor Pastorum*; but in any case it will stimulate their thought and quicken their interest. It will help them to realize more vividly the wisdom and tenderness of the methods employed by Almighty God in the education of His children."—*Guardian.*

ON THE ACTION OF EXAMINATIONS CONSIDERED AS A MEANS OF SELECTION. Crown 8vo., 6s. 6d.

"In this able and thoughtful book Mr Latham has brought the long experience of a successful College tutor to bear on a subject of more than merely scholastic or academic interest...... How far does this great engine Examination, as at present applied, work satisfactorily for the interests of education and of the public service? This is the central question which Mr Latham discusses.—He writes easily and clearly."—*The Times.*

CAMBRIDGE
DEIGHTON BELL AND CO.

Made in the USA
Lexington, KY
01 February 2011